Understanding Combat
Related Post Traumatic
Stress Disorder

 W9-BRT-243

Property of
Broadview University
Orem Campus

Understanding Combat Related Post Traumatic Stress Disorder

WALTER F. MCDERMOTT

McFarland & Company, Inc., Publishers

Jefferson, North Carolina, and London

Library of Congress Cataloguing-in-Publication Data

McDermott, Walter F., 1946–
Understanding combat related post traumatic
stress disorder / Walter F. McDermott.
p. cm.
Includes bibliographical references and index.

ISBN 978-0-7864-6946-8
softcover : acid free paper ∞

1. Post-traumatic stress disorder. 2. Post-traumatic stress
disorder — Treatment. 3. Soldiers— Mental health — United
States. 4. Veterans— Mental health — United States. 5. Combat —
Psychological aspects. 6. Psychology, Military. 7. Soldiers— United
States— Biography. 8. Veterans— United States— Biography. 9. Post-
traumatic stress disorder — Patients— United States— Biography. I. Title.
RC552.P67M383 2012 616.85'21— dc23 2012008064

British Library cataloguing data are available

© 2012 Walter F. McDermott. All rights reserved

*No part of this book may be reproduced or transmitted in any form
or by any means, electronic or mechanical, including photocopying
or recording, or by any information storage and retrieval system,
without permission in writing from the publisher.*

Front cover image © 2012 Shutterstock

Manufactured in the United States of America

*McFarland & Company, Inc., Publishers
Box 611, Jefferson, North Carolina 28640
www.mcfarlandpub.com*

To the tens of thousands of Americans
who died fighting in the Vietnam War,
especially to those men who died alone.
You will never be forgotten.

TABLE OF CONTENTS

PREFACE

This book is about the invisible wounds of war: Post Traumatic Stress Disorder (PTSD). In a semi-memoir format, it provides an explanation of the historical development of PTSD, its myriad symptoms and the scientifically verified psychological and medical treatments for the disorder. In the United States and Great Britain alone there are hundreds of thousands of war veterans suffering PTSD symptoms. Our current Mideast wars are generating thousands of new PTSD cases. Because it is a psychological hidden wound, veterans afflicted with PTSD may find it difficult to understand the troubling symptoms of their disorder. Combat veterans and their families can learn to better understand PTSD by reading this book.

I wrote this book from a unique perspective: I am a Vietnam combat veteran and clinical psychologist who has treated combat PTSD veterans for more than 28 years. I served in an artillery battery assigned to the 9th Infantry Division in Vietnam's Mekong Delta from 1969 to 1970. For most of my psychological career I worked as a staff psychologist at the Jacksonville, Florida, VA Outpatient Clinic's Mental Health Unit. This combination of experiences enables me to analyze PTSD symptoms from a personal perspective as well as a professional one.

Combining the basic tenets of cognitive psychotherapy and my own military experience, I developed and refined many unique therapeutic ideas and insights. These innovative therapeutic concepts are described in detail and in plain language. For example, the reader will learn that the Bible's fourth commandment is usually mistranslated, an awareness of which can help some combat PTSD veterans ease pathological guilt over killing the enemy. An early chapter addresses those unsung victims of combat stress, the spouses of PTSD veterans. It helps them comprehend this alien combat disorder by detailing its similarities to the negative psychological aftereffects of a sadly more familiar trauma: rape. The book also

1

reports the relevant scientific research on the diagnosis and treatment of PTSD, including exciting new investigations into the neurobiological foundation of PTSD.

The book's contents are important to all enlightened American citizens who are concerned about the detrimental mental effects our current Mideast wars are producing in our returning soldiers.

I would like to take this opportunity to thank my wife, Judith, and my daughter, Colleen, for their help in editing, but most of all for their affection and support throughout this project. They and my son-in-law Adam are my main balcony people. I would also like to thank Dr. John Bates and Dr. David Sovine for their encouragement and advice at the start of this project and their support throughout.

1

INTRODUCTION

Mike's personality changed after he returned from his transportation unit's tour in Iraq. His wife, Debbie, was the first to notice the differences. Throughout the years that she had known him, Mike had always been a lighthearted, cheerful guy who enjoyed having fun. Now he rarely smiled and was frequently irritable. When he returned from his job at the post office, he would hide away in the den and start drinking beer. He did little else besides drinking beers while watching television, which most of the time was tuned to the military channel. He stopped playing with their five-year-old son Ben, who would now ask why Daddy was always so mad. Debbie was worried about his drinking, but dared not confront him about it; anyway, it seemed that the alcohol helped him sleep. Most nights she heard him thrashing and moaning in his sleep. Mike frightened her when he awoke from a nightmare screaming and flailing his arms. But when she tried to talk to him about his nightmares, he claimed he could not remember any.

Mike no longer socialized with friends or attended family gatherings. Debbie tried to encourage him to get out more, but he refused, even refusing to do what they had always enjoyed together, playing pool. She was worried that there was something mentally wrong with Mike. She prayed that he would go to the Veterans Administration's Mental Health Clinic for help, but every time she tried to talk to him about her worries, Mike would become enraged. He would shout that he was not crazy and that he would be fine if people would just leave him alone. Mike's rage was so frightening that Debbie learned to keep quiet, but when alone, she secretly cried about Mike and her fears about their family's future.

Cases like Mike's are far too common today in the United States, as more and more soldiers return home from the latest of their war zone tours in Iraq or Afghanistan. Families want their veteran's psychological difficulties evaluated and treated, but the veteran often refuses. Part of the difficulty male combat veterans have in seeking help for their war-related symptoms is their belief that it is not a manly thing to do. Military training indoctrinated them into accepting the traditional male gender role, which insists that a real man is tough and strong. Normal emotions such as fear or sorrow are not acceptable; anger is the only acceptable emotion. The U.S. military's attitude traditionally has been that it is a sign of weakness for a soldier to seek psychological help. Active-duty combat veterans also worry that their being treated for mental problems could hurt both their military and future civilian careers. One concern is that military or civilian coworkers would find out and then lose confidence in them. But this traditional concept of real manhood is misguided. The combat veteran has already proven his masculinity by enduring and surviving the hell of war. If he seeks psychological treatment to better deal with war's emotional aftereffects, it does not make him effeminate. He reaches out not because of mental weakness or unmanly tendencies, but rather because of his exposure to the gruesome horror of modern war. No one goes through that hell without being scathed.

There is, however, new evidence that today's U.S. military establishment is attempting to change its attitude against soldiers seeking mental health care. On November 25, 2008, a front-page article in a national newspaper publicized that even Army generals have been seeking treatment for mental health problems after their own service in the Mideast War. The article reports how General Carter Ham, one of the United States dozen four-star generals in the Army, sought psychological treatment for PTSD after returning from a 2005 tour in Iraq. It states that General Ham's willingness to speak publicly about his PTSD represents a major "shift for a military system in which seeking help has long been seen as a sign of weakness.... It's also a recognition of the seriousness of combat stress which can worsen to become Post Traumatic Stress Disorder." General Ham is quoted as saying, "It's OK to seek help. It doesn't mean you are a bad person, and it certainly doesn't mean you are a bad soldier." The article also reports that Brigadier General Gary Patton sought treatment for his combat stress after serving in 2004 as a brigade commander in Anbar Province, Iraq. He suffered from insomnia, difficulties concentrating and hyperarousal while driving. General Patton insists, "You're not going crazy. I'm not going to say it's normal, but they [symptoms] are expected outcomes of being exposed to this kind of trauma over an extended period of time." The article goes on to quote Brigadier General Keith Gallagher, who commanded Army health care facilities throughout Europe. He thinks that soldiers should consider mental health treatment as no different than receiving medical treatment for a pulled muscle: "I've got pain. I'm going to get help."[1]

One reason why many combat veterans do not acknowledge their war-related psychological problems is because they externalize these postwar difficulties by projecting the blame on others. They think that the problems are not due to their emotions and behavior, but rather, due to the emotional problems of others, such as an arrogant boss or an unsympathetic wife. When the problems persist, they simply change jobs or divorce their spouses and remarry. Initially there is always a honeymoon period, during which the veteran feels better and his life appears to have improved. This positive honeymoon is due to the excitement and challenge of the new situation, but eventually the same old problems reappear. Conflicts with the new boss or the new spouse occur. Again the veteran responds by changing jobs or divorcing. But how many times does the combat veteran have to change jobs or spouses before understanding that the problem is not other people but within? One Vietnam veteran married seven times. A Korean War veteran worked at 200 different jobs. Still their PTSD symptoms persisted.

Another barrier against recognition of a combat veteran's emotional problems is that these problematic emotional aftereffects are not easily seen. Post-combat psychological problems are the hidden, invisible wounds of war. Coworkers or casual acquaintances of the troubled combat veteran see that he has the correct number of arms, legs, and eyes; so they expect him to be fine. A veteran seriously troubled by emotional problems is not easily retrained to work a computer or even a typewriter. The psychologically troubled veteran's wounds encompass his entire being; they limit his or her ability to function in any work or social arena. Invisible emotional wounds of war do not evoke the same level of recognition in society as the physical wounds.

The current technical term for psychological problems caused by war is Post Traumatic Stress Disorder (PTSD). PTSD experts agree that the foundation for psychological recovery after suffering a traumatic event is education about recovery for traumas. It behooves all veterans diagnosed with combat-related psychological problems and their families to learn as much as they can about their psychological disorder. Reading and studying this book on PTSD is a positive first step towards recovery. It can help veterans and their families better understand this condition by providing information on the nature of the disorder, its symptoms and most importantly, the recommended treatment options. This volume will be most helpful if it can motivate the combat veteran to become involved in psychotherapy (talk therapy), which is the effective psychological treatment for PTSD.

But this book is not a substitute for psychotherapy. The volume is not designed as a do-it-yourself psychotherapy workbook. No book can be a substitute for actual psychotherapy because it cannot provide the healing human relationship that is the foundation of psychotherapy. The process of psychotherapy is like learning to play a musical instrument. Studying a book on playing the piano will aid the student's knowledge of the process. However, it is unrealistic to think that just by studying a book the student will learn how to play the piano well. Just as there is no substitute for the hard work of practice under the guidance of a skilled piano teacher, this PTSD book is no substitute for the hard work of psychotherapy with a skilled psychologist who has been competently trained in the treatment of war-related PTSD.

2

HISTORY OF COMBAT DISORDERS

Over the centuries wise men have known that war may cause chronic psychological problems in the minds of returning soldiers. In the sixteenth century William Shakespeare demonstrated his insight into the emotional aftereffects of war with his play *The First Part of King Henry IV*. In Act II Lady Percy gives voice to the silent complaints that worry all soldiers' wives as she confronts her husband, the warrior Knight Henry Percy, surnamed Hotspur:

> For what offence have I this fortnight been
> A banish'd woman from my Henry's bed?
> Tell me, sweet lord, what is't that takes from thee
> Thy stomach, pleasure and thy golden sleep?
> Why dost thou bend thine eyes upon the earth,
> And start so often when thou sit'st alone?
> In thy faint slumbers I by thee have watch'd
> And heard thee murmur tales of iron wars,
> Speak terms of manage to thy bounding steed,
> Cry "Courage! To the field!" ...
> Thy spirit within thee hath been so at war, ...
> That beads of sweat have stood upon thy brow[2]

In the United States the first description of exhaustion symptoms in soldiers exposed to combat stress was after the Civil War, when in 1871 Dr. Mendez DaCosta described what he thought was a cardiovascular condition known as *soldier's heart*.[3] Since then military psychiatrists have called these problematic effects of combat stress various names: *Shell shock* was used during World War I, because the source of the condition was mistakenly thought to be a type of brain damage resulting from exposure to the concussions of exploding artillery shells. During World War II and the Korean War, the diagnostic term was *combat exhaustion*. This diagnosis evolved as military psychiatrists realized that even documented heroes, men with prior awards for valor, could become psychological casualties after exposure to prolonged combat. Their conception was that this disorder was similar to physical fatigue, a kind of energy drain where the soldier's psychological adaptive resources had been depleted. The corollary was that every man, even a decorated hero, may reach his breaking point.

A major difficulty with World War II-era military psychiatrists' understanding of combat fatigue is that they considered the aftereffects of combat, again similar to physical fatigue, as only temporary. Standard treatment for combat fatigue consisted of removing the soldier from the front lines, providing hot showers, hot meals and sedative-enhanced sleep. After a day or two of such therapy the soldier was returned to his unit to continue fighting. Regrettably, for many soldiers this limited treatment was not enough; they remained overwhelmed by their battlefield horrors. For these chronically troubled soldiers, their psychiatric diagnosis was changed because American military psychiatrists were still under the spell of Sigmund Freud's psychoanalytic theory. Dr. Freud emphasized imaginary childhood traumas rather than actual adult traumas like war. These inaccurate diagnoses resulted in ineffective treatments.

During the 1970s, Veterans Administration psychologists and psychiatrists recognized that they were treating psychological symptoms of Vietnam veterans that were directly related to combat stressors that had occurred years before. Informally it was termed *post–Vietnam syndrome*. Diagnostic understanding advanced in 1980 with the publication of the *Diagnostic and Statistical Manual of Mental Disorders*, third edition (DSM-III) by the American Psychiatric Association. The manual is the diagnostic bible of psychiatry, and within its third edition was, for the first time, a diagnostic classification which acknowledged that post-trauma psychological problems could be long lasting. The new name for the disorder introduced then is still in use; it is Post Traumatic Stress Disorder, most often referred to by its acronym PTSD. It consists of three subcategories: Acute, when the onset of symptoms is immediate, *delayed onset*, when symptom onset is at least six months after the stressor, or *chronic*, when symptoms persist longer than six months.

Let's examine the terminology. *Trauma* means any extremely dangerous event that involves the threat or fact of serious physical harm or death, be it military combat, rape or torture. *Post-trauma* means after the trauma. *Post-trauma stress* means the stress, specifically the emotional and social symptoms, that persists long after the trauma. It is a *disorder* because "the disturbance causes clinically significant distress or impairment in social, occupational, or other important areas of functioning."[4] Post Traumatic Stress Disorder is defined as the psychological symptoms that may disturb a person after being exposed to a severely dangerous experience, such as combat in a war.

The validity of PTSD as a true biological disorder has been established through animal experiments that illustrate many of the prominent symptoms of the disorder. One type of experiment subjects animals, usually rats, to inescapable and unpredictable electric shocks. After repeated exposure to such painful stressors, the rats demonstrated chronic physiological arousal, overproduction of stress chemicals, generalized fear behaviors, exaggerated startle responses, and chronic sleep disturbances. "These effects closely resemble the syndrome of PTSD in humans and may imply that the uncontrollable and unpredictable nature of monumental trauma plays an important role in the etiology (causes) of PTSD."[5] Psychiatrist Dr. Van Der Kolk of the Massachusetts Mental Health Center agrees that animals given inescapable shocks display PTSD-like symptoms: "There is a very good animal model of inescapable response. Tortured animals show hyperactivity, hyperarousal, and they continue to react even to minor stimuli as if they were being re-exposed to the same shock."[6]

An alternative animal model for PTSD comes from elaborate experiments that train animals in fear. The animals are conditioned, to react to an initially neutral stimulus, such as a light or a tone, with a fear response by pairing the neutral stimulus with an inescapable electric shock. After repeated pairings of light and shock, the animal learns to react with fear even when the light is presented by itself. The traumatized animals display hyperstartle and hyperarousal overreactions. This type of fear conditioning has been found in all animals tested, including a number of different species, such as fish, birds and lizards, as well as mammals such as rats, rabbits, dogs and monkeys. The research psychiatrist Lawrence Kolb observed that "The long-term behavioral and physiological hyperactivity of these animals was remarkably similar to that noted in the chronic PTSD of combat veterans."[7] We will learn later how fear conditioning plays a critical role in the combat related PTSD of humans.

3

SYMPTOMS AND
DIAGNOSIS OF PTSD

The diagnostic criterion for PTSD is rather unusual in psychiatry in that it defines the cause of the disorder, which is technically termed its *etiology*. PTSD requires an emotionally overwhelming traumatic event that the person must have suffered through before the disorder can be diagnosed. The 1980 DSM-III states: "the essential feature is the development of characteristic symptoms following a psychological traumatic event that is generally outside the range of usual human experience."[8] This "outside the range" requirement was included to separate PTSD from reactions to common human stressors like divorce, the death of a loved one, the loss of a job or a severe illness. Military combat in Vietnam, Iraq or Afghanistan surely qualifies as such an extreme event.

Once the psychologist has verified that the veteran has survived such an extreme event, current symptoms can be examined. Only when the combat veteran demonstrates the following set of symptoms is the PTSD diagnosis made. In the diagnostic manual the various PTSD symptoms are separated into three clusters. The first group requires that the veteran reexperiences the traumatic event through either intrusive thoughts about the event, or nightmares of the event, or flashbacks in which the veteran feels like he or she is reliving the event. During these reexperiencing episodes, the veteran is subjected to uncomfortable psychological distress and intense physiological arousal. The second symptom group requires that the veteran avoids reminders of the trauma by either deliberately trying not to think about it, or avoids places and people that serve as reminders of it. Trauma victims frequently display a limited range of emotional expressions, lowered interest in formerly "significant activities" and a sense of a shortened future. The third symptom group requires that the traumatized veteran experiences chronic physiological arousal as evidenced by difficulties sleeping, outbursts of anger, hypervigilance (the technical term for always being alert and on guard for danger) or difficulties concentrating. Finally the PTSD diagnostic criterion requires that the above set of symptoms is severe enough to cause the veteran significant interpersonal difficulties at home, at work or in social situations for over one month (see table 1).

Table 1. Diagnostic Criteria for Post Traumatic Stress Disorder (adapted from American Psychiatric Association, 1994, pages 427–429)

A. Exposure to Trauma
  (1) Veteran experienced, witnessed or was confronted with events that involved death, serious injury or threat of injury to self or others
  (2) Veteran's response involved intense fear, helplessness, or horror.

B. Trauma Persistently Reexperienced as One of the Following:
  (1) recurrent and intrusive distressing recollections of the event
  (2) recurrent distressing dreams of the event
  (3) feeling and acting as if the traumatic event were recurring
  (4) psychological distress at exposure to cues that resemble aspects of the traumatic event
  (5) physiological reactivity on exposure to cues that resemble aspects of the traumatic event

C. Avoidance of Stimuli Associated with Trauma and Numbing of Responsiveness as Indicated by at Least Three of the Following:
  (1) avoiding thoughts, feelings or talking about the trauma
  (2) avoiding people, places or behaviors associated with the trauma
  (3) inability to remember aspects of the trauma
  (4) diminished interest or participation in significant activities
  (5) feelings of detachment or estrangement from others
  (6) limited range of emotions
  (7) sense of foreshortened future (not expecting a normal life or life span)

D. Increased Arousal Indicated by at Least Two of the Following:
  (1) difficulties falling or staying asleep
  (2) irritability or angry outbursts
  (3) difficulties concentrating
  (4) hypervigilance
  (5) exaggerated startle response

E. Symptoms Persist for Over 1 Month

F. Symptoms Cause Impairments in Social, Occupational or Other Important Areas of Functioning

G. Specify If:
  Acute: duration of symptoms less than 3 months
  Chronic: duration of symptoms more than 3 months
  With Delayed Onset: onset of symptoms is at least 6 months after traumatic event

4

POST TRAUMA PTSD RATES

In 1994 the American Psychiatric Association revised their DSM-III diagnostic manual into a new edition: *The Diagnostic and Statistical Manuel of Mental Disorders, Fourth Edition* (DSM-IV). Included in the fourth edition changes was a revised definition for Post Traumatic Stress Disorder. No longer was the direct experience of an "outside the range" trauma the only experience that could generate PTSD. The DSM-IV PTSD trauma definition was expanded to include indirect vicarious experience of a trauma: "the person experienced, *witnessed or was confronted with* an event or events that involve actual or threatened death or serious injury" [italics added]. There was also an addition for the first time of the individual's reaction to the trauma as a requirement for the diagnosis: "the person's response involved intense fear, helplessness, or horror."[9]

With the additional requirement of a specific emotional reaction to the trauma, the diagnostic manual shifts the focus from the severity of the trauma alone to an interaction between the trauma and the individual soldier's reaction to it. One helpful way of conceptualizing a soldier's reaction to combat stress is to consider his or her individual set of stress-coping skills. Some soldiers possess many such skills, such as emotional stability or physical vitality, and consequently they are able to handle combat stress relatively well; others may possess few such coping skills. It is like money stored in a bank account; some people are rich, others are poor. But no matter how rich, one cannot continually withdraw and withdraw from an account without eventually draining it to zero. Similarly, no matter how many adaptive resources a soldier possesses, he or she cannot continually draw and draw upon them to deal with chronic stress without eventually depleting them. If soldiers continually spend their energy and skills to cope with ongoing stressors, they will eventually go broke. For example, Vietnam Prisoners of War (POWs) were physically strong, mentally healthy officers; yet they were all broken by the repeated bouts of gruesome tortures inflicted on them by their brutal Vietnamese guards. Their capitulation due to severe torture became a source of intense guilt for the POWs.

Currently no one fully understands why one combat soldier develops PTSD and another does not. Psychological experts think the disorder is a result of the interaction of the soldier's personality and his or her war-related traumatic experiences. Using this concept, one may develop a simple interaction model that can generate predictions as to who will develop combat PTSD after a trauma. Some soldiers possess characteristics that help them adjust to the stress of combat; these individuals are called *good adapters*. A few of these assets are basic ones, such as intelligence and robust physical health, that help the soldier cope with many types of stressors. There are also specific assets that help the soldier adapt to combat stress. Specific coping assets for combat could be, for example, superior eye-hand coordination that enables the soldier to be an accurate shot, or having an extensive civilian history of tracking and hunting. *Poor adapters* are defined as soldiers who possess fewer basic and specific coping skills. Both types of adapters could possibly be exposed to various levels of combat. One may simply define only two levels of combat: *heavy combat,* defined as extremely dangerous fighting, such as making direct frontal assaults on enemy positions, and *light combat,* defined as less dangerous types of combat duty, such as occasional fighting from a reinforced guard bunker at a large war-zone military base.

This model interaction of soldier with level of combat generates predictions as to who will develop PTSD. The best-case scenario is the one that predicts the fewest cases of future PTSD. This scenario occurs when a good adapter is subjected to only light combat. The worst-case scenario is the one that predicts the most cases of future PTSD. This scenario occurs when a poor adapter is subjected to heavy combat. The other two adaptation-combat level combinations predict numbers of future PTSD cases that lie somewhere in between the two extremes (see figure 1).

Figure 1. Soldier X Combat Level Interaction Model

	Light Combat	*Heavy Combat*
Good Adapters	Best Case	
Poor Adapters		Worst Case

Scientific evidence supports the assertion that chronic severe stress may overwhelm the adaptive resources of soldiers, even strong ones. Sophisticated research performed by Dr. Robert Ursano at the U.S. Air Force's School of Aerospace medicine investigated the psychological adjustments of 253 Vietnam POWs. Six of the men had been part of the Air Force's astronaut program. As part of their training the pilots had been subjected to complete psychiatric evaluations, including a comprehensive battery of psychological tests. This earlier data enabled Dr. Ursano to compare the psychological health of the POWs before and after their tortuous captivity. His research team conducted comprehensive psychological testing and psychiatric evaluations of all the POWs upon their return to the United States. This type of pre and post trauma research design is considered by behavioral scientists as ideal. Dr. Ursano diagnosed psychiatric disturbances in these veterans even though they were intelligent, motivated, patriotic, emotionally stable and successful pilots: "Despite thorough evaluations showing no detectable psychiatric illnesses or predispositions, socially advantaged, mature, healthy adults previously selected for their psychological health developed diagnosable illnesses after their POW experiences."[10] The U.S. military establishment was so moved by Vietnam POW's horrific captivity and their psychiatric difficulties afterwards that they liberalized the captivity conduct rules for all subsequent POWs. Dr. Ursano's research results are potent argument against the critics who claim that veterans diagnosed with PTSD were unstable personalities before the military, consequently their psychiatric problems had little to do with their combat stressors.

Many soldiers' families worry that because their loved one was involved in war zone combat, he or she was traumatized by it. These families think that combat exposure inevitability leads to PTSD. Fortunately, scientific research has proven that their worries are unfounded. Large-scale epidemiological studies have repeatedly demonstrated that it is only a minority of combat soldiers who subsequently develop PTSD. Epidemiology is the study of the percentage of individuals in any particular group who are affected by a particular disease or disorder. The Research Triangle Institute's comprehensive five-year study of the epidemiology of PTSD in Vietnam veterans concluded that only 15 percent of the veterans who were exposed to Vietnam combat were diagnosed with PTSD.[11]

The RAND Corporation completed a large epidemiological study of Iraq and Afghanistan combat veterans in 2008. Their results indicated that 20 percent or one out of five service members returning from Mideast deployment reported symptoms of PTSD or major depression. Unfortunately only half of these soldiers sought treatment.[12] So simply being exposed to possibly fatal combat does not entirely explain the development of the post-trauma disorder. A majority of soldiers exposed to combat stress do not develop PTSD; only about one out of every five to seven combat soldiers do. Psychologists who are experts in PTSD think that combat does cause a mild to moderate stress response in just about every soldier; however, for the majority of combatants the effects are only temporary. It appears that most combat soldiers recover within roughly three months after a trauma. But somehow, in soldiers with PTSD the normal recovery from combat process is blocked. Thus PTSD can be classified as a disorder of nonrecovery. It is an abnormal reaction to combat stressors, because most soldiers do recover and do not develop the full set of clinical symptoms. Therefore Post Traumatic Stress Disorder cannot be defined as "a normal reaction to an abnormal situation," as some psychiatrists and veteran advocates claim.

5

FAMILY DIFFICULTIES

Combat-related Post Traumatic Stress Disorder is at times infectious. Family members may contract it from their PTSD veteran. Combat veterans need to understand that their psychological problems disrupt their family's harmony and balance, a process know as secondary traumatization. The spouses and children of PTSD veterans are at elevated risk for developing psychological problems themselves. The veteran's problems become the family's problems, especially for the spouses. Any member's serious illness would disrupt a family's equilibrium. For example, if a veteran's wife were diagnosed with breast cancer, it would disrupt the entire family. Family transmission of trauma effects has been documented with the Vietnam PTSD veteran. In 1992 the Research Triangle Institute interviewed a national representative sample of 1,200 Vietnam veterans and 376 of their spouses or co-resident partners. The study concluded that "Compared with families of male veterans without current PTSD, families of male veterans with current PTSD showed markedly elevated levels of severe and diffuse problems in marital and family adjustment, in parenting skills and in violent behaviors."[13]

There are a number of ways in which the veteran's PTSD difficulties can disrupt marital and family equilibrium. One common outcome is that the PTSD veteran's dramatic combat nightmares interfere with the spouse's sleep, causing him or her to experience insomnia. One Vietnam veteran's wife complained that she was having nightmares of Saigon. Of course she had never traveled overseas, but this case illustrates how a veteran's spouse can so identify with the veteran's problems that he or she imitates them. Many such couples have had to work out a compromise like sleeping in different beds or rooms. Another significant marital stress results from the PTSD veteran's social isolation. In general women tend to be more socially inclined than men. The combat PTSD veteran's wife will nearly always desire a more active social life than her husband. In couples' psychotherapy, the attempt would be made to have the PTSD veteran realize that if he wanted to stay married, he would have to work out some type of compromise with his wife's social needs. Fortunately when sufficiently motivated, it is often possible for couples to do so. For example, some couples worked out a successful compromise where they would go out to dinner on a regular schedule, but only to a familiar restaurant and only at a table where the veteran could sit with his back to a corner. This problem of the PTSD veteran's social isolation will be examined in more detail later in this volume.

The Research Triangle Institute study also concluded that violent behavior is a significant problem within the Vietnam combat PTSD veteran's family. Combat veterans act out their anger towards their spouses far too often. Wives or girlfriends would at times present at our clinic with bruises on their arms and faces. The abused wife would be referred to Hubbard House, which is a local shelter that provides protection and social services for battered women. Counselors there would work with the wife to establish a safe environment for her and her children, sometimes even having them move to their community safe house. Hubbard House female counselors would occasionally refer veterans to us for treatment of their violent behaviors. One of their counselors reported that they had found the combat veteran's abuse of his wife was not the type they usually encountered. Their usual wife abuser came from a disordered subculture where young males are taught by their older male relatives to beat their wives to demonstrate dominance. However, this was not the situation for violent PTSD veterans. Their spousal abuse appeared to be a product of the fact that the spouse happened to be *the closest target* for acting out their anger. This distinction in no way reduces the veteran's responsibility for his or her behavior or our condemnation of the violence. Anger management training is the priority issue in psychotherapy with the abusing veteran until his spouse reports improvements in the veteran's self-control. (See the chapter on anger and violence for details of anger control therapy.)

The Research Triangle Institute's final conclusion was that poor parenting skills were a major difficulty for combat PTSD veterans and their families. Frequently the children of the male PTSD veteran viewed their fathers as emotionally distant because his social isolation discouraged much interpersonal contact. He would not be there for them when they needed a father's advice on their own emotional issues. In these troubled families it was mainly the mother who provided guidance and discipline. Or the opposite sometimes occurred where the PTSD veteran would be a strict disciplinarian of the children, possibly enforcing Saturday room inspections with rigid punishment of minor transgressions. In effect the PTSD veteran would become a drill sergeant to his children. This harsh approach generated an intergenerational transmission of PTSD symptoms. The children, especially the boys, frequently modeled the father's behavior, becoming emotionally insensitive and physically violent.

However, the psychological interaction between veterans and their families is two directional. A family's reaction to post-war changes in a combat veteran's personality profoundly influences his or her civilian readjustment. There are a number of negative family attitudes and behaviors that impede the veteran's readjustment. A family's incomprehension of the severity of the veteran's problems leads to the expectation that the veteran can heal spontaneously within a short time period. Routinely families then become angry with the veteran when the expected quick healing does not occur. A lack of psychological support increases the severity of the veteran's PTSD symptoms, and mild symptoms may deteriorate into a full-blown Post Traumatic Stress Disorder. A few Vietnam PTSD veterans reported stories of their family's unthinking callousness, for example, how family members laughed at Fourth of July picnics when the veteran jumped wildly in response to firecrackers thrown nearby. The family accepted society's negative attitude towards victims. Rejection from his or her own family damages the PTSD veteran's psyche worse than any other rejection, be it coworkers, classmates or friends. This pain makes the combat veteran feel totally cut off from people. Family callousness can stimulate anger, further social withdrawal, and even severe depression. Disapproving families make the mistake of blaming the victim for his or her psychological problems. It is especially true today in the United States because there is no longer a draft; combat veterans are now all volunteers. Family members can vent their anger by demanding why the veteran joined the military in the first place. In contrast, if the combat veteran's family is emotionally comforting and supportive to their PTSD veteran, they will be enhancing recovery, reducing emotional distress and contributing to his or her positive self-esteem.

6

THE VETERAN'S SPOUSE

Considering that veterans, who fought in Iraq or Vietnam, have trouble comprehending their PTSD problems, imagine how difficult it is for spouses who have never been in the military or in combat to understand PTSD. Early attempts at educating spouses, including showing them Vietnam War movies, failed. They became easily bored with the films; the usual reaction was "oh well ... yawn ... another war movie." Combat and its stressors were simply too far removed from their own world of personal life experiences. But the wives could understand and relate to the stress of a sadly more familiar trauma: rape.

Ask a woman who has never been raped if she is afraid of being raped. She is likely to answer, "Yes ... a little" in a rather unemotional, matter-of-fact manner. She will report that she takes reasonable precautions to prevent it from happening; however, this fear is not intense nor does it dominate her life. Ask a woman who has been brutally raped if she is afraid of being raped again. She will probably answer "Yes!" in a highly charged, emotional manner. Indeed there is a high probability that she organizes and restricts her entire life around precautions to insure that she is never raped again. The fear of rape may dominate her life.

Imagine a possible history of a rape victim's traumatization; we will call her Ann. Imagine that Ann was badly beaten and raped after she had gone out to a nightclub. Afterwards she sought out an emergency room for treatment, and then the hospital called in the police. Police rape investigations have greatly improved, but all too often in the past the male police officer would interrogate the female rape victim with minimal compassion. Many men in our society do not easily empathize with victims, especially female victims. Besides gathering details of the crime, the police may have asked about the amount of alcohol Ann had consumed that night or if she had flirted with anyone. They may have inquired about why she was wearing such a short skirt or such a revealing blouse. Such questioning could easily deteriorate into an accusation, suggesting that Ann's behavior or outfit was the cause of the rape. What makes this type of interrogation especially damaging is that it occurs during the psychological shock the victim experiences after such a major trauma. Ann's sense of security is shattered; her confidence that she can safely function in her world has deteriorated. Ann's psychological disorientation leaves her completely vulnerable to such harsh questioning. The callous police interrogation could plant a seed of doubt in her mind. She may begin to question herself: "Yes ... why did I drink so much and why did I pick this outfit?" As if she wears an attractive outfit or flirts to deliberately attract a rapist—clearly an absurd idea. The self-doubt can lead to lowered self-esteem, growing possibly into depression and self-hatred, sometimes even to the extreme of suicidal thoughts.

No one would be surprised if Ann afterwards would not go out to nightclubs or limited all her social activities, staying at home as much as possible. Post-rape fears are like cancer cells; once established, they grow enormously and spread widely. If a young white man raped Ann, she will at first avoid young white males. But over time and without treatment, Ann's fears will likely spread to older Caucasian men and then to lighter-skinned Hispanics. It may then spread to all Hispanics and possibly to all men. We would not think Ann crazy if she became angry with younger men, which grew into a distrust and hostility towards all men. Her friends would not be shocked to learn that Ann has rape nightmares, or that she suffers from intrusive memories of the assault that automatically come into her mind. Her friends may learn that Ann feels vulnerable and insecure much of the time, feeling especially fearful at night. She may be so terrified that she comes to believe that she needs a weapon to protect herself.

Now what happens if our female rape victim had a boyfriend or a husband? Most women would understand when Ann has difficulties relating emotionally to him. If she is fortunate, he will be supportive and comforting. Otherwise a husband may also question Ann's behavior that awful night. His doubts will strain their relationship. He may consider her damaged or soiled somehow, which will, of course, increase her anger and depression. Unfortunately, relationship problems may occur even when the husband is genuinely compassionate. There will come a time when he will want to be physically close to her. Imagine yourself as Ann. In her mind, who does she see when her husband or boyfriend first approaches her sexually? Her post-trauma fears will force her to respond as if he were the rapist. She will become quite upset and distressed with his sexual overtures because they remind her of the rape. It is indeed a daunting challenge for rape victims to reestablish normal sexual relationships. Only those victims who are fortunate enough to have a loving and understanding husband or who receive effective psychological treatment, have the possibility of resuming a healthy adult sexual relationship.

If a PTSD veteran's wife can relate emotionally to how a rape victim like Ann feels, then she can learn to relate to what her husband is going through. His psychological reactions are quite similar to Ann's; he, too, will be deeply fearful, angry, socially inhibited and probably depressed. Possibly his readjustment will be more difficult because he had to endure multiple episodes of combat traumas. Post-traumatic stress is cumulative; repeated traumatic episodes make recovery more difficult. It is as if the combat PTSD veteran has been raped psychologically over and over again. He needs all the affection, understanding and support his wife can provide so that he may finally come home from his war.

Whenever marital problems surface during psychotherapy with a PTSD veteran, initial therapeutic efforts center upon improving the couple's communication. Many marital conflicts settle through more open and effective communication between the husband and wife. The couple can be taught that messages sent may be interfered with, like static on a radio signal, resulting in message distortion. Consequently the message received may not be the intended message. To guarantee that messages heard while arguing over marital conflicts are the intended ones, troubled partners can be taught the technique of repeating back to the partner whatever message they heard sent by their partner. Only after the other partner agrees that what was heard was exactly the message intended would the first partner then be allowed to respond with his or her own message. This technique sounds more complicated than it really is. After a little basic coaching this communication technique is quickly acquired. For practice, each of the partners can be told to write a list of up to seven of their most troublesome marital problems. Then the challenge is to compare the individual lists and have them agree upon a list of their top three marital problems. As they discuss their problems, they can be continually encouraged to apply the paraphrasing technique. Subsequent couples therapy sessions would be devoted to an analysis and the development of potential solutions of their mutual top three marital problems.

Most PTSD experts agree that one of the best things a combat PTSD veteran's partner can do to help their veteran is to learn about combat traumas and their effects on veterans. Psychotherapeutic efforts concentrate on educating the spouse. If the spouse's relationship predates the veteran's military service, one of the first tasks is developing realistic expectations. Spouses hope that the psychological treatment will resurrect the veteran's premilitary personality. These spouses need to be taught that the psychological damage of combat stress can be so devastating that a complete return to their veteran's pre-trauma personality is unlikely. But on the other hand, because of capable psychiatric and psychological treatment, spouses can look forward to a calmer veteran with fewer and less severe symptoms. Continued psychoeducational efforts focus upon developing the spouse's understanding of PTSD and its effects.

Because PTSD veterans prefer to live an isolated lifestyle, the couple's social life is usually problematic. Combat veterans possess a high tolerance for social isolation, but their spouses often do not. Spouses complained at our clinic that they had neither friends nor a social life. The veterans would not go shopping with their spouses or eat out at restaurants; many would not even accompany their spouses to family holiday gatherings. Given the epidemic of divorce among our Vietnam PTSD veterans, where two to three divorces is the norm, each married PTSD veteran is fortunate to have a spouse who tolerates her or him. A major treatment goal here is to have the veterans learn to accommodate to the social needs of their spouses. They had to understand that if they did not adjust, their marital relationship was in trouble. In couples' psychotherapy the search would be for an acceptable compromise: perhaps the veteran could attend family holiday parties for only an hour or so before leaving alone; perhaps the couple could agree to eat out occasionally at a corner table in a quiet restaurant where they both enjoyed the food.

To help strengthen marital relationships, our Vietnam-era combat PTSD psychotherapy groups would periodically celebrate partner appreciation sessions. First of all the wives or girlfriends would be invited to attend this special group therapy session. Each veteran had to agree to wear "the uniform of the day," which was his "Sunday best" dress clothing. The day before, we would clean and attractively decorate the group's meeting room. At a partner appreciation opening ceremony, all of the members were required to share with the group a few positive remarks about their wives or girlfriends, before presenting them with a bouquet of red roses. During the ensuing couple's group session, the discussions centered upon positive historical aspects of their relationships such as how the couples met and what exactly attracted them to each other. At the end of the session, all partook in a delicious catered meal. Many a teary wife expressed afterwards how thankful she was for the partner appreciation meeting, because this was the first social event she had shared with her husband in a long time.

7

PSYCHOTHERAPY

Combat PTSD veterans question, "Can my problem be fixed?" Thankfully there is reason for hope; healing from trauma can happen. The solution lies not in wishing that the problem would just fade away, but rather through directly addressing the problem with the correct psychological and psychiatric treatments. There are two major types of treatment for PTSD. The first is talk therapy, formally known as psychotherapy, which is the treatment of emotional problems through psychological techniques. The other primary treatment is psychopharmacology, which relies on medicines, ideally, prescribed by a psychiatrist. Both of these treatments and especially their combination have been shown through scientific research to be effective in reducing the symptoms of PTSD in combat veterans. Clinical treatment experience has proven that combat PTSD does not have to deteriorate into a permanently disabling condition. The troubled lives of PTSD veterans do not have to be the only lives they know. Veterans are not helpless victims; they are soldiers that can learn how to fight this new enemy. However, the PTSD veteran has to be motivated to change his life. The critical question is whether the PTSD veteran is ready to fight for his psychological health. Is he ready to confront his demons? If not now, when?

Psychotherapy is a partnership between a patient and therapist, dedicated to the work of analyzing the patient's psychological problems in order to discover solutions. The essence of psychotherapy is the development of a positive emotional relationship between the patient and the psychotherapist. Because PTSD is caused by an overwhelmingly horrible emotional experience, it is reasonable to expect that a positive emotional experience generated by this relationship could provide a powerful healing effect. This special healing relationship is called the therapeutic alliance, which supplies the corrective emotional experience. The therapeutic alliance is much like a teacher's partnership with a student. For real learning to occur, the teacher must strive to effectively communicate knowledge, but that work alone is not sufficient. The student too must be responsible for his or her share of the work. Students must pay attention in class, ask questions, complete homework assignments and study the material for actual learning to occur. The more effort the student applies to this work, the more knowledge he or she will acquire. This type of joint effort partnership is also required in psychotherapy. The psychotherapist must strive wholeheartedly at listening, analyzing and communicating, but that is not enough for the healing of the patient's emotional disorder. The psychotherapy patient must be responsible for his or her share of the hard work. Patients must be willing to reveal their inner world in order to wrestle with their emotional demons. Psychological recovery from combat traumas through psychotherapy is a difficult, but not impossible undertaking; like most important opportunities in life, the more energy one applies to the effort, the more benefits one receives.

A profitable way of thinking about strategies for coping with life's problems is to consider the game of poker. When playing five card draw poker, initially the dealer gives every player a five-card hand. Of course every poker player wants to be dealt a super hand, such as four aces, because winning is easy when possessing such a hand. But those types of excellent hands are rarely dealt out. Usually players receive average or weak hands on the initial deal. But even when dealt a weak hand, the smart poker player can still win the game. Winning at poker is not entirely based upon the hand initially dealt, but rather it depends more on how skillfully the player plays out all of the cards. The same strategy applies to the traumatized combat veterans. There is no doubt that destiny has dealt them a poor hand; there is no doubt that undergoing combat trauma is a bad deal. But that does not mean that veterans are condemned to a lifetime of emotional turmoil. Whether combat PTSD veterans can achieve the good life is not based entirely upon the bad deal of their trauma, but rather on how well they manage the burden. Mental health does not depend only on their trauma; it is more dependent upon how well the veteran fights the negative emotional aftereffects. Admitting psychological difficulties and then obtaining appropriate psychological and psychiatric treatment is the first step in playing a weak hand skillfully. Only then can the combat veteran win the goal of PTSD recovery.

For psychotherapy to succeed, the PTSD veteran must be ready to discuss traumatic memories with a therapist. However, this is difficult because thinking and talking about traumas is exactly what most veterans have been avoiding. Why? Because the ugly memories trigger a reexperiencing of the painful emotions connected to them. Many combat veterans simply try to forget about their traumatic experiences. But forgetting about them is impossible. How do you forget the unforgettable? One of the first duties of the psychotherapist is to motivate the combat veteran to commit to disclosing his or her traumatic memories. Ironically, the psychotherapist must convince the veteran to discuss the very issue he or she fears and does not want to talk about.

The only PTSD psychotherapeutic strategy that has any chance of succeeding is one that directly confronts the traumatic experiences. Avoiding, at all costs, talking or thinking about a trauma is like a young man running away from a bully. When a boy runs away from a bully, the boy becomes weaker and the bully becomes stronger. This happens because the only way the boy can mentally justify the decision to run is to overestimate the bully's power and to underestimate his own. Similarly, by running away from traumatic memories, combat veterans increase the power these memories have over their minds and weaken their ability to tame them. Yet more than one boy has learned the pivotal lesson that for whatever reason — he may have felt cornered with no other option or realized that he has friends that can help in the fight — when he turned and confronted the bully, the bully was not as tough as the boy had feared. Those who directly confront a bully weaken the bully and strengthen themselves. More than one PTSD veteran has learned through psychotherapy that by directly confronting painful traumatic memories, the power these memories held over his or her mind weakened. They began to realize, for example, that after the hard therapeutic work of confronting traumas, the frequency and severity of their nightmares had significantly decreased or that when reminded of traumas, their anxious arousal had decreased.

Combat PTSD veterans need to understand that they pay a steep price for their problem-avoidance strategy. Experts in trauma care agree that when a combat PTSD veteran avoids treatment, it makes the disorder worse, and therefore more difficult to treat. Post-trauma stress is like a cancerous tumor that, if not detected and treated early on, will spread throughout the body, making successful treatment unlikely. Recent research demonstrates that toxic stress chemicals such as cortisol increase and become more difficult to regulate when the PTSD disorder becomes chronic.[14] Chronic PTSD nearly guarantees that the veteran will continue to overreact to even mild stressors over his lifetime. A fender-bender car accident could result in a veteran becoming so angry that he or she loses control and physically assaults the other driver. It also guarantees that combat veterans' bad habits, which are their ineffective methods of dealing with their PTSD symptoms, will become stronger as they continue to use them. Psychologists use a concept called *habit strength*, which is defined as the strengthening of a habit the more frequently it is performed. Strengthening of a bad habit makes it harder to break. For example, a two-pack-a-day cigarette smoker will have a harder time quitting than a one-pack-a-day smoker because the former's smoking habit strength is stronger. The PTSD veteran's bad habits, such as social avoidance, irritability, and insomnia, become stronger as they continue to occur. Consequently these bad habits become harder to break. Furthermore, chronic PTSD allows veterans time to develop new bad habits, like feeling so fearful that they think they need to carry a weapon for protection. A combat veteran's attempt to avoid dealing with PTSD by simply trying to forget about it does not make the PTSD symptoms disappear. Continual trauma avoidance or denial only makes the PTSD symptoms worse.

Motivating the combat PTSD veteran to speak about unspeakable horrors is always a tough challenge. If PTSD veterans were taught to understand the true nature of medical treatments, their motivation for change may increase. In medicine the uncomfortable reality is that many effective treatments are painful, such as surgery or dentistry. The mature dental patient endures the short-term pain of a dental procedure for long-term gain. The patient realizes that the pain of an infected tooth is much worse than the pain of having a cavity filled. By not avoiding dentists his or her overall lifetime total pain level will be reduced. A similar argument applies to psychotherapy for combat PTSD. Troubled combat veterans must learn to tolerate the short-term discomfort of confronting traumatic memories in order to reduce the long-term emotional pain caused by these demons. They will be better able to do so if they possesses a realistic understanding of what happens in PTSD psychotherapy.

A PTSD veteran beginning psychotherapy should have realistic treatment expectations. Many want the traumatic memories to somehow disappear. These veterans were taught that the magic treatment to make these indelible memories simply disappear does not exist. Others expect to return to their prior personality, to that nice man or woman they were before they marched off to war. This too is an unrealistic expectation. Surviving intense combat traumas fundamentally changes soldiers. Veterans diagnosed with PTSD are not going to return to the innocent person they may have been before their war. However, their combat traumatization does not have to completely define their personality forever. Effective psychological and psychiatric treatment establishes emotional equilibrium within the PTSD veteran. Reduction of painful symptoms is both a meaningful and realistic treatment goal. Another therapeutic goal is to be able to recall traumatic memories without emotional distress. Effective treatments not only reduce damaging PTSD symptoms, but also enhance psychological growth, thus improving the veteran's overall quality of life. It will help the veteran establish an identity that is not stuck in the traumatic past. Psychological and psychiatric treatments free up psychic energy, allowing veterans to concentrate on their current life, building it into the quality one they deserve.

Some poorly informed psychotherapists tell their PTSD patients that they will get worse in psychotherapy before they get better. But that message is counterproductive; it is the wrong way to conceptualize the process of psychotherapeutic change. Initially the PTSD veteran may appear to become worse as negative emotions are expressed, but what is actually happening is that the negative emotions, which were hidden below the surface of consciousness, are now surfacing. It is only when these emotions are openly revealed that can they be directly confronted and dealt with. Wives have asked why the psychotherapist has to talk about Vietnam with their Vietnam War PTSD husbands. They have complained that after psychotherapeutic sessions their husbands would come home irritable and snappy. These wives were blaming their husband's bad mood on the PTSD psychotherapy. In response the wives were asked to imagine a situation in which a medical doctor is lancing a patient's infected boil. Just then an unsophisticated relative comes into the room and sees the putrid pus coming out of the boil. He yells at the doctor to stop. A kind physician would simply smile and explain to the naive relative that he or she was not causing the pus; it was always there hidden below the surface. The physician would explain that the healing process consisted of piercing the boil, which allowed the pus to drain out to the surface where it could be cleaned away. The same explanation applies to psychotherapy directed at traumatic events. Psychotherapy did not cause the veteran's negative emotions; they were always there festering below in the unconscious, connected to traumatic memories. The essence of the psychotherapeutic healing process forced trauma memories along with their accompanying negative emotions to surface in the Vietnam veteran's conscious mind, where he could learn to better cope with them.

Effective Psychotherapy

Once the combat PTSD veteran commits to psychological treatment, he or she is then faced with the dilemma of choosing the best one from the different types of psychotherapies available. Given the many therapeutic options, it is easy to become confused over which one would be the most helpful. Obviously expert guidance on this question would be useful. Fortunately the mental health community acknowledged this need and produced the required guidance. In 1999 the *Journal of Clinical Psychiatry* established the "Expert Consensus Guidelines for the Treatment of Posttraumatic Stress Disorder" by surveying worldwide over a 100 psychologists and psychiatrists who are considered PTSD experts. All of these renowned scholars were asked their expert opinions of what were the most effective psychotherapeutic techniques for the psychological treatment of PTSD. The aggregate consensus made up the guidelines. Their recommended psychotherapies for the treatment of adults suffering from PTSD were *cognitive therapy, exposure therapy,* and *anxiety management skills training.*

The PTSD experts were also asked about a newly developed therapy called *eye movement desensitization reprocessing* (EMDR) as well as the traditional therapies of *hypnotherapy* and *psychodynamic therapy,* which is a modern variation of Dr. Sigmund Freud's psychoanalytic therapy. The experts "did not rate these techniques highly for the treatment of PTSD."[15] Their poor ratings for these three therapies were influenced by the fact that the scientific research supporting these particular psychotherapies is weak. For example, in EMDR the therapist's two fingers are rhythmically moved across the patient's field of vision because, supposedly, the subsequent eye movements accelerate processing of emotional material. Yet controlled research studying this crucial EMDR technique found that a fixed eye position reduced PTSD symptoms in Vietnam veterans more than the standard eye movement technique.[16]

Exposure therapy is often referred to as reexposure therapy. Unlike EMDR, exposure psychotherapy is backed by considerable scientific research. Its defining characteristic is the confrontation of the PTSD veteran's symptomatic avoidance of trauma memories by directly addressing the veteran's traumatic experience. Upon creating a solidly supportive therapeutic relationship, the exposure therapist then encourages the patient to disclose traumatic history by applying various techniques. The therapist attempts to increase the patient's motivation through such efforts as the educational ones previously described. An exposure psychotherapist would also directly engage the powerful emotions released as the combat veteran discloses his or her traumas. Doing so is a delicate task requiring much psychotherapeutic skill because these painful emotions are the cause of the veteran's avoidance of trauma memories in the first place. Yet the exposure therapist insists that the veteran confront the painful memories fully because, as we have learned, avoiding them impedes healing and recovery.

The primary therapeutic focus in exposure therapy is on stimulating combat veterans into symbolically reliving their trauma. Many well-intentioned psychotherapists underestimate their veteran's ability to handle the negative emotions triggered by recalling trauma. Consequently these therapists avoid discussing the topic during psychotherapy with PTSD veterans. Such avoidance is a major therapeutic error because these psychotherapists are basically giving up on their traumatized patients. Their psychotherapy is inadequate because they are not applying what scientific research has demonstrated to be one of the most effective psychotherapeutic techniques for the treatment of PSTD: exposure therapy. Psychotherapists of this type may articulate apparent justifications for their trauma avoidance, but one can still question their motives. What commonly occurs is that these psychotherapists are shocked by the grisly tales combat PTSD veterans tell them. The veterans' accounts are so gruesome that they generate emotional discomfort within the psychotherapist. This emotional distress is so uncomfortable that the therapists refuse, either consciously or unconsciously, to hear any more of the stories that caused it. Psychotherapists of this type are placing their own emotional comfort ahead of their patients.

The best course of action for the informed combat veteran suffering from PTSD is to not engage in a psychotherapeutic relationship with trauma-avoidance psychotherapists. Early on in therapy the PTSD veteran should ask the psychotherapist if he or she plans on using a type of exposure approach. If the psychotherapist is not fully committed to exposure therapy, then the PTSD veteran would be well served to consider switching therapists. If already involved in psychotherapy, then the therapist should be asked, "Why aren't we talking about my horrible experiences in Vietnam?" or, "Why aren't we talking about the hell I went through in Iraq?" Do not accept the argument that the therapist is concerned mainly about the veteran's present day adjustment and does not want to dredge up the past. PTSD veterans and their families need to understand that the primary goal of exposure psychotherapy is help veterans get unstuck from their terrible pasts in order to be able again to freely and totally live in the present.

Within the category of exposure therapies there are a number of valuable subtypes. One subtype called *narrative therapy* consists of combat PTSD veterans simply telling and retelling their trauma story in their own words. Sometimes an exposure psychotherapist will ask the veteran to write out the traumatic tale in as much detail as possible. Completing a written account of a traumatic tale can be a potent therapeutic exercise in itself. The goal of both of these endeavors is for the PTSD veteran to better understand what exactly happened. This understanding occurs by the therapist aiding the veteran in elaborating and organizing his or her trauma memories. Through the psychotherapist's questions, the veteran will be able to better make sense of it. Through exposure therapy the veteran's trauma memories become less fragmented, eventually becoming more organized and integrated into his or her personal memory system. At first therapeutic progress will probably be slow and difficult, but with continued and concerted effort it may become easier. Although more helpful than nonexposure psychotherapies, basic narrative therapy is not highly recommended because it lacks a theoretical background defining exactly how to process the patient's narrative. It appears to be a rather common sense approach rather than one based on a scientific theory that would guide therapy by explaining exactly how to reorganize the disordered memories.

Another exposure therapy subtype is called *flooding* or sometimes termed *implosion therapy*. It is called flooding because patients are exposed to their anxiety-provoking memories at maximum intensity while escape is somehow prevented. The therapeutic goal is to have intense anxiety flood over the patient until he or she breaks on through, the so-called implosion, to a realization that the uncomfortable memories are no longer frightening. It is based upon a psychological learning theory, which argues that the flooding experience enables the patient to disconnect the previously learned connection between traumatic memories and fearful arousal. This decoupling of the fear from the memory is called extinction; the painful connection is extinguished. Flooding may be effective for some psychiatric patients, but it has serious limitations for combat PTSD veterans because it generates quite uncomfortable therapy sessions. It requires reliving trauma-based painful emotions at maximum intensity; accordingly it will not be helpful for the veteran who is unable to tolerate such high levels of emotional intensity. Therefore, flooding is not recommended for the PTSD veteran who is severely depressed or suicidal; nor is it appropriate for the angry or guilt-ridden veteran. Another limitation is that flooding requires a highly skilled psychotherapist who is able to continually monitor the veteran to ensure that the intense levels of generated emotionality do not trigger a severe flashback. Flooding psychotherapy for combat PTSD must be considered risky and should only be cautiously applied.

Why make PTSD psychotherapy deliberately more painful than it has to be? A preferable approach to extinguishing the combat veteran's acquired emotional responses to traumatic memories is a gradual one. A gradual approach towards trauma generates a reduced level of emotion, which allows the veteran a chance to adapt to small increases in fearful arousal without being overwhelmed. There exists a type of behavioral therapy called *systematic desensitization* that provides such a formal incremental exposure to fearful stimuli like traumatic memories. This desensitization technique of gradual exposure is flexible enough that it can be adapted for application with other psychotherapies. For example, the technique of gradual exposure could be blended into a primary therapeutic technique such as cognitive therapy. One of the therapeutic goals is to limit the combat PTSD veteran's in-session distressing emotional arousal. Extensive efforts need to be made to prepare the veteran psychologically for even gradual exposure therapy. It is a good idea that all exposure therapy sessions end with a relaxation training exercise to reduce anxious arousal. (See the chapter on fear and anxiety for a description of relaxation therapy.)

8

COGNITIVE PSYCHOTHERAPY

Cognitive therapy is a powerful scientifically based type of psychotherapy that is a major theoretical force in contemporary psychology and psychiatry. Cognition is a technical term for thinking, broadly defined as everything that goes on in the human brain. Thus cognitive therapy focuses upon all types of thinking processes, including expectations, assumptions, imagination, problem solving and language. The following section is an introduction to this type of psychological treatment; a complete explanation of cognitive therapy is beyond the scope of this volume. The interested reader who requires a fuller description is referred to Dr. David Burns' bestselling book, *Feeling Good: The New Mood Therapy* (revised edition, 1999) or to Dr. Aaron Beck's *Cognitive Therapy and the Emotional Disorders.* The authors are psychiatric experts who describe in a clear and detailed manner both the underlying theory and the application of this effective method of psychotherapy.

Not only is cognitive therapy one of the PTSD psychotherapies recommended by the Expert Consensus Guidelines, it is also recommended as a best practice by the International Society for Traumatic Stress Studies. In the year 2000 their task force reviewed extensively the scientific research in PTSD to establish their best practices guidelines. *Best practices* is the term used for medical treatments that scientific research demonstrates as producing the highest probably of beneficial treatment results. The Society's task force concluded that "Cognitive therapy has been effective in reducing post trauma symptoms and receives support" from well-designed scientific studies.[17] They classified cognitive therapy into a broader category called *cognitive-behavioral therapy* (CBT), a type of psychotherapy that includes anxiety management skills, such as relaxation training, along with its cognitive components.[18]

Cognitive psychotherapy is conceptually based upon the principle

33

that the personal meaning of an event, that is how one thinks about an event, determines one's emotional reaction to the event. In other words it is not what happens to you, but how you think about what happens to you, that will determine your feelings about the event. This basic concept has been understood by wise men since ancient times. Epictetus, a first-century Greek philosopher, taught that we are disturbed not by things themselves, but by the view we take of them.[19] The Buddha himself is quoted as saying: "We are what we think. All that we are arises with our thoughts. With our thoughts we make the world."[20] William Shakespeare wrote in his tragic play *Hamlet*, "for there is nothing either good or bad but thinking makes it so."[21]

Consider how difficult human emotions are to modify or control. Now consider how relatively easy it is to change what we think; we change our minds all the time. We change our minds, that is, how we think about things, as we experience new things as we age. The old veteran master sergeant thinks differently about combat and the military than when he or she was a private. We frequently change our minds due to receiving new information, such as when someone is educated. All would agree that college graduates who do not think differently than when they were freshmen have wasted their time and money. In fact there are numerous advantages associated with the flexibility of changing our minds. A buyer who has made a choice is foolish for not changing his or her mind after a salesman demonstrates a cheaper product with better features.

What is particularly appealing about cognitive therapy is that it primarily focuses upon the truly human, our ability to think and use language. Cognitive therapy is not one of the emotionally oriented psychotherapies that have been all too popular in the history of psychology. Their therapists only emphasize feelings, asking their patients "How do you feel? What do you feel?" or advising them to "Get in touch with your feelings." But humans are complex beings, comprised of much more than feelings. Emotions are part of our primitive evolutionary past; we share them with all mammals. Dogs can become angry, cats can be afraid, and monkeys have been known to appear sad. But no other animal, not even another advanced primate such as a chimpanzee, can replicate what we do each day, which is to reason and think symbolically. Evolutionarily advanced human brains enable us to read, to write, to solve math problems and to plan for our future. Humans are neither the strongest nor fastest animal, we can neither fly on our own nor swim underwater for hours; yet, humans dominate the earth and all other animals. Why? Humans dominate because we possess the most complex brain of any primate, enabling us to be the thinker, the most intelligent animal on earth.

Cognitive therapy states that our ability to think enables our brains to build an internalized model of the world. We actually organize brain cells, technically called neurons, into elaborate neural circuits that map the world in our minds. But to be useful, our map must fit the territory. If you only have a map of Miami and you are trying to travel across Jacksonville, your map is of little use. If you attempt to follow your map, it is quite likely that you will become lost. In other words, humans build a model of the world in their minds. Consider an aeronautical engineer designing a new airplane. First he or she will build a model of the plane because it is easier and cheaper than building the full-scale plane. The model allows the engineer to efficiently run various wind tunnel tests. However, it is imperative that the model be an exact replica of the actual plane. If the model's wings extend at a different angle than those on the real plane, then any tests run with the model will lead to inaccurate predictions of how the actual plane will handle in the wind. Like the engineer's model, it is crucial that our internal map of the world exactly replicates the actual world. If our internal maps are inaccurate, then we will have trouble finding our way or making accurate predictions in the real world.

Another useful way of conceptualizing the human ability to think and model the world is to consider thinking as a form of self-talk. Realize that self-talk, our internalized monologue, is not a symptom of mental instability. Psychotically deranged people may appear to be talking to themselves when they verbalize out loud; however, they are not actually talking to themselves. What they are really doing most of the time is conversing with their hallucinations. Normal people do talk to themselves much of the time, in many different situations and in many different forms. For example a person may self-coach, when performing a difficult task for the first time, by saying "Be careful. This is the tricky part," either out loud or internally. In this case the self-talk aids in focusing his or her attention upon the complex task. Or a person may self-question as a type of memory aid: "What did she want me to buy? Oh yes, a gallon of milk." Most people do not realize how often they use private speech or how powerful it is in influencing their feelings and behaviors. The fundamental question is not do you talk to yourself, but rather. what exactly do you say.

To further explain the theory, cognitive therapists employ what is known as the A-B-C analysis. Dr. Albert Ellis, a pioneering psychologist in the field, first developed this cogent explanation. The "A" stands for the event or the situation a person is in; the "B" stands for the person's evaluation or interpretation of the event; the "C" stands for the person's emotional reaction to the event. When people express statements such as "What you are doing makes me so angry," they imply that an external event, that is the other person's annoying behavior, directly caused his emotional reaction, the anger. The implication is that event A directly leads to the angry emotion C (see figure 2).

Figure 2

```
>--------------------------------------->
A              B           C
Event          to          Emotion
               OR
Action         to          Consequence
```

But this idea of an immediate and direct connection between an event and its emotional consequence is inaccurate. Exactly how is it possible that anyone can make another person angry? What anger buttons does one push on the other person? What strings does one pull? How does anyone directly alter another person's brain chemistry to trigger anger? Simply put, they cannot. What really happens is that someone else's belligerent behavior ("A") is interpreted by the person as threatening ("B"), which then triggers the person's anger ("C") (see figure 3).

Figure 3

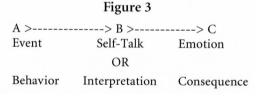

```
A >--------------> B >------------> C
Event          Self-Talk        Emotion
                  OR
Behavior     Interpretation     Consequence
```

Confusion over what really took place occurs because our evaluations of events are usually done automatically in our unconscious. Our powerful brains perform these types of threat evaluations so quickly and efficiently that we are not fully aware of the process. The meaning one gives to an event occurs below conscious awareness, which makes it appear on the surface that event "A" is directly causing emotion "C." In reality, "B," which is the person's interpretation of the suspicious behavior or event, is causing the emotional reaction "C." Therefore, for combat veterans to change their negative emotions associated with an event, they must learn how to change their interpretation or beliefs about the event. That is exactly what cognitive therapy provides: a method that teaches veterans how to question, in order to change, their automatic evaluation of events. Cognitive therapy is not simply the power of positive thinking, as some have argued, but rather the superior power of applying reality-based, accurate thinking.

Cognitive therapy for combat PTSD is a form of psychotherapy that emphasizes how combat veterans think about their traumatic experience. Thinking here is broadly defined; it includes all the processes that go on at the highest levels within the veteran's brain, such as memory recall, imaginative fantasies, problems solving, and self-talk. The technical term that categorizes all these advanced brain functions is *cognitions*. As previously explained, cognitive therapy is based upon the theory that what happens to an individual is not as critical for producing emotional reactions as how that individual thinks about the event. The basic principle is that cognitions determine emotions. Frequently patients at our clinic would demonstrate this very idea. For example, a male veteran complained that his wife of many years was divorcing him. When asked about his reaction, he answered that he was upset because "I am afraid of being lonely with no one to talk to. It is sad eating alone and anyway I don't even know how to cook. This divorce is a total disaster." Soon afterwards, another veteran reported during a psychotherapy session that his wife of many years was divorcing him. When asked about his reaction, he answered, "This divorce is great. Now I will be able to drink and eat whatever I want, whenever I want. Now I can chase after pretty women. I can't wait until the witch leaves." Here were two veterans going through the same situation, but having totally different emotional reactions to the experience. Why were there two different emotional reactions associated with the same event? They had different emotions because each of the veterans thought about and thus interpreted their divorces differently.

Clinical application of the principles of cognitive therapy would have me helping PTSD veterans examine their thinking to discover which conclusions were unrealistic or incorrect. The therapeutic goal was to teach veterans how to challenge and restructure their dysfunctional thoughts that were causing negative emotions. Because combat traumatization drastically impacts a veteran's thinking, with experience I learned to modify and extend the standard present-day orientation of cognitive therapy to include an examination of the veteran's thinking about the trauma itself. We would explore memories of traumatic experiences to discover distorted beliefs concerning the trauma and its emotional aftereffects. This modification of the usual present-day orientation of cognitive therapy proved to be quite effective. A renowned psychologist has developed a similar version of cognitive therapy, which also emphasizes an examination of cognitions associated with past traumas. Dr. Patricia Resick, at the Center for Trauma Recovery in St. Louis, modified standard cognitive therapy for rape victims to include attention being paid to the interpretations of the victim's trauma. She calls her approach *cognitive processing therapy* (CPT). She advises her patients to access their memories of the rape in order to discover any dysfunctional beliefs they may have about themselves or the event. Dr. Resick's modification was intriguing enough to attract psychologists working out of the Department of Veteran's Affairs (the VA) National Center for Post Traumatic Stress Disorder. They have successfully applied cognitive processing therapy to traumatized combat veterans.[22]

Cognitively oriented treatment of combat PTSD provides veterans with the set of psychological tools required to fix their problem. It appeared as if combat PTSD veterans' problem-solving tool box held only one tool before — a hammer, which symbolizes the one behavior that is most commonly used to cope with PTSD: avoidance. If all veterans have in their problem-solving toolbox is a hammer, then every problem looks like a nail. Possessing only one tool severely limits the number and types of problems that veterans can solve. But if veterans add more tools, such as a saw, a drill and pliers to his toolbox, then they dramatically increase their ability to fix and build. This is an excellent way of conceptualizing how cognitive therapy works; the cognitive psychotherapist teaches PTSD veterans the questioning and reasoning skills that are the tools they need to limit their trauma-based symptoms. Or in military terminology, the cognitive therapist provides veterans with the necessary weapons required for winning the battle against their PTSD disorder.

9

Shattered Assumptions

An especially devastating effect of combat traumas on a soldier is the clash between the traumatic experience and the soldier's previous pre-combat beliefs about the world. Ronnie Janoff-Bulman, in her book entitled *Shattered Assumptions: Towards a New Psychology of Trauma*, elegantly describes this clash. In it she argues that within the core of our cognitive internal world, we hold basic views of our external world and of ourselves. Her basic views concept is exactly the same idea that has been previously described as our internal model of the world. The soldier may not be aware of his basic views because they are held deep in the unconscious mind. Yet these internal world models possess the power to organize our experiences and to influence our behaviors. Dr. Janoff-Bulman contends, " in general we believe in a benevolent, safe world, rather than a malevolent, hostile one.... The world in this context is an abstract conception that refers to both people and events. When we assume that other people are benevolent, we believe that they are good, kind, helpful and caring."[23] She argues that we think this way because most of us are fortunate enough to live in a circumscribed, secure world where, generally, people are good. Dr. Janoff-Bulamn argues that extreme traumas such as brutal rapes shatter the basic security beliefs of the victims.

My own naive protective belief before Vietnam was that the war would be a fair fight, kind of like a deadly football game. Our team of uniformed soldiers with our weapons would be on one side of the battlefield and the uniformed enemies with their rifles would be on the other side. We would then attack each other, and may the best soldier win. Having played high school and college football provided me with some confidence that I could handle this type of battle. I was not at all prepared for the grotesque realities of guerrilla war, specifically its plain-clothed enemies, women soldiers, surprise ambushes, enemy suicide squads, booby traps and most horribly, children exploited as offensive weapons. These repulsive horrors quickly destroyed all my previous protective notions of a fair fight or any belief that there could be honor and glory in war.

Currently American soldiers in the Mideast, like most young Americans, go into battle feeling the strength of their vitality, believing that they are invulnerable, perhaps even immortal. Yes, they realize people die in war, but that only applies to someone else. They know that they are young, strong and tough; so they conclude, "Death won't touch me." But after their first taste of combat, after seeing their comrades, just as tough and strong, blown apart or brutally maimed, their illusion of personal invulnerability is shattered. They are forced to deal with the new harsh reality that they are in fact not invulnerable, that they too could possibly be killed. They develop a solemn resolve to do everything they can to prevent that tragic outcome. The combat soldier's previous internal model of life and the world is shattered; prior beliefs and assumptions do not fit into this new gruesome reality. But what replaces it?

Sadly, a soldier's broken world model is not replaced with wisdom; instead it is replaced with flawed and distorted dysfunctional beliefs. Too often the replacement conclusions are the products of a primitive all-or-none thinking of the following type of flawed logic: "The entire world is a dangerous war zone.... I need to be afraid, to be very afraid ... I can't trust anyone ... I must always be alert for danger." These all-or-nothing beliefs are inaccurate generalizations that reflect veterans' incomplete and superficial processing of their combat traumas. Trying to survive in a war zone allows soldiers little time or opportunity to seriously reflect upon what has happened to them. Usually little has been learned from battle and little has been integrated into a more comprehensive world model or life philosophy. This is especially true for unfortunate soldiers who are overwhelmed by the horror of deadly combat. Traumatized soldiers' emotional and intellectual growth is blocked; they become stuck in their trauma. The traumatic combat experience may become the organizing principle of their entire lives, the central point around which everything else in life revolves. Even their self-identity may become defined by it: they are nothing but trauma survivors. This self-image defined by victimhood is commonly infused with a sense of incompetency, helplessness and guilt.

There are a few major themes that underlie most post-combat, trauma-distorted beliefs. A devastating one results from dealing with a lethal enemy out to kill, a confrontation that destroys the combatant's previous trust in others; it is replaced by a chronic, isolating mistrust. For example, in Vietnam a young American infantry soldier at first learned to mistrust Vietnamese civilians because he could not distinguish them from the peasant-garbed Vietcong enemy. Then he learned to mistrust the allied soldiers of South Vietnam (they were know as ARVNs, an acronym for Army of the Republic of Vietnam) that he was fighting beside because their widespread incompetence and cowardliness could be just as deadly to him as the Vietcong. This suspicious mistrust frequently spread like a cancer, growing to include the soldier's leaders, the noncommissioned sergeants and commissioned officers, because their incompetence or cowardliness could also prove fatal. Any previously comforting trust in authorities was replaced by a hostile antiauthority resentment. As the pathological distrust grew, it even engulfed the other soldiers in his unit, whose mistakes under fire could cause his death. Finally the mistrust grew to include most American politicians, whom the soldier came to realize had been blatantly lying to the American people about the realities of the Vietnam War.

The Vietnam soldier's suspicious mistrust of others becomes so entrenched in his mind that it does not simply stop upon returning home to the United States. His pathological attitude continues and invariably leads to social conflicts with wives, children, coworkers and friends. The combat veteran suffering from PTSD would rather err on the side of mistrusting someone who is a nonthreat rather than trusting someone who turns out to be an enemy. It is kind of like training a guard dog for a home. Most owners would rather the dog makes the mistake of not allowing a friend to enter than allowing in a dangerous intruder. PTSD combat veterans have learned to keep their guard up at all times because the penalty for not doing so had proven to be disastrous.

The resulting suspicion and mistrust is a common but always challenging obstacle in psychotherapy with combat PTSD veterans. It interferes with the building of a positive therapeutic relationship, which is the foundation of effective psychotherapy. The skilled cognitive therapist strives to establish the therapeutic alliance, which then allows the therapist to challenge the veteran's generalized mistrust. The logic supporting the therapist's questions is something like the following: "Mistrusting most people or everyone may seem like the safe and smart thing to do, but you pay a steep price. You miss the help you may need from someone you can trust. For example, even though many ARVNs did not deserve your trust, by mistrusting them all, you missed the ones who were courageous enough to fight at your side and possibly save your life. It is the same with civilians here in the world; you may need the help of the trustworthy ones. Now this does not mean that you should trust everyone; that approach is just as foolish as not trusting anyone. The crucial question is: whom can you trust and how do you know you can trust them?"

Hopefully such reasoning would stimulate a therapeutic discussion of how the veteran could tell if someone was worthy of trust. One practical philosophy of interpersonal trust is predicated on the rule that trust is demonstrated by how people behave, not through what they say. Therefore, one must observe what others do and not be fooled by what they claim. This philosophy recognizes that there are many glib con artists who manipulate people with their fine words. These frauds generally say what they think people want to hear. For example, one of these con men may repeatedly claim that he loves his aging mother, but close observation of his behavior indicates that he rarely visits or even phones his mother. Another man may rarely verbalize his love for his mother, but observations prove that he phones his mother regularly and visits her often. Which man truly loves his mother? Of course the answer is the man who acts on his love, not the one who merely claims that he loves his mother.

An effective cognitive psychotherapist strives to discover exactly what meaning each PTSD veteran gives to his or her combat trauma. In other words, what are PTSD veterans telling themselves about their traumatic experience? The cognitive therapist examines veterans' trauma-based thinking, searching for unrealistic distortions that should be challenged. For example, a common post-trauma, distorted belief held by many PTSD veterans is "My world is fearfully dangerous and I am weak and powerless to deal with it." How would a cognitive therapist confront this mistaken belief, this sense of incompetence? The therapist would begin by encouraging PTSD veterans to gradually expose themselves to their anxiety-producing traumatic memories. Let us assume that a veteran had been caught in an enemy rocket barrage. The cognitive therapist would ask the patient to relive the experience in his or her imagination and share what emotion is evoked. Possibly the veteran would disclose shame at being so terrified by the rocket barrage that he or she lost bladder control. After acknowledging the veteran's courage at recalling such a terrifying memory, his therapist would empathize with the intense terror. The therapist would then explain that the veteran's negative self-image has been learned; therefore, new learning could change it. The therapist then sets the stage for this therapeutic learning by providing the necessary challenges to the veteran's damaged self-beliefs: "Who would not feel afraid when you are nothing more than a mere target for deadly rockets, a sitting duck on a vast shooting range? Could it be that your shame is understandable; that it is a type of frustration that anyone would feel in that horrible situation where the reality is that you could not effectively fight back? Could it be that in that terrifying attack you learned what it is like to be totally helpless?"

Another powerful strategy that cognitive psychotherapists routinely apply is to help PTSD veterans develop a new perspective about their trauma, one that is broader and more encompassing. The goal is to develop a more accurate view that will enable the veteran to cope better with the civilian world. In our rocket attack example, the skilled cognitive psychotherapist would then ask if, perhaps, there were other attacks when the veteran was not so overwhelmed with fear. Possibly the veteran recalled a time when he was assigned to a mortar team and they were attacked again by enemy rockets. During this attack the veteran had helped work the mortar tube to return fire. The cognitive therapist would comment on how it appears that when the veteran had a weapon such as the mortar to fight back with, he was not as terrified. If the veteran does accept the accuracy of this observation, his cognitive therapist might then venture the comment that the veteran's current self-image of being helpless is perhaps due to his belief that he does not have the needed weapons to fight in the civilian world. If the veteran can agree with this insight, he is well on his way to learning how cognitive psychotherapy provides these necessary weapons. He is learning how to question and rethink his unhealthy and distorted beliefs along with the accompanying negative feelings. Veterans learn in therapy that it is possible to change the personal meaning of a traumatic experience by reexamining and rethinking it, and therefore reducing the accompanying emotional pain.

After such a therapeutically powerful session, it is necessary that the psychotherapist warn the PTSD veteran that there is a chance that he will have a combat nightmare that night. However, the veteran needs to understand that the nightmare does not mean he has relapsed or regressed. What the nightmare really means is that the veteran has breeched his prior defenses of always avoiding traumatic memories. The frightening memories are arising easier to his conscious mind, as they must for him to reexamine and rethink them in order to recover from his PTSD. Any residual physiological arousal triggered by such an emotional session can be reduced through the application of behavioral techniques such as relaxation exercises and deep diaphragmatic breathing exercises. (See the chapter on fear and anxiety for details of relaxation training.)

The flawed assumptions that PTSD combat veterans have learned to believe after trauma are numerous. Below are listed a few common examples of these misconceptions, followed by brief cognitively oriented therapeutic comments.

(1) *I should have seen that enemy shooter.* The use of the wording "should have" indicates that the PTSD veteran is interpreting his or her combat trauma behavior as something to feel guilty about. An effective cognitive therapy tactic is to encourage the veteran to change this "should have" interpretation to "would have" or "could have," to discover where the more accurate assessment may lead. For example: "I *would have* seen the shooter ... if I had not been so tired ... or if my wounds had not hurt so much ... or if I had not be so distracted by the noisy explosions."

(2) *I need to be alert and as on guard as I was in Nam.* This assertion is an example of hypervigilance, one of the defining symptoms of PTSD. It reflects an irrational belief that the veteran's neighborhood or barrio is as dangerous as a war zone. It is what cognitive psychologists classify as catastrophic thinking, which is a type of reasoning that makes a bigger deal out of a situation than what is realistically called for. It is figuratively making a mountain out of a molehill. Even if there were people being attacked or shot in the veteran's community, it is highly unlikely that they were hurt by heavy machine guns or mortars as they would have been if it were an actual war zone. PTSD veterans who believe in this distortion need to learn how to make distinctions within their typically overinflated and inaccurate conclusions. For example, veterans can recognize that their neighborhood is moderately dangerous, yet far less dangerous than a true war zone. (See the chapter on anger and violence for more information on the perception of danger.)

(3) *It is better to avoid problems than to face them directly.* This dysfunctional belief produces the characteristic PTSD avoidance symptom. As previously explained, avoiding a problem is like running away from a bully: the problem grows stronger as the veteran become weaker. It is only by turning to face their PTSD problems do veterans have any chance of defeating them.

(4) *What happened in your past mainly determines how you behave today.* Unfortunately this irrational belief is widely held, even by people who do not suffer from PTSD. Of course we are influenced by our past

experiences, but we need not be forever chained to them. Cognitive psychotherapy will help break those chains. It is difficult to do so, but difficult does not mean impossible, especially with the right type of help from a skilled cognitive psychotherapist.

(5) *I can't get emotionally attached to anyone because they may be dead tomorrow.* This conclusion is an overgeneralization; in effect the veteran is predicting that his or her future life will be exactly like the past. The concept illogically equates the dangerousness of a war zone with the limited risk level of civilian life. Because veterans suffered the painful loss of soldier friends during the war does not mean that they will inevitably lose every civilian they feel any affection for. Targeting war-related grief would be a primary therapeutic goal in cognitive therapy with this combat veteran. (See the chapter on depression and suicide for more information on coping with grief.)

(6) *I can't handle this stress."* Or *"I can't handle_____(fill in the blank).* If veterans brainwash themselves with this type of negative self-talk, then their conclusion could be accurate, because this distortion will prevent them from even attempting to make a reasonable effort to deal with the stress. It reflects the PTSD veteran's overly developed sense of personal incompetency. A more realistic and therapeutic self-coaching message would be "I haven't learned how to handle this stress yet." Cognitive psychotherapy will teach the PTSD veteran the thinking skills needed to cope with stress.

(7) *I feel afraid, so I must be in a dangerous situation.* This type of illogical thinking is called *emotional reasoning,* which is when a person uses primitive emotions to judge reality. But emotions, a primitive product of our evolutionary heritage that we share with all mammals, are a poor judge of reality. When combat veterans feel afraid, it does not necessarily mean that they are in a hazardous situation. Because of all their wartime practice at being afraid, combat veterans become too good of an expert at triggering fear. PTSD combat veterans need to learn in psychotherapy how to use their intelligence to judge the true threat potential of a situation rather than relying only on feelings. (See the chapter on anger and violence for a detailed explanation of emotional reasoning.)

(8) *Why me? Why is God punishing me?* This complaint is based on the illogical assumption that bad things should not happen to good people.

Yet negative events do occur randomly, thus they may happen even to people who do not deserve them. In cognitive therapy the response would be something like: "Why not you? Do you have a special contract with God? Or do you own some special kind of insurance? The reality is that you are just as likely as anyone else to have bad things happen." This response may seem harsh, but it is designed to shock veterans, to disrupt their mental equilibrium, increasing the possibility that they would be willing to rethink their irrational and dysfunctional belief.

A prime example of tough-minded, adaptive thinking and reasoning that can help overcome nightmarish situations is that of U.S. Army Major Rhonda Cornum, who was captured during the first Gulf War. When asked about her reaction to the sexual abuse she endured as a POW in the hands of Iraqi soldiers, the courageous Major Cornum answered,

> I asked myself, "Is it going to prevent me from getting out of here? Is there a risk of death attached to it? Is it permanently disabling? Is it permanently disfiguring? Lastly, is it excruciating?" If it doesn't fit one of those five categories, then it isn't important.[24]

There is much to be admired in this heroic woman's thinking. Major Cornum was able to use her superior intelligence to survive a potentially fatal captivity with an undefeated spirit. Her reasoning demonstrates the power of the cognitive approach to coping with potentially traumatic situations. She is truly a psychological warrior.

One of the final goals of cognitive psychotherapy with PTSD combat veterans is to teach them how to challenge any of their potentially pathological beliefs on their own. This task is accomplished by systematically demonstrating how to logically challenge their own dysfunctional beliefs through the following types of questioning:

(1) What is the concrete factual evidence for and against this belief?

(2) What is another plausible way of interpreting this situation? Is there a broader, more encompassing perspective that could be adaptively applied to this situation?

(3) What is statistically the most likely outcome of this situation?

(4) What are the advantages of modifying the belief? What are the disadvantages of continuing to hold on to the belief?

(5) What realistic advice would you give to a loved one who held this belief?

After guidance by the psychotherapist and repeated practice, PTSD veterans learn how to creatively restructure their unhealthy beliefs into more adaptive and reasonable ones. Initially, therapeutic progress may be slow, but with motivation and continued effort, the pace of learning accelerates. Through the skillful application of cognitive psychotherapy, combat veterans suffering from PTSD eventually learn how to change their own minds, how not to be stuck in their trauma, and how to define themselves as someone other than a trauma victim.

10

FEAR AND ANXIETY

Today in America when patients are concerned about physical symptoms, they visit a medical doctor for diagnosis and treatment. But when they suffer from psychological symptoms, they have to visit an entirely different type of healer, either a psychiatrist or psychologist, for diagnosis and treatment. The existence of these two different types of physicians is one example of Western medicine's long tradition of considering the mind and the body as separate entities.

This cultural tradition, known as dualism, goes back at least to seventeenth-century Europe, when the powerful Catholic Church was acknowledged as owning the arena of the human mind, which they called the soul. The French scientist and mathematician René Descartes received permission from the church to study human cadavers only because he claimed that he could study the human body as a type of machine that follows the laws of physics. He argued that the human soul, in contrast, did not follow the laws of physics; therefore, it is separate from the body. Descartes thus began our tradition of dualism, the separation of mind from the body, which became permanently entrenched in Western medicine and science. The problem, however, is that *this concept of dualism is totally inaccurate.* The human being is a unity. The human mind and body are not two separate entities; they are totally interconnected in one being. Our bodies are composed of multiple organs; one of these physical organs, the brain, directly controls all the others. The vast majority of today's psychologists, neuroscientists, and psychiatrists define the mind as the functioning outputs of the brain. Without a brain there exists no mind.

Given this biological unity, it is not surprising that within every human disorder there exists a mind/body connection. Physical problems routinely cause psychological difficulties. An avid skier who breaks her leg in a fall will feel sad or even depressed over her inability to pursue the pleasures of her sport. Similarly, a person with a purely psychological problem will experience physical manifestations of that disorder. For example a grieving widow will suffer from sleep difficulties and lack of energy. Understanding this mind/body connection enables one to recognize that what many consider to be the purely psychological problem of PTSD emerges directly from a biological foundation. In the following section, the central biological bases of PTSD — the physical manifestations of fear and anxiety — are explored.

Post Traumatic Stress Disorder is in essence a disorder of fear and a disorder of memory. Combat veterans suffering from PTSD have survived an overwhelmingly fearful experience, the memory of which continues to haunt them. Post Traumatic Stress Disorder occurs because the PTSD veteran has had too much practice at being afraid. Psychologists call this type of chronic fear an anxiety disorder. The difference between fear and anxiety has to do with the source of the threat. With fear the threat source is external to the person: for example, a rapist with a gun. An outside observer would be able to see the threat, thus would understand why the victim was exhibiting such signs of fear as screaming. On the other hand, in anxiety the source of the fear is internal; it is being produced inside the person. An observer would not see a threat and consequently would have trouble understanding why the anxious person was exhibiting such fear behaviors as sweating, rapid breathing or tensing of muscles. The soldier's heart racing in a deadly firefight is a display of fear. A few days later, when the soldier remembers the firefight with a racing heart, he or she will be exhibiting a symptom of anxiety. The memory of the firefight is producing signs of anxiety, a kind of internalized fear.

Post Traumatic Stress Disorder should not be categorized as a psychological condition only. It is also a biologically based disorder caused by the body's stress response system continually being overstimulated. Veterans' original fear in combat triggers their stress-response system, which is their body's method of coping with the life-threatening situation by generating increased physical energy. When combat PTSD veterans symbolically relive their traumatic experiences, be it by an intrusive memory or by a combat nightmare, they immediately become anxious and feel the accompanying biological symptoms, such as an accelerated heart rate, increased respiration and muscle tension. In biology when animals energize themselves in the face of threatening predators, it is said that the animal has triggered the *fight or flight response*. A cat arching its back and snarling when confronted by a large dog is exhibiting the fight or flight response.

Some animals, such as the bear, will fight when threatened, while others, such as the rabbit, will flee when threatened. Animals that are camouflaged will freeze in total paralysis when threatened because most predators' eyes are especially sensitive to movement. Freezing makes the animal almost invisible to the predator. Dr. Joseph LeDoux contends that "Actually, a better term might be the freeze-flight-fight response, since freezing often occurs first."[25]

In contrast human beings possess a larger repertoire of options when threatened; we may freeze, fight, flee, or flow, depending upon the particular circumstances. Because of the human's response flexibility, rather than the *fight or flight response*, this basic human survival reflex is more accurately labeled as the *emergency alarm response*. This alarm reaction exists in modern humans because of our evolutionary history. We are the direct descendants of only those prehistoric ancestors who possessed the ability to quickly generate massive amounts of physical energy when attacked by predators. Those prehistoric humans who could not generate the emergency energy to fight harder or run faster when attacked died. Consequently these unfortunate ones were not available to breed offspring.

The next section explores the biology of the emergency alarm response in detail. Even though the explanations will be technical at times, it is important for combat PTSD veterans to understand how their fears and anxieties are biologically based. Understanding how a flashback is an acquired biological fear response rather than a sign of psychological weakness or mental illness can help PTSD veterans feel more normal and be less self-critical.

In combat, soldiers at first perceive the enemy with their sensory organs and the brain areas that respond to sensation. These higher level zones of the brain then send this sensory information to a central, older region of the brain, known as the *limbic system*, where threat information is emotionally processed. Within the limbic system there is a small almond shaped organ known as the *amygdala*, which upon receiving threat information immediately triggers the body's freeze-fight-flee response. The amygdala starts the emergency alarm response within a fraction of a second, which is nature's way of recognizing that failing to quickly react to serious threat is risky. In a jungle ambush a few seconds' delay in reaction time can mean the difference between the soldier's survival or not.

The launched emergency alarm response is a massive energizing of the body's systems to deal with the threat. The alarm will increase the soldier's heart rate and cause blood to be directed away from the skin and stomach to the brain and muscles, where the most energy will be required. Body functions nonessential for immediate survival, such as digestion and reproduction, are shut down. The alarm causes the lungs to breathe in more oxygen, resulting in as much as a fivefold increase in oxygenated blood delivered to the muscles and brain. During the alarm, blood pressure is increased as blood vessels are constricted. Through its nerve connections, the alerted amygdala stimulates the adrenal glands to flood the soldier's blood stream with adrenaline, a natural chemical that increases and then sustains the soldier's muscle strength and reaction speed. The emergency alarm increases blood sugar levels and causes the release of blood clotting chemicals into the bloodstream to prevent excessive bleeding. The threatened soldier's senses become more efficient: for example, the pupils will dilate, making vision sharper. The soldier will be able to see, hear and even smell better — changes that have obvious survival advantages. Because of the emergency alarm response the entire body is brought to a state of high energy, ready to meet the soldier's needs to fight or flee the enemy. The bottom line is that our body's response to deadly threats is highly adaptable, helping soldiers survive in the jungles of Vietnam and in the deserts of Iraq.

Unfortunately the emergency alarm response can also be maladaptive, when it incorrectly responds to nondangerous stimuli as if they were dangerous threats, in effect generating a false alarm. To understand how an emergency alarm could turn out to be a false alarm, one needs to understand what psychologists call the *conditioned emotional response* (CRE). First of all consider the typical psychological experiment of fear learning in rats. A caged rat is presented with an auditory tone a second before it is mildly shocked on its leg. The rat's fear response to pain causes it to freeze in place. After a few pairings of the tone with the electrical shock, the rat will begin to freeze in fear at the tone, even when it is not followed by a shock. The rat has learned what psychologists call a conditioned response; its natural alarm to painful shocks has been enlarged to include being triggered by the sound of a tone.

Conditioned fear responses are one of the most essential types of learning; nature uses it to ensure survival of animals in unpredictable and dangerous environments. Through such emotion-based learning the animal develops an emotional memory. The tone becomes a warning signal, which the rat can then use to initiate efforts to avoid the painful shock. But the rat will not only use sounds; it will try to learn and remember as much as possible about the painful situation. The rat will thus use its vision or any sensory experience possible to learn what is associated with the danger, be it a cat or an electric shock. If the rat can learn and recall the associated stimuli as danger signals, it can react vigorously to them the next time they are encountered. When it uses its conditioned response learning by reacting to the sounds and smells associated with a cat, the rat significantly increases its chances of avoiding danger and surviving.

Fear conditioning in animals is so similar to what happens to soldiers in battle that the eminent psychiatrist Dr. Lawrence Kolb thinks that PTSD could be due to conditioned emotional responses.[26] Consider an enemy ambush in Iraq or Vietnam. The mortality threat of the ambush causes the fear and biological arousal of the emergency alarm response. Veterans report that during an ambush they noticed many specific details surrounding the battle. A wide variety of associated stimuli have the potential of becoming triggers for the soldier's subsequent emergency alarm responses. This learned association occurs because, as mentioned, all our senses become sharper when the emergency alarm reaction is triggered, not only vision but also hearing and smell. It is obviously to the soldier's advantage to learn all he or she can about things that precede and predict an ambush, so as to avoid them in the future. Experienced combat soldiers in Vietnam learned to sniff the air, searching for the enemy's odor. These men were utilizing every possible source of information they could about their enemy in order to survive. On the opposite side, North Vietnamese soldiers would try to smell American soldiers, who often used deodorants and aftershave lotions, odors that were in sharp contrast to the natural jungle smells.

An animal's ability to remember sensory stimuli connected to threats as a warning signal is such a survival advantage that nature makes it happen quickly. Many times all it takes is a one-time pairing between the associated sensory stimulus and the mortal danger for the learning connection to be established. The ultimate reward of survival firmly strengthens this critical connection. Remember this evolutionary fact: those prehistoric humans who could not quickly learn to associate sensory warning signals with dangerous predators, such as bears or wolves, were easily killed by these creatures. Our ancestors were those who were able to quickly learn this vital survival connection.

Unfortunately this conditioned fear learning may cause problems for combat veterans when they return home from the war zone. A wide variety of stimulus cues in the civilian environment may trigger the uncomfortable emergency alarm reaction, even though in reality there is no danger. Their previous fear conditioning triggers false alarms. Vietnam PTSD veterans complained of reliving crippling fears that upon later analysis were triggered by exposure to such diverse stimuli as uncooked meat in a grocery counter, police in uniforms, unexpected encounters with Vietnamese, jungle foliage, fireworks or firecrackers, and the odor of hot diesel fuel or Vietnamese spices. Another complication for combat veterans is the human brain's ability to establish associations that are much more abstract than any animal's simple connection of a sound to a dangerous threat. A few Vietnam combat veterans came to the clinic complaining of feeling periodically anxious, but for no obvious reason. Their lives seemed to be reasonably successful, with decent jobs and a good family. After extensive review of their military histories we concluded that these men were suffering from a type of anniversary emotional response. Their anxiety occurred only near the anniversary of some traumatic combat event such as the death of a friend. These veterans had learned to connect their emergency alarm reactions to such abstract concepts as anniversary dates or seasons of the year.

The resulting emergency alarm responses triggered by these diverse cues are false alarms, automatically causing the PTSD veteran the uncomfortable feeling of intense fear when there is no real threat. This type of problem is inherent in all alarm systems. For example, home alarm systems that have sophisticated motion detectors set to a sensitive level to react to burglars could be triggered by such nonthreats as small animals running or tree limbs swaying in the wind. Nevertheless most homeowners would rather have a false alarm triggered by an animal than miss an alarm when a burglar breaks into their homes. The ultimate deciding factor for the motion detector's setting is the relative costs of a true emergency versus a false alarm. A neighbor's home alarm system produced many false alarms, each of which caused the police to be summoned. The irritated police stated that they would start charging for every false alarm they responded to. After that threat, the neighbor set the home alarm system to a less sensitive setting. PTSD veterans could pay a high price in terms of serious medical problems, such as hypertension or cardiac disease, if their emergency alarm response is repeatedly triggered by false alarms.

It is difficult enough to control fear when the PTSD veteran knows the environmental cue that stimulates a false alarm. Control is immensely more difficult if a cue triggers a false alarm unconsciously, outside of the veteran's conscious awareness. To fully comprehend this idea it is necessary to understand that the human mind encompasses much more than what we are consciously aware of at any time. The human unconscious mind is defined as the deeper layers of the mind, where information is stored and processed outside of our awareness. For example, it is where memories are stored when we are not thinking of them; it is where we search when we are trying to recall someone's name. It is also where dreams and nightmares are generated. The existence of the human unconscious is universally accepted in both psychology and psychiatry. Of special interest is the fact that humans can learn things with their unconscious mind and not be aware of what they have learned. For example, the elaborate muscular coordination necessary for such advanced motor skills as swimming or diving is learned without direct knowledge of which specific muscles are required for performing the skill. Thus the skill is acquired outside of the conscious mind, within the athlete's unconscious mind.

Conditioned fear learning can also occur unconsciously. Scientific experiments conducted by the eminent American psychologist Joseph Le Deux have firmly established that fear conditioning can occur in humans even though the triggering cues never reach conscious awareness.[27] An especially powerful type of emergency alarm cue is odor—for example, the smell of diesel fuel. Combat veterans report that the most potent of the olfactory cues is the stench of dead and decaying bodies, the "smell of death." "Doc, I will never forget that ugly smell, the smell of death ... I can't get it out of my mind." Odors may trigger fear because the olfactory nerve connects directly into the limbic system and the amygdala, which are the areas of the brain that are directly involved in emotional learning. Dr. J. Douglas Bremner writes: "Smells, therefore, have a direct pathway to the primitive fear responses, without conscious control. They represent a direct link to primitive emotional responses to threat."[28]

This phenomenon of unconscious fear conditioning explains why many PTSD combat veterans reexperience traumatic fears without knowing what exactly is triggering their emotional discomfort. The odor of rotting meat in a supermarket could trigger an emergency alarm reaction even thought combat veterans do not realize their combat traumas have taught them to connect the putrid odor with threatening danger. Although they are actually safe, they respond to the false alarm as if it were a real alarm. This lack of understanding may have devastating effects on veterans, who consequently cannot predict nor control their fears. Generally this ignorance leads them to the mental distortion of emotional reasoning: "I feel afraid, so I must be in a dangerous situation." This illogic causes social suspicion and further withdrawal. It routinely leads PTSD veterans into developing another fear, the depressing one that they are losing their minds. All combat PTSD veterans who feel afraid without knowing the reason why need to be reassured that they are not losing their minds nor going crazy, but that their combat traumatization caused a true physical change within, the rewiring of primitive fear circuits in the brain that now signal false alarms.

Unfortunately, as many PTSD veterans have come to realize, unconscious fear conditioning can endure for years. A bit of my own history will illustrate the unconscious nature and durability of this type of fear learning. After returning from the Vietnam War, I enrolled at Indiana University to pursue my graduate studies in clinical psychology. Frequently my new wife and I would walk hand-in-hand, enjoying the many social events held on the university campus. At dinner one night my wife asked why I had painfully squeezed her hand that day as we were walking through the campus crowds. Worried and puzzled, I apologized immediately, but I had no idea what she was talking about. Attempting to make some sense of this problem, I asked my wife to alert me immediately if I ever squeezed her hand too hard again. She agreed and subsequently alerted me when it happened. Now alerted, I began to pay closer attention to what was going on in the crowds as we passed through. By paying better attention to the people around us at the moment of her complaints, I eventually recognized that I was squeezing her hand only when I saw an Asian in the crowd. My tensing of my hand muscles was part of an automatic fear reaction to a visual cue, the almond-shaped eyes of an Asian, which the Vietnam War had conditioned me to associate with mortal danger. It is necessary to reemphasize that my fear reaction occurred completely outside of my conscious awareness. Fortunately I was able to extinguish this conditioned fear response with self-directed reexposure therapy. I became friends with an American graduate student who was of Japanese descent. Socializing with him broke the connection in me between people who looked Asian and danger. Yet my other conditioned fears from the Vietnam War have persisted over the years. Every Fourth of July I suffer a barely controllable, automatic fear reaction whenever I hear the loud crashing of fireworks or the unexpected bang of randomly thrown firecrackers.

To summarize, parts of the combat PTSD veteran's brain have been rewired into a rigid and unconsciously automatic system for the identification and processing of threat information. The veteran's brain circuits have been set at a sensitive level that frequently results in false alarms, which occur when an emergency alarm response is triggered by an essentially safe cue.

11

PSYCHOLOGICAL TREATMENTS FOR FEAR

A reasonable question is what can be done about the combat veteran's fears and anxieties that are the core symptom of PTSD? The recommended psychological treatments consist of two stages: first focusing on the body and then on the mind. The first stage works primarily upon the hyperarousal that is the biological core of the PTSD fear response. This treatment consists mainly of teaching veterans deep breathing and relaxation exercises to reduce their muscular tension and to calm overall arousal. The second stage is advanced cognitive psychotherapy that is designed to help PTSD veterans recalibrate the brain circuits that trigger their emergency alarm responses or, better yet, to learn how to extinguish their learned fear reactions.

The following section examines the biology of the combat veteran's emergency alarm response. A major function of this alarm is to stimulate the part of the central nervous system that controls the body's automatic functions; it is called the sympathetic branch of the autonomic nervous system (ANS). The sympathetic sub-system's job is to stimulate other biological systems that are so critical for survival that they occur without conscious control — systems that control basic functions such as heart rate, blood pressure and respiration. Most of our biological systems work in a balanced manner; for example, to move our forearms upwards towards our shoulders, we have to tense our biceps while relaxing our triceps. In contrast, to straighten out our forearms, we have to tense our triceps and relax our biceps. Similarly the human ANS also contains a sub-system that balances out the sympathetic branch's arousal; it is called the parasympathetic branch of the ANS. Its job is to lower the physiological markers of hyperarousal. For example, the parasympathetic system lowers heart rate, lowers blood pressure, and decreases respiration rate.

Dr. Herbert Benson, an associate professor at Harvard Medical School, calls this parasympathetic effect the *relaxation response.* "While the fight-or-flight response is associated with the over activity of the sympathetic nervous system, there is another response that leads to quieting of the same nervous system.... This is the Relaxation Response, an opposite, involuntary response that causes a reduction in the activity of the sympathetic nervous system."[29] The relaxation response brings our bodies down from the medically dangerous high gear of sympathetic arousal to a lower gear.

Consider driving a brand new Cadillac. It could be mechanically sound, but if you only drove the car in high gear, you would damage it. At first you would only notice the car's poor performance; but if you continued to stress it by driving in high gear, eventually the car would break down mechanically. The human body is a significantly more complicated system than any car, but like a Cadillac, if it is run mainly in the high gear of hyperarousal, eventually there will be a biological breakdown. Eventually that individual will begin to suffer from such medical problems as high blood pressure or even heart disease. To counter his or her emergency alarm hyperarousal, the PTSD veteran needs to learn how to trigger the balancing relaxation response, which will then reduce muscle tension, heart rate, and blood pressure. Luckily the veteran does not have to concentrate on each specific physiological change, but rather, he or she simply triggers the relaxation response, then automatically all the specific reductions will fall into place.

Relaxation Techniques

The easiest way for hyperaroused PTSD veterans to trigger the parasympathetic relaxation response is for them to control their breathing, making sure that it is slow diaphragmatic breathing. Breath control is the best way to exert influence on the usually uncontrollable autonomic nervous system because breathing is both automatic and voluntary. Most of the time our breathing is involuntary. We do not have to think about it; it happens automatically even when we sleep. But because it is such a critical life-sustaining function, nature has endowed us with a fail-safe back-up system for breathing. Humans possess the ability to overrule its usually automatic functioning and place respiration under voluntary control. We all can force ourselves to breathe faster or slower as we wish. This breath control ability has obvious survival value in special emergency situations, such as holding our breath when swimming underwater or when exposed to poisonous gases. In contrast humans cannot easily control their heart rates, which is basically an automatic function. But because our lungs are closely connected to our hearts in what is known as the cardiovascular system, as we slow down our respiration rate, we will also be automatically slowing down our heart rates.

People think that the best way to increase the flow of oxygen to their bodies is to quickly inhale and exhale by pumping their shoulders and expanding their chest. But they are wrong; really effective breathing is not simply getting air in and out of their mouth and lungs. Effective breathing only occurs when an individual transfers oxygen from the numerous tiny air sacs in the lungs to the capillaries of blood that surround these air sacs. It is only after it is transferred to the blood that oxygen can then flow to the entire body. This transfer of oxygen is not instantaneous; it takes a second or two for the oxygen to bridge the gap between the lung's air sacs and capillaries. Consequently the most effective and efficient type of breathing is slow, deep breathing that allows time for the oxygen to transfer. The deepest type of breathing happens when people use their diaphragm. The diaphragm is a sheet of smooth muscle that divides the midsection in half, separating the lungs and chest from the stomach area. It can be profitably thought of as the bottom of the lungs. When a person inhales deeply, the diaphragm flexes downward, pushing the stomach area out as well as expanding the lungs. In contrast to shallow chest and shoulder breathing, diaphragmatic breathing forces a person to employ the bottom two lobes of the lungs. It is the most efficient manner of breathing, delivering a full measure of oxygenated blood to the rest of the body with each breath. As the diaphragm stretches, it sends an "all is well" signal to the brain, which in turn signals the entire body to slow down and relax. Slow diaphragmatic breathing is as effective a tranquilizer as the medication Valium in relaxing the body; moreover it takes effect faster without any negative side effects.

To learn diaphragmatic breathing, practice by placing one hand on your belly and the other hand on your chest. As you inhale deeply, try to push the hand on your stomach out and at the same time keep the other hand on your chest stable. The goal is to have the chest remain still as the belly expands into what looks like a beer belly, and then contracts. This approach is sometimes called belly-breathing, but that term is not technically correct because you are not really using the stomach or belly. What you are really doing is expanding and contracting your internal diaphragm, which forces the stomach to move in and out. As you slow the rate of your diaphragmatic breathing down, you will become more and more relaxed. The ideal way to practice this technique is to do it in a quiet space for about ten to fifteen minutes. The more frequent the practice sessions, the faster hyperaroused PTSD veterans will learn how to use breathing to drop their body's arousal from high gear tension to a low gear relaxation.

Another recommended self-control technique for achieving a state of calmness is a muscle-based relaxing approach known as progressive relaxation. It was developed in the 1930s by a Harvard physiologist and physician named Edmund Jacobson. By that time he had already invented the electromyograph (EMG) for measuring a muscle's tension level. In his book *Progressive Relaxation* Dr. Jacobson writes that many of his chronic patients were not aware of how high their muscular tension levels were.[30] These patients had lived with high levels of muscle tension for so long that they had learned to tolerate it. Apparently they adapted to their elevated tension levels; it had become accepted as normal. Dr. Jacobson learned that in order for these patients to become aware of muscular tension he had to have them deliberately tense their muscles beyond their usual norms. He would then teach them to deliberately relax their tense muscles. This tensing and relaxing of specific muscle groups is the basis for his progressive relaxation technique. By tensing muscles beyond their normal levels, the patient becomes aware of how uncomfortable muscular tension can be. These higher levels of tension make it easier for the patient to learn the crucial skill of letting go of tension. The higher the muscle tension, the easier it is to reduce it. Dr. Jacobson would have his anxious patients practice the skills of tensing and relaxing skeletal muscles sequentially from their toes up to their scalps. His practice sessions were long and frequent. However, present day psychologists have shortened his training program considerably, yet are still able to successfully teach the healthy skill of relaxation. The best way to learn progressive relaxation is under the individual guidance of a trained therapist.

Another way to achieving total body relaxation without tranquilizers is the application of a technique called *autogenic training*. It was developed by Dr. Johannes Schultz in the 1930s and popularized by Dr. Wolfgang Luthe in the 1960s.[31] Its effectiveness comes from its reliance on self-instructions to train the body to relax. With this emphasis on self-talk, autogenic training is similar to cognitive therapy. Dr. Schultz originally studied hypnosis; eventually he wondered if he could obtain the same types of results without employing hypnotism's mysterious trappings. He asked patients what they felt while in the hypnotic trance state; their most frequent answer was that they felt heavy and warm. Dr. Schultz did indeed discover that his patients, while lying down in a dark quiet environment, could release tension and achieve a deep calm feeling by telling themselves quietly that their various muscles were heavy and warm. Their feelings of relaxation comfort do make biological sense; when muscles are no longer fighting gravity, they feel heavy and when the smooth muscled walls of blood vessels relax, the vessels expand, resulting in increased circulation and therefore a sensation of heat.

Dr. Schultz insisted on passive concentration as a central autogenic technique. He recommended that tense patients not force the calming physical changes in a driven manner, but rather simply allow them to happen. It is like falling asleep; a person cannot force himself to fall asleep. The more one tries to force sleep, the worse the situation becomes. One can only fall asleep by letting go of the effort, by confidently allowing the natural process of sleep to occur. Dr. Schultz also developed patient self-directed instructions that focused upon other biological systems and functions: for example, "My breath is calm and effortless," "My solar plexus is warm," "My forehead is cool," and "I am calm." These standardized self-instructions form the core of autogenic training. After the training the patient is able to voluntarily shift his body from an uncomfortable state of stressed arousal to a comfortable state of calm relaxation.

A skilled relaxation therapist would advise PTSD veterans to mix and match any or all of these standard relaxation techniques in order to develop a technique that is personalized for maximum effectiveness. Many combat PTSD veterans reported considerable benefit after adapting relaxation training into their lives. Scientific research in the field supports their claims: "The evidence that relaxation training has useful properties, particularly in alleviating symptoms of stress, has been substantial. Those (techniques) with the most empirical documentation to date have been: progressive relaxation; autogenic training."[32]

Physical Exercise

There is a behavioral method for reducing the damage of PTSD stress. It is regular physical exercise, a dynamic health generator that is underappreciated and, therefore, underutilized. As one example of the mind/body connection, a strong body makes for a strong mind. A combat veteran with mental problems can help reduce their effects by strengthening his or her body. Regular physical exercise is a powerful prescription for mental and physical health because it burns up the stress chemicals overproduced in PTSD veterans. Physical exercise decreases elevated heart rates and elevated blood pressure, two of the most dangerous physical symptoms associated with PTSD. Scientists now know that regular physical activity increases our brain's capacity to produce its own "happy" chemicals, which are internal opium-like compounds, know as endorphins, that improve mood. "Emerging new research in animals and humans suggests that physical exercise may boost brain function, improve mood, and increase learning." Mice who exercised were found to have almost double the number of brain cells in the brain regions responsible for memory and learning when compared to inactive mice.[33] PTSD veterans who experience elevated arousal, amnesia or depression can look forward to a reduction in these troubling symptoms if they exercise regularly. A physician colleague declared once that if he were able to put all the health benefits that exercise provides for us in pill form, he could sell the pill for five hundred dollars.

I recommend that veterans consult their primary care physician before attempting any exercise routine. After doctor approval, veterans need to find some type of physical activity that they find enjoyable or at least pleasant. There are so many different ways to exercise that it is inconceivable that a veteran could not find an enjoyable one. Veterans could run, bicycle, swim, row, lift weights, or engage in a popular sport like basketball, baseball or tennis. One increasingly popular activity is yoga, which strengthens the body as well as calming the mind. Exercising to counter PTSD stress does not have to be expensive nor require elaborate equipment. One of the best ways to start becoming more physically active is simply to take a walk. Walking is not just another form of exercise; it is the human form of locomotion. We are the monkeys that were made to walk. Human hips and legs are specially designed for walking on two feet. No matter how heavy, old or out of shape, veterans should always try to walk. There is a saying in medicine: "If you don't use it, you will lose it." When individuals can no longer walk to the bathroom or the kitchen, their loss of independence is severe enough to become a nursing problem. The probability increases significantly that they will end up being cared for in a nursing home — not an agreeable outcome. Army and Marine veterans may remember how fit they became during basic or boot camp because of those regular twenty-mile training marches. One air-borne veteran still hiked ten miles every day; of course he was exceptionally fit and appeared much younger looking than his actual age. About ten percent of the inactive veterans to whom we recommended walking took heed of the advice. Invariably each one of these now active veterans reported back that they felt better physically and mentally because of their new habit of regularly walking.

Cognitive Therapy

Once PTSD veterans have learned how to lower their fear-induced physical arousal, they are then ready to learn the advanced skill of recognizing and then challenging the cues that trigger their emergency alarm reaction. The best way to achieve this goal is by applying the principles of cognitive therapy.

Let us review the basic concepts of the human emergency alarm response. Evolution supplied us with a method of responding to imminent mortal danger by energizing our bodies to deal with the threat. Whether it be fleeing the beast or fighting the enemy, our emergency alarm reaction is an adaptable response, aiding us in overcoming the danger by providing the needed energy for fleeing or fighting. But this adaptive response can deteriorate into a maladaptive one under certain circumstances. It becomes maladaptive when the threat is not a short-term one, but rather a long-term threat. When the danger is prolonged, such as repeated bouts of combat during a short period of time, the emergency response is continually turned on, causing chronic elevations of the combatant's physiologic reactions, such as heart rate and blood pressure. Another negative result is that the stress chemicals that are released by the emergency alarm continue to circulate throughout the battle. Chronic elevations of stress chemicals in the soldier's body could cause such serious problems as a weakening of the immune system. If the threat arousal exists long enough, the soldier's adaptive energy becomes depleted, setting the stage for possibly developing PTSD. As explained, the emergency alarm response also becomes dysfunctional when it triggers frequent false alarms.

If a PTSD veteran overreacts alarmingly to a policeman as if the officer were an enemy soldier, it is apparent that the veteran needs to learn how to reset the reaction setting of his or her emergency alarm system. The theory and application of cognitive psychotherapy can provide significant help. Remember that the foundation of cognitive therapy is the principle that thinking determines how one feels emotionally. This concept is not recognized as important by most people because much of their evaluations and interpretations happen so quickly that they are not aware of them. Dr. Aaron Beck, a pioneer in the field, calls this type of rapid unconscious analysis *automatic thoughts*. Imagine yourself walking down a street in your community. Suddenly you spot a man who has owed you money for months and has not returned your calls. You immediately become angry and start running towards him. However, as you approach him you realize that the man is just someone who resembles your debtor. Immediately you calm down and stop running. Your emotions during this situation changed significantly based upon your evaluation of the oncoming man's identity. Because people are not aware of these automatic calculations, they only notice the emotional result, be it fear or anger. Much of the power of cognitive therapy comes from its emphasis on learning how to become more aware of these rapid and unconscious evaluations. The primary goal of the cognitive psychotherapist is to help patients become more conscious of their automatic thinking and then to challenge any dysfunctional automatic conclusions.

These basic cognitive therapy concepts can be applied to a reexamination of one of the most common irrational conclusions of anxious PTSD veterans. It is called emotional reasoning; the basic assumption is that if someone feels something strongly, then it must be true. For example, if we feel afraid, then we must be in a dangerous situation. A correlation to this incorrect belief is that if we feel an intense level of fear, then the situation must be that much more dangerous and threatening. The incorrect reasoning is that the stronger the feeling, the more accurate it must be in judging reality. However, the problem is that feelings are primitive; we share them with other mammals. Dogs can be angry, horses can be afraid and chimpanzees can even be sad; but no other animal, not even other primates, can do what humans do regularly. No other animal is able to think rationally, plan for the future or solve math problems. Feelings are so primitive that they cannot accurately reflect reality; emotions lack the complexity required to inform us as to the way things really are. Consequently emotions cannot provide a solid foundation upon which to build our mental models of reality. People used to feel quite strongly that the world was flat and that the sun revolved around the earth. Yet they were completely wrong. A young woman may feel perfectly safe in a lit parking garage, not realizing that there is a rapist hiding behind the next car. Her feelings of safety inaccurately reflect the dangerous reality of the situation. Many a young man has paid the ultimate price for his feelings of invulnerability and safety while driving his automobile at an exceedingly high rate of speed.

In contrast, the problem for combat PTSD veterans is that they feel afraid even when they are in a safe and secure environment. The source of this dysfunctional emotionality lies in the veteran's many conditioned fear responses. Recall how PTSD veterans have learned through their combat traumas to associate initially neutral stimuli with threat and danger. Subsequent future exposure to these "safe" stimuli can trigger the veteran's emergency alarm response. The sound of a truck backfiring may cause a PTSD veteran to hyperstartle.

A skilled cognitive psychotherapist would educate the combat veteran who is suffering from intense fears and anxiety about his or her conditioned fear responses. He would explore the veteran's combat history to discover their source and then explore how they are currently interfering in the veteran's civilian life. The therapist also teaches the veteran about emotional reasoning and how to discount emotions as evidence of reality. When fearful, veterans need to understand that the existence of this emotion does not provide valid evidence that they are in a dangerous situation. The cognitive therapist teaches the veteran how to recognize and consider reality-based factors as valid indicators of danger. PTSD veterans need to learn how to use reality-based rethinking to help them control uncomfortable fears. In biological terms the feelings of fear generated by conditioning within the brain's older limbic system need to be inhibited by signals literally coming down from the most advanced sections of the human brain, the cerebral cortex. In neuroscience this ability of evolutionarily newer, more advanced sections of the brain to regulate its older, primitive parts is called top-down control. The brain's ability to do so can be quite dramatic.

To understand the human brain's potential for top-down control, consider the following thought experiment. How would you react if you accidentally touched a red-hot stove? Of course you would not have to think about what to do, but rather you would reflexively pull back your hand. But what if, at that exact second, a known serial killer put a gun to your head, warning you convincingly that if you moved your hand from the stove, he would kill you? Could you keep your hand on the stove even with the intense burning pain? Yes, you could because top-down control would enable you to do so. Of course you would feel the fear and pain, but your reaction would be controlled when the advanced regions of your brain identified the bigger issues of life-or-death survival in the face of this threat. At the same time that your emergency alarm response is being triggered by your limbic system, the deadly threat information is also being sent to the cerebral cortex, which is the brain's most recently evolved region. The cerebral cortex is the layer of the brain where the most complex information processing occurs. In the cerebral cortex, real-time threat information is extensively processed and combined with memory data. It is where humans weigh evidence, consider various options and make decisions. The final decision is then sent back down to older regions of the brain such as the limbic system, where it modulates and refines the body's response to any particular emergency.

Teaching PTSD veterans to change their automatic assessments of danger is a difficult therapeutic goal to reach. But difficult does not mean impossible. If the PTSD veteran's motivation is high, then there is a reasonable chance that this goal can be achieved. Hypervigilance, a defining symptom of PTSD, keeps veterans constantly on the alert, scanning their environment for any and all potential threats. The cognitive therapist strives to teach PTSD veterans to at least consider that their initial impression of a threat could possibly be in error, a false alarm. Veterans need to learn that their first massive emotional reaction to a perceived threat is probably overblown. After Sherlock Holmes reached his initial theory of who committed a crime, he then searched for confirming or nonconfirming evidence. He did not consider his first theory as a fact, but only as a reasonable first guess that had to be confirmed or denied depending upon whatever further evidence he could discover. Sherlock Holmes' evidence-based approach to crime detection made him the successful literary detective he was. A clever scientist will also use an evidence-based approach to research. The scientist first of all develops an initial hypothesis, a first best guess, concerning a phenomenon based upon extensive reading. Then the scientist performs an experiment to test the hypothesis. If the experiment produces negative evidence with results that are different than predicted, the scientist will change the hypothesis to reflect the new evidence. The scientist will change his or her mind based upon evidence. In the manner of the good detective Sherlock Holmes or the intelligent research scientist, PTSD veterans need to learn in therapy how to take a deep breath and reconsider their initial impression that there exists a dangerous threat. They must learn to routinely ask themselves: What is the evidence? What are the facts that I am basing my emotional reaction upon?

One reliable source of reality-based evidence, if available, is the veteran's family. Alarmed PTSD veterans could consider if their spouse and children are also frightened by the situation. Or are family members more alarmed about their veteran's behavior? Such crucial evidence is always important. If family members are not available, the veteran could consider the emotional reactions of nearby strangers. How are they reacting to the situation? Is the veteran the only person who appears to be reacting with fear in the situation? Another question a veteran should ask when feeling threatened: Is there another way of viewing the situation? Veterans may generate alternative interpretations by enlarging their perspective somehow, looking at the bigger picture. Many times this may mean changing their primary focus from themselves to include all others in the situation. The critical question is always "What is the evidence?" combined with a willingness not to be wedded to your first conclusion. Intelligent PTSD veterans are the ones who have learned in cognitive therapy to be willing to change their mind when confronted with new information that discredits their old ways of thinking.

Combat PTSD veterans do not want to be as mentally stuck as American generals were during the Korean War. For whatever reason, probably political, a number of our high-ranking generals in Korea believed that the Chinese communists would not come to the aid of their North Korean comrades. The official line was that "there are no Chinese soldiers in Korea." Yet front line American infantry soldiers saw tall enemy soldiers in strange non-Korean uniforms shooting at them. When they reported this fact to their higher-level officers, they were basically ignored because "there are no Chinese soldiers in Korea." A few of the ignored infantry soldiers became so angry that they then set out to capture a few of these non-Korean uniformed soldiers. After succeeding, they sent the Chinese prisoners up the chain of command to central headquarters to show the generals. Eventually the word came down from the generals that these prisoners were only Chinese advisors, because "there are no Chinese soldiers in Korea." It seemed as if the generals, living in their never-never land of rear bases, had said to themselves, "We have our minds made up, don't try to confuse us with real evidence." Of course we now know that they were terribly wrong; soon afterwards vast numbers of Chinese soldiers attacked and overran Allied front line positions, slaughtering many Americans and South Korean soldiers. The lesson learned is that refusing to change one's mental maps in the face of contrary evidence is a recipe for disaster. When our mental maps no longer fit the territory, we need to redraw them to fit the new reality.

12

MEMORY DIFFICULTIES

Recall that Post Traumatic Stress Disorder is defined as both a disorder of fear and a disorder of memory. The 1980 Diagnostic and Statistical Manual, Third Edition's (DSM-III) listing of criterion symptoms for PTSD included memory impairments. However in the revised 1994 Diagnostic and Statistical Manual, Fourth Edition (DSM-IV), memory impairment is no longer listed as a criterion symptom. The only memory symptom listed in the DSM-IV is the inability to remember details of the trauma, which is listed as a type of avoidance symptom. This type of memory difficulty reflects psychoanalytic thinking in which generally remembering a trauma, but not the specific details, is considered to be the result of a patient's use of an unconscious defense mechanism called *repression*. It is defined as the process of forcing painful memories out of the conscious mind into the deep layers of the unconscious. Repression is thought of as a kind of deliberate, but unconscious, forgetting to avoid thinking about uncomfortable memories.

Why the psychiatric experts removed memory difficulties as a defining PTSD symptom remains unclear. Their downgrade of memory in the 1994 DSM-IV may reflect the fact that during the 1980s most Vietnam War PTSD veterans were complaining not of amnesia (the technical term for memory problems), but rather complaining of remembering too much. PTSD Vietnam veterans were tormented by a type of hypermemory, experienced as vivid visual images of their combat traumas. These visions appeared either in the form of frequent nightmares of traumatic experiences or traumatic memories that intruded into their minds during the day. Usually their stated goal was simply to forget about these troubling memories. But their efforts at forgetting failed, because "How do you forget the unforgettable?" These veterans were encouraged to establish, instead, a more realistic goal, one of being capable of remembering their traumas without becoming emotionally distressed. It was only when Vietnam veterans had aged into their fifties, during the late 1990s, that their memory complaints began. This trend was also reported in published research. In 2005 a team of scientists studying older veterans at the Bronx, New York, VA hospital concluded that the memory difficulties of aging PTSD combat veterans were "likely reflecting aspects of both combat exposure and aging."[34]

The memory complaints of midlife Vietnam PTSD veterans partially reflected the worries and anxieties that all aging Americans feel about their memory lapses. They worried that momentary memory lapses, or what are sometimes called geriatric moments, were early signs of diseases like Alzheimer's, a devastating disease that causes memory and thinking deterioration. Reassurances were routinely offered because studies have shown that younger people have as many memory lapses as older people, but that they do not worry about them as much. When reassurance was not enough to reduce the veteran's amnesia worries, then formal memory testing would be initiated. Specially developed assessment instruments, known as neuropsychological tests, were used to measure an individual's memory performance on specific tasks, like the learning and recalling of a list of words. The individual veteran's results were then compared with large group averages to help determine the existence of any amnesia.

Since most were combat veterans, they would also be interviewed and evaluated for PTSD along with the memory testing. Sometimes it was discovered that the veteran's memory functioning was within the normal range, yet the veteran displayed enough symptoms to be diagnosed with PTSD. In a follow-up meeting the good news of normal memory was shared, but there was also a recommendation of treatment for the diagnosed PTSD. If the combat veteran agreed with the recommendation, then both psychological and psychiatric treatment would be initiated. For those PTSD veterans who responded successfully to the mental health treatments, it was gratifying to observe not only how their memories improved, but also how their overall intellectual functioning would improve, as demonstrated by such factors as improved job performance.

A few of the combat PTSD veterans who were administered memory and intellectual tests at our clinic did demonstrate memory difficulties, especially in the learning and recall of new information. Again, our results were replicated in research performed at a Department of Veterans Affairs medical center in another part of the country. Dr. J. Douglas Bremner's team at the West Haven, Connecticut, VA Medical Center administered a broad range of intellectual tests to 26 combat veterans diagnosed with PTSD. Their results revealed that the PTSD veterans had significantly more difficulties in recalling logical paragraphs, both immediately and after a delay, than the control group. Interestingly the memory deficit was found only in memory of verbal information, but not in visual memory or general intelligence.[35]

It is notable that at our clinic another cognitive skill was found more often than memory to be significantly below normal in PTSD veterans. This impaired skill was attention, defined as an individual's ability to focus on a particular target stimulus. Attending can be a difficult mental skill to sustain. When teachers order students to pay attention, they are acknowledging the mental cost and effort required to attend, especially in the face of any type of distraction. It became apparent after these test results of limited attentional ability that what many combat PTSD veterans were complaining about, what they were calling memory difficulties, were in actuality attention and learning difficulties. The explanation provided to these veterans was based upon the following reasoning: "You cannot forget what you never learned in the first place. Think about what happens when you are introduced to a new person whose name is a difficult one, like Mr. Samuel Kulokowski. If you ran into him a few days later and did not know his name, you would probably say, 'I am sorry, but I forgot your name.' But you would be wrong. You had not forgotten his name: you had never learned it in the first place. We are fooling ourselves when we expect to remember a difficult name like Kulokowski after hearing it only once. Most names are difficult to learn because they are unique and abstract. This makes it hard to find something common and concrete to connect to them, which is one of the most effective memory strategies. To remember anything, you must pay attention to it and then repeat it often, using as many different senses as possible. To remember that new name you must hear it, say it, write it, see it, then review it and connect it. The more energy you put into learning the name, the more likely you are to remember it."

To attend, to concentrate, and to remember are mental skills that are difficult to do under the best of circumstances. It becomes nearly impossible to perform these skills so when a person is distracted. For PTSD veterans, their performance of these mental skills is hindered by interference from primitive emotional factors. Emotional conflicts associated with PTSD, the anger and the fear, can churn and agitate so much inside the individual PTSD veteran's mind that it interferes with his or her ability to learn and remember. Ongoing biological arousal can divert anyone from attending to any new information they need to learn and recall. The discomfort of living in high gear, the physical overdrive of PTSD, can monopolize a veteran's attention. The accompanying characteristic PTSD symptom of hypervigilance may also act as a distraction. If PTSD veterans are constantly engaged in searching the environment for potentially dangerous threats, then they are limited in their ability to pay attention to other important information. If they cannot fully attend to and concentrate on new information, they will be unable to learn the information. Later they will be unable to recall it, not because of a memory problem, but rather because they never truly acquired the information in the first place. One of the primary psychotherapeutic goals in PTSD treatment is to help combat veterans learn how to calm their hyperarousal and hypervigilance; only then will they be capable of focusing his attention on acquiring vital new information.

A PTSD veteran worried about memory difficulties may wonder what part of the brain is affected. The region of the brain that has been found to be involved in the establishment of memories is called the hippocampus. It is a small, sea horse shaped organ found deep within the region of our brains located under the side of our head, beneath our ears. Specifically the hippocampus is part of the older section of our brains called the limbic system. Doctors think this is the site for memory processing because when the hippocampus is somehow damaged through disease or injury, then that patient has difficulties forming new memories. These unfortunate patients cannot remember new telephone numbers or what they ate for breakfast. Our two hippocampi (we have one beneath each ear) have also been found to be a brain organ extremely sensitive to stress. In the 1990s Dr Robert Sapolsky and his research team at Stanford University performed experiments in which they deliberately stressed male vervet monkeys by caging them with a female. The female vervets would immediately and continually attack the male monkey. This unnatural living arrangement so stressed out the male monkeys that many died. Upon autopsy the scientists found that the male vervets had enlarged adrenal glands and gastric ulcers, pathological changes that meant that these stressed monkeys had been releasing unhealthy amounts of stress chemicals. They also found that part of the male vervets' brains had been damaged, specifically the hippocampus.[36]

Studying the above stressed monkey research led Dr. J. Douglas Bremner, who was the medical director of the West Haven, Connecticut, VA's PTSD inpatient unit at the time, to speculate that his PTSD combat veterans' amnesia may have been related to their high levels of stress. He hypothesized that the veterans' chronic hyperarousal and hypervigilance was resulting in massive amounts of stress chemicals being released into their brains, causing hippocampal damage. In order to test his hypothesis, Dr. Bremner scanned the brains of his PTSD veterans with a *magnetic resonance imaging* (MRI) machine. He then compared these MRI scans to the brain scans of a control group, who were a group of construction workers matched to the veterans across a number of factors such as alcohol usage and educational levels. He discovered that the average PTSD veteran's brain regions implicated in developing new memories, the hippocampi, were significantly smaller than the hippocampi of the average construction worker in the control group. He also found that the smaller the veteran's hippocampi, the more problems the veteran experienced with short-term memory. Dr. Bremner's pioneering research produced some of the first evidence that traumatic stress may cause damaging effects on combat PTSD veterans' brains and thus their memories.[37]

However the jury is still out on the question of whether the hippocampi of combat PTSD veterans are smaller because of damage due to their traumatic stress. Other neuroscientists argue that PTSD veterans possessed smaller hippocampi even before they were subjected to combat stress. They argue that the smaller volume of the hippocampi was due to the veterans' genetic heritage, a biological variation that placed them at higher risk for developing PTSD. The argument is based upon an identical twin study performed by Dr. Mark Gilberston and his colleges at Harvard Medical School and the Manchester VA Medical Center. Dr. Gilberston compared hippocampal MRI brain scans of 40 men who saw Vietnam combat (17 had PTSD and 23 did not) to the MRI brain scans of their identical twins who did not see military service. He found that the hippocampi of the PTSD veterans and their identical nonmilitary twins were all smaller than those of non–PTSD veterans and their identical twins. Since the PTSD veterans' identical twins also had smaller hippocampi, but had not been exposed to Vietnam combat, then combat stress could not logically be the reason for their reduced hippocampal size. Rather than stress chemicals causing the small hippocampi, Dr. Gilberston concluded that smaller hippocampi were a preexisting genetic risk factor for the development of PTSD.[38]

My own interpretation of the research is that the extensive existing animal and human research data demonstrating hippocampal damage due to stress chemicals has not been overturned by the findings of one human twin study. It is my considered professional opinion that severe and repeated traumatic stress does cause human brain damage in the hippocampus. Only future well-designed, long-term human identical twin research will resolve the argument.

All combat PTSD veterans need to know about the exciting good news coming out of human brain research. Up until only a few years ago, young doctors and neuroscientists were taught that the human brain grows new neuron cells only in childhood. The adult brain was thought of as being a stable, fully formed, computer-like organ, unable to change by growing new cells. But then in the late 1990s there was a huge breakthrough in brain research, at first only with animals, but then onward to humans. Dr. Fred Gage and his research colleges at the Salk Institute in Southern California injected dying cancer patients with radioactive markers. After the patients died their brains were examined for neural cells that contained the injected markers, because its presence would mean that the affected neural cells had formed since the injections. Dr. Gage succeeded in finding such cells, thus proving that the adult human brain has the ability to grow new cells. The good news for PTSD veterans is that the brain region that demonstrated this recent neural growth was the hippocampus.[39] This fact leads to the exciting possibility that veterans may be able to reverse the devastating effects of PTSD stress on their brains. The human hippocampus may be induced to repair itself by growing new cells in damaged regions. Brain research is providing even more good news. There is evidence to suggest that the new class of psychiatric antidepressant medications known as the SSRIs (an acronym for selective serotonin reuptake inhibitors), including such popular medications as Paxil and Zoloft, may indeed generate their beneficial effects by promoting new cell growth in the hippocampi of patients who take these medicines.[40]

Our investigation of the combat veteran's memory complaints has included only the negative influences of psychological disorders like PTSD. Yet there are other possible causes for a combat veteran's amnesia. For one, if she or he were unfortunate enough to have suffered a mild head injury such as a concussion, it is possible that higher order mental functions, including memory, could be impaired by the injury. These types of head and brain injuries are all too common in combat veterans returning from Operation Enduring Freedom (OEF) and Operation Iraqi Freedom (OIF), where improvised explosive devices (IEDs) are the terrorists' weapons of choice for attacking soldiers riding in their military vehicles. The resulting explosions frequently cause what has been called the signature injury of the current Mideast wars: traumatic brain injury (TBI). In fact three out of four combat-related injuries in Operation Iraqi Freedom are due to such explosions.[41] (See the chapter on traumatic brain injury for more information on this topic.)

Another common cause of memory difficulties in combat veterans is the overuse of drugs, either legal or illegal. By far the most abused substance in the military is alcohol. It is a well-known fact in addiction medicine that chronic alcohol abuse can not only damage the alcoholic's liver, but also damage the brain. The resulting brain cell deaths can be numerous enough to cause amnesia and possibly the more serious dementia. Dementia is defined as a disorder characterized by a number of mental impairments including memory, problem-solving and decision-making difficulties. A common excuse of many veterans is that they do not drink alcohol, only beer, but they are fooling themselves. Beer is alcohol. In terms of alcohol content, one glass of beer equals one shot of liquor (be it whiskey, vodka, or gin) or one glass of wine. Drinking beer is just as damaging to a veteran's brain as drinking liquor. As for other substances, the chronic abuse of just about any illicit street drug will cause amnesia and probably dementia: for example, speed (amphetamine), cocaine (especially in the "crack" form), heroin or opiates, (See the chapter on substance abuse for more information on this topic.)

13

NIGHTMARES AND FLASHBACKS

Humans have always been fascinated by their nightly dreams. In the Bible dreams are considered divine revelations, even prophecies. Unfortunately a traumatized veteran's sleep is not filled with divine messages; instead it is filled with dreadful nightmares. Sleeping difficulties due to trauma-related nightmares was the number one symptom motivating combat veterans to seek treatment at our clinic. Estimates of nightmare frequency in individuals suffering from all types of PTSD range from 60 percent to as high as 90 percent.[42] Many veterans complained that they were unable to return to sleep after being awakened by nightmares. Others were unable to initiate sleep due to their anticipatory fears of more nightmares. They would all complain that their nightmares infected their daily lives with the intense fear or rage they felt upon awakening. After their initial assessment, these sleep-deprived veterans were referred to psychiatry for a sedative evaluation and advised to begin psychotherapy.

Over the last few decades, scientists have devoted intense research efforts on investigating sleep and dreaming. They discovered that while asleep, the human brain cycles through four distinct stages and then a period know as REM sleep. REM stands for rapid eye movement, because an observer can detect the dreamer's eyes moving under their closed eyelids. When sleepers were awakened during REM sleep, they invariably reported that they had been dreaming. Research has also demonstrated that sleep disturbances, especially during the REM period, caused a variety of negative effects. One early study found that subjects deprived of REM sleep became anxious and irritable.[43] There is evidence that Israeli authorities abuse their prisoners with sleep deprivation, causing a disruption of both emotional and cognitive functioning.[44] Animal studies have established that REM sleep is involved in the animal's processing and strengthening of daytime memories. Human studies from Israel have reported that when subjects were deprived of REM sleep, their memory performance deteriorated.[45] These studies suggest that one possible explanation for the attention and memory difficulties, as well as the elevated anxiety and irritability, of combat veterans diagnosed with PTSD is their chronic sleep deprivation, due to nightmares interrupting their REM sleep.

The most influential psychological theory on the purpose and function of dreaming is Dr. Sigmund Freud's psychoanalytic theory. His book *The Interpretation of Dreams,* published in 1900, is considered his masterpiece. Dr. Freud himself thought it contained the most valuable of his many insights into the human psyche. Dr. Freud wrote that dreams are the "royal road to the unconscious," the best method of understanding the unconscious. A dream's surface story line, known in psychoanalysis as the manifest content, does not have to follow the laws of physics nor standard reality. In a dream veterans could walk out their home's front door and immediately find themselves in the middle of the Vietnamese jungle. Underneath the dream's surface lies the dream's latent content, the true meaning of the dream. With their bizarre plots and hidden meanings, dreams pack a powerful emotional impact. Dr. Freud's revolutionary insight was that the dream's latent content reflected a symbolic wish fulfillment for the dreamer. He theorized that the dreamer possesses an instinctual desire that is unfulfilled in reality; however, in the dream it is symbolically satisfied.[46] Consider the "wet dreams" of an adolescent male. He is frustrated by his sexual desires; yet, by dreaming of a sexual encounter, he experiences symbolic satisfaction through his nocturnal emission.

An analysis of one of my own dreams will illustrate the psychoanalytic style of dream interpretation. A few years ago a series of repetitive semi-nightmares haunted my sleep. They all involved the theme of me losing my automobile. In my dream I had driven to an unfamiliar city and parked my car either on a back street or in a large parking garage. After some activity, I attempted to return to my car, anxiously searching for but unable to locate the automobile. The manifest content of the dream, which is its story line, is my desperate hunt. No matter how far I walked nor where I searched, through strange and frightening stairwells and alleys, I could never find the garage or my car's parking place. These dreams did not awaken me, thus they were not serious nightmares; but I was uncomfortably anxious upon awakening. Consequently I tried a psychoanalytic self-analysis. Applying Freud's wish fulfillment concept, I considered the question "What wish would be fulfilled by my dream?" One answer was a wish to no longer possess an automobile. As I thought about the idea, a light bulb came on in my mind; I really did not want to own a car. My analysis provided the insight that I was not like most American males who loved and pampered their automobiles. This was the dream's latent content, which in psycho-analytic theory is the true meaning behind the dream's manifest content. I recognized that I considered cars much too expensive, unreliable and bur-densome. If there were a realistic alternative for my work commute, I would not own an automobile. My favorite mode of transportation is my mountain bike; I wished that I lived close enough to my job that I could bicycle to work. Once I had successfully translated this message from my unconscious, the dream was no longer needed. This anxiety dream never reoccurred.

Interestingly the horrors of World War I altered Dr. Freud's basic con-ceptualization of dreams. Austrian military psychiatrists were noting how shell-shocked World War I veterans were suffering from repetitive night-mares of their battle traumas. Dr. Freud eventually realized that post-trauma nightmares were a separate entity from the usual wish fulfillment dreams. These terror nightmares, which awaken the sleeper, failed at one of the basic functions of dreams, which is to enable the dreamer to continue sleeping. Dr. Freud came to the conclusion that post-trauma nightmares were repeated attempts by the dreamer to retrospectively master the orig-inal combat trauma and to control the anxiety it produced.

Most traumatized veterans are both puzzled and angered by their nightmares returning again and again to haunt them. These vivid replays of gruesome war traumas were frightening because the veterans were lit-erally reliving the horrors of combat in their sleep. The psychoanalytic explanation is that their unconscious mind was trying, in a peculiar way, to master the trauma through repetition. Since the unconscious is the primitive level of the mind, it is limited indeed in its mental resources for complex and flexible problem solving. The only tool the unconscious nightmare does possess for solving the trauma problem is blunt force rep-etition. Its single strategy is the elementary one of "If at first you don't suc-ceed, try, try again." The unconscious mind is like a goat battering its horns against a brick wall. They both have only one plan of attack: repeat-ing the direct frontal assault. Usually they both fail, but they continue to try. Neither is sophisticated enough to conceive of a workable alternative strategy, like climbing over, digging under or going around the barrier.

Surprisingly, a few PTSD veterans at our clinic denied ever experi-encing combat nightmares; but their spouses, like Shakespeare's Lady Percy in *Henry IV*, knew better. These spouses recognized that their partners were having nightmares by their screaming or thrashing around while asleep. Some spouses had actually been hurt by their partner striking out during a nightmare. Dr. Freud's belief was that these types of individuals were defending themselves from the terror of their nightmare by repressing the nightmare; he thought that they were forcing the terror memories out of their conscious mind into their unconscious, where they could not be easily accessed. Consequently the veteran would not remember the nightmare. This avoidance of emotionally painful memories indicated that these fragile veterans suffered from a severe level of PTSD. Other combat veterans admitted that they experienced nightmares, but were unable to recall many details. This amnesia also reflects a type of repression that is an avoidance of emotionally charged memories. They were advised to place a pen and paper near their bed. Immediately upon awakening, they were to write down anything they could recall from the nightmare. It did not have to be the entire story; any detail from the dream — a color, a feeling or an image — should be noted, because it could then be used as a hook in psychotherapy to recall other memories from the nightmare.

By repressing their nightmare memories, veterans are depriving themselves of an opportunity for emotional healing. In his book on Freud, Dr. Erich Fromm, the eminent American psychoanalyst, quotes from the Talmud: "A dream which has not been interpreted is like a letter that has not been opened."[47] All dreams contain valuable messages from the dreamer's unconscious mind to themselves, about themselves. Repression has been described as the damming up of emotional memories. Like water exerting immense pressure on a dam, blocked trauma memories exert pressure to break through into the dreamer's conscious mind. Most often it is combat veterans who deny or repress their nightmares, in a vain attempt at forgetting their traumas, who suffer from the most frequent and dramatic nightmares. The bottom line is that a memory-avoidance strategy simply does not work. Avoiding traumatic memories does not make them vanish; they are much too emotionally powerful. Instead, the more energy exerted on pushing trauma memories out of the veteran's conscious mind, the more they push back through frequent disturbing nightmares.

Nightmare Treatments

Rather than avoiding nightmares, the only effective strategy for solving the nightmare problem is to directly confront them. Within the context of a trusting and supportive therapeutic relationship, a skilled psychotherapist strives to convince veterans diagnosed with PTSD of the benefits of openly examining their nightmares. When a psychoanalytic-type therapy is utilized, therapist and veteran search for and then analyze the particular meaning the nightmare has for the veteran. Usually combat nightmares are replays of horrific battles; each one needs to be examined to discover the emotional theme underlying the nightmarish event. What are the veteran's unresolved emotional issues? Does the veteran associate guilt, anger or fear with the nightmare? Given all the other horrid battles the combat veteran endured, why was this particular nightmarish event so especially upsetting? One helpful technique is to explore the symbolic aspects of the nightmare, treating the nightmare as a kind of visual poetry. What associations does the veteran make with probable symbols in the dream? Often times the veteran reports that the nightmare does not accurately depict all the details of the actual battle. These distortions or omissions must be closely examined to discover their meaning. What message is the nightmare sending by these distortions of the actual battle details? Is there some wish that is answered by the omission? For example, a young civilian who was actually killed in the battle may somehow survive in the veteran's nightmare rendition of events.

When cognitive psychotherapy is the therapy of choice, the therapist brings into play the power and flexibility of the veteran's conscious reasoning abilities to bear upon the nightmare problem. The veteran and therapist form a therapeutic alliance to search for the distorted and dysfunctional beliefs that the veteran may have applied to his or her behavior during the fight depicted in the nightmare. For example, is the veteran applying perfectionist standards to his or her behavior? If so, this perfectionism is challenged by questioning the rationality of such a rigid and exacting standard. One cognitive therapy technique developed by me was designed to have the veteran symbolically master the nightmare. The veteran is directed to consider how he or she wishes that the actual battle had turned out. The veteran is then told to rework the nightmare's plot by creating a new ending, one that reflects the preferred version. This therapeutic exercise encourages PTSD veterans to think about their nightmare traumas in a different and therapeutically creative way. It helps them clarify unresolved emotional issues. It teaches that they possess more control and influence over their dreams than they had realized. Veterans reported that verbalizing their reworked nightmare story was a positive emotional experience. Therapeutic discussions would then concentrate on what their thinking was now about the battle. Other cognitive therapists call a similar nightmare rewriting technique *imagery rehearsal therapy*. After the reworking they have their PTSD patients review the altered outcome dream story in their minds while in bed just before sleep. These cognitive therapists claim that this rehearsal may change the usual nightmare that evening. Recent psychological research has demonstrated there is reason to hope that these types of cognitive therapy treatments can limit the chronic nightmares of PTSD patients. A 2007 study published in the *Journal of Traumatic Stress* examined the effects of nightmare-oriented imagery rehearsal therapy on 27 civilians diagnosed with PTSD due to sexual assaults. The study's results demonstrated that "At the 6-month follow-up assessment, 84 percent of treated participants reported an absence of nightmares in the previous week. Significant decreases were also reported in the symptoms of depression and PTSD."[48]

Desperate veterans frequently want their PTSD nightmares to stop totally, but their wish is unrealistic. A more realistic therapeutic goal is to have the nightmares occur less and less often. Learning to cope with PTSD nightmares is like learning to ride a bicycle. At first the beginner falls frequently, but with the help of a coach and motivated practice, the length of time between falls become longer and longer. Likewise for PTSD nightmares; as veterans learn to restructure their traumas and to integrate them into a new life model of recovery, the nightmares gradually decrease in frequency. Those combat PTSD veterans who did heal through cognitive psychotherapy reported exactly this pattern of nightmare improvement. Their combat nightmares gradually became less and less frequent. Indeed the increased time between nightmares becomes an accurate gauge of the veteran's rate of healing. But even as an expert biker may still fall upon encountering a road hazard, PTSD veterans need to be taught that nightmares may reoccur intermittently. Occasionally, when stressed out by a present-day civilian crisis or on the anniversary date of a trauma, they may reexperience a combat nightmare. They need to learn not to interpret the reoccurrence as a total catastrophe; it does not mean that the veteran has psychologically regressed to a pretreatment state. Such a reoccurrence simply means that the veteran has hit another bump on the road of life. The best response is to remount and continue the healing journey.

Flashbacks

The following section explores a more pathological type of trauma reexperience than a nightmare, namely the dissociative state or what most combat PTSD veterans call the flashback.

Dissociation is defined in psychiatry to mean a splitting of consciousness, a defect in mental integration, when one mental process separates from normal consciousness and operates on its own. A milder form of disassociation occurs when traumatic memories break into the PTSD veteran's conscious mind, even when the individual does not want to think about them. This is known in psychology as an intrusive memory. A trauma memory's ability to invade a PTSD veteran's thinking demonstrates its emotional charge, a power to forcefully demand conscious attention. Some psychologists theorize that intrusive memories are memories that do not easily fit in with the veteran's other memories; they are not integrated into his or her normal memory system. Consequently the veteran's unconscious mind forces them back into the conscious mind in another attempt to force the PTSD veteran into dealing with them — that is, making sense of them, giving them meaning within the background context of all his or her other normal personal memories.

Interestingly many PTSD veterans reported that they have often experienced intrusive memories and sometimes even the more serious dissociative state, a flashback, while driving along a highway. These veterans were all American men who typically loved their cars and loved to drive them. Traveling America's highways even without any real destination was for them a favorite form of stress reduction. They had driven so many years that it evolved into an overlearned skill, one that was almost automatic; therefore, driving did not require the full capacity of their minds. Their conscious attention was not fully engaged while driving on a straight and dry highway. This subconscious style of driving made it easier for emotionally charged combat memories to demand attention by breaking into their conscious minds.

Civilian drivers on a highway experience a similar, but milder, phenomenon when they are surprised at realizing they have gone a considerable distance without full awareness of the actual drive. What they do recall is that they were involved in an animated conversation with a passenger or were listening so intently to the radio that they were driving on automatic pilot. There is something hypnotic about driving on a highway, especially at night when the headlights limit your attention to only a few things such as the broken lane lines. A mild trancelike state of consciousness makes the veteran's conscious mind more vulnerable to invasion by emotionally charged memories. Obviously this could be quite dangerous; family members have complained that their PTSD veteran had a far away look in the eyes while driving straight through red lights without realizing it. We all need to keep our conscious attention fully engaged on the task at hand while driving. For combat veterans the possibility of causing a fatal crash should be another motivational factor to encourage them to seek psychological help for their PTSD.

In the pathological flashback, the traumatic memory is so emotionally charged that, when sufficiently stimulated, it overpowers the veteran's normal conscious awareness. During his flashback, combat PTSD veterans regress into living totally within their traumatic memory, a change of consciousness that obviously interferes with their ability to react normally to present day reality. Engulfed from a few minutes to possibly hours, the troubled veteran reexperiences the painfully traumatic memory as if experiencing the event in the present.

The flashback is automatically triggered by present day reminders that relate directly to the veteran's combat trauma. The unanticipated environmental cue could be a sight, a sound or even a smell that triggers the traumatic memory within the veteran's psyche. These flashback memory scenes are vivid and lifelike, but they can also be fragmented and confusing. The accompanying emotionality is uncomfortably intense and frightening. It is as if the veteran is experiencing a terrible frightening nightmare during the day, a daymare. Psychologists theorize that the daymare flashback is a special type of emotional memory, one that has its own unique nerve circuitry in the deeper layers of the brain, separate from the normal memory circuits. This regression to living within a traumatic memory is a serious breakdown in the integration of the veteran's conscious mind, one that can lead to dire consequences. One PTSD Vietnam veteran reported suffering his first flashback while driving a fully loaded semitrailer truck down a Southeastern highway. Even though he was living within his trauma memory, he was still able to drive the truck straight ahead. But when the highway curved, he continued to drive straight, right off of the road. His truck fell on its side; fortunately the truck did not hit anything nor was anyone hurt. However, because of the incident, he lost his license to drive semitrailer trucks, a loss that motivated him to seek psychological treatment.

Flashbacks may also include the combat veteran's acting out his trauma memory through inappropriate behaviors. Often it was a police officer, with uniform, weapon and authority, who triggered these types of flashback. One PTSD veteran started talking in Vietnamese to the uniformed police officer that had pulled him over for speeding; he became so fearful that he ran away from the scene. A particularly dangerous flashback was experienced by a Vietnam War PTSD veteran who, when heavily armed police approached his house to arrest him for drunken assault and battery, disassociated into his Mekong Delta combat memories and fought the police. He was fortunate because, instead of imprisonment for attempted murder, the judge sentenced the Navy veteran to psychiatric treatment at our outpatient clinic.

Psychological treatment for PTSD dissociative states such as flashbacks is similar in form to the treatment of nightmares. What is required is a type of reexposure psychotherapy, where the combat veteran and psychotherapist examine the war memories relived during the dissociative flashback. Similar to the treatment of nightmares, the psychotherapeutic goal is not to forget, but rather, to discover the hidden meaning within the flashback memory. Why was this particular combat experience so emotionally powerful? What are the unresolved emotional conflicts associated with it? Does the veteran have unresolved issues of guilt or shame? What is the veteran's self-talk about this emotionally painful experience? As always the psychologist's job is to challenge the PTSD veteran's dysfunctional interpretation of the trauma and to help generate a healthy, reality-based alternative. A supplementary goal is to search for the environmental cues that triggered the dissociative flashback in order that they can be anticipated and avoided in the future. It is difficult work, but the payoff is well worth the effort. The frequency of the PTSD veteran's dissociative episodes decreases significantly as traumatic memories are consciously analyzed in therapy.

14

SOCIAL AVOIDANCE

Of the three major Post Traumatic Stress Disorder symptom clusters, possibly the most psychologically damaging are the symptoms listed under the chronic avoidance cluster. Under this cluster a combat veteran diagnosed with PTSD demonstrates evidence of "persistent avoidance of ... people that arouse recollections of the trauma ... markedly diminished interest or participation in significant activities ... feeling of detachment or estrangement from others."[49] These avoidance behaviors frequently lead to a profound social isolation that causes the psychological damage.

Vietnam War veterans known as Bush Vets illustrate perfectly how social avoidance symptoms can result in an abnormally isolated lifestyle. Jungles in Vietnam were nicknamed the "Bush." These Bush Vets shunned any civilian world contacts by disappearing deep into various American jungles. Some Bush Vets lived in tents they erected in the tropical jungles of Hawaii.[50] Dozens lived during the 1980s in Pompano Beach, Florida, where again the local vegetation resembles the jungles of Vietnam. They inhabited backwoods, military-style encampments, exiled from mainstream society.[51] One of the most colorful of these Bush Vets is a self-described mountain man who attended one of our clinic's PTSD group therapy sessions. After phoning in for permission, he arrived for the session conspicuously dressed in a homemade buckskin outfit, complete with moccasins. He was accompanied by two large, pure white Alaskan Huskies, who had to be tied into the bed of his pickup truck. A Vietnam combat medic, he was a big hit with the PTSD group members because he was living out their fantasies. He revealed that he had lived in the Wyoming wilderness for years and was currently building a new, larger log home entirely by himself. He claimed to hunt deer for food, skinning them to make his buckskin clothing. His only companions were his two dogs and his horse. Twice a year he would return to civilization for medical care and a chance to sell his buckskin creations. A few months later this same veteran was featured on a Discovery channel television program investigating contemporary mountain men. Again dressed in his full buckskin regalia he recounted his life alone in the mountains. He gave a tour of his new log home, complete with a deep root cellar for food refrigeration, and the raised Indian burial shrine he had built as the last resting place for his horse. He claimed that he was too busy to be lonely, and besides he had his dogs. Strange as it seemed, this indeed was a twentieth-century combat veteran living in a time warp back to the mountain man lifestyle of the nineteenth-century American wilderness.

From a mental health perspective the problem is that social isolation and avoidance are contrary to our basic nature as social beings. We humans share with all our primate cousins a primary need for continual interactions and relationships with our kind. There are animals that are solitary creatures, such as the rhinoceros, the polar bear or the tiger. At the zoo one does not find herds of tigers or rhinoceroses. Even baby rhinos, which weigh hundreds of pounds at birth, stay with their mothers only three or four months before they wander off by themselves. In contrast monkeys and chimpanzees live together in large colonies. Like all our primate cousins, we humans are born into and raised by families. This social world is fundamental within our basic human nature.

It is so basic that the prominent American psychiatrist Harry S. Sullivan advocated a social view of mental health. His interpersonal theory was based upon the enormous dependency human children have on their parents and family. Without their care the children would not survive; thus human relationships are essential. Dr. Sullivan defined mental illness as a pattern of inadequate or inappropriate interpersonal relationships.[52] Consequently a rough measure of an individual's psychological health is the number and quality of his or her relationships. The number of friends an individual has, the closeness to family, and the quality of these relationships are all indicators of better mental health. Intelligent prison wardens understand the powerful psychological consequences when this human social need is not met. They learned that they could not break strong, willful inmates by physical punishment alone, but even the strongest inmates had their spirits broken by prolonged solitary confinement. The social isolation of solitary confinement is psychologically abnormal. Keep prisoners confined in solitude long enough and they will deteriorate into wretched loneliness and possibly severe mental illness. In desperation some solitary confinement prisoners have attempted to make friends with their prison guards, or failing that, attempted to make pets of the rats and roaches that infested their cells. Thus our need for others is essential for good mental health.

It is not only Vietnam veterans who isolate themselves. One Korean War PTSD veteran disclosed that he lived alone on a small plot of land in rural Florida. Along the perimeter of his land he had built a six-foot-high chain-link fence, and then installed barbed wire across the top of the fence. He also planted large bayonet palms all along the outside of the fence as a natural but impenetrable barrier. Every night before he could sleep, he had to patrol the inside perimeter of his fenced land armed with his revolver, accompanied by his large German Shepherd guard dog. His fears centered upon the possibility that someone would break into his home. But who would be crazy enough to break into such a fortification? He had, in effect, built himself his own prison, where he was the prison warden and the only inmate. Other PTSD veterans would simply watch television or lie on their couch all day, every day, instead of engaging in any social activities. They may be comfortable in their detached lives, but at what price? Their lifestyle fails the dead man test, which states that if a dead person could do what they were doing, then it could not be much fun, nor could it be much of a life. One could make a dead person lie on a couch all day or stare at the television from a recliner. What is the quality of life when one lives only within the confines of a house or an apartment? They are denying not just their humanity, but also their more basic primate nature. The authorities could cement shut their front doors and it would not change their lifestyle one bit. These withdrawn PTSD veterans were also inmates in prisons of their own construction.

A serious question at this point is what are the causes of this social impoverishment on the part of combat veterans diagnosed with PTSD? The answer lies within the fierce emotions of anger, fear and mistrust. For Vietnam combat veterans it began with a guerrilla war where the enemy wore civilian dress instead of military uniforms. It became difficult, if not impossible, for the American soldier to distinguish the Viet Cong from civilians. They were all dressed the same and looked alike. What starts in the war as a fear and anger at the enemy grows into a mistrust of all the Vietnamese people because it is the safest strategy. It is safer for the soldier to mistrust a civilian and be wrong than to trust someone who turns out to be an enemy. The consequences of such an error are fatal. The Vietnam veteran's fearful mistrust spread like a cancerous tumor upon their return to include all American civilians.

This was especially true for the Vietnam veterans who experienced the shock of having been spit upon at the airport or having been called a baby killer. Many times their own family rejected them because family members believed the big lie perpetuated by the war's critics that veterans were the real cause of the Vietnam tragedy. The saddest stories heard at our mental health clinic were those of the Vietnam veterans who disclosed the thoughtless cruelty their families displayed towards them. For example, a veteran had firecrackers thrown behind his back at a family Fourth of July picnic so that family members could all laugh at the veteran's exaggerated startle reaction.

After these types of incidents, Vietnam combat veterans came to believe that they could not trust anyone. They found themselves highly anxious when people were near and intolerant of social interactions. Much of it had to do with the fear of further attacks, but part of it was also a fear of their own anger and desire to violently counterattack. The only coping strategy that successfully reduced their emotional turmoil was to avoid others: for example, to shop for food and other necessities in the middle of the night. Many would not even attend family functions like Thanksgiving or Christmas dinners. One Vietnam veteran found that the only job he could tolerate was stacking shelves in a grocery store alone at night. These PTSD veterans behaved as if everyone was potentially a dangerous enemy. For some others their social isolation was caused by the intense grief they felt after the deaths of their fellow soldiers. The pain caused by a friend's death was simply too severe to repeat, consequently they developed the habit of never again allowing themselves to become emotionally attached to other soldiers. Upon returning home they continued this habit, staying emotionally distant from others. These combat veterans suffered feelings of detachment and estrangement. They learned that the only time they felt calm and secure was when they were alone. Upon being awarded PTSD disability payments, a few of the veterans built houses in underpopulated rural areas, preferably in the middle of thickly wooded forests; most of them entertained the dream of escaping to such an isolated retreat.

Group Psychotherapy

The best solution for the characteristic social avoidance of combat veterans diagnosed with Post Traumatic Stress Disorder is to enroll them into a group psychotherapy program. However this symptom of social isolation makes recruitment for such a social treatment difficult. At our clinic veterans would resist the group therapy recommendation with a few common arguments. Some demanded the well-known treatment of individual psychotherapy because they desired the increased attention they thought was inherent in this traditional therapeutic arrangement. Another frequent argument was "I don't need to listen to someone else's problems. I have enough of my own." Others argued that they were loners who would not fit in; the counterargument was "don't worry, you will be in a room full of loners." Too many veterans flatly refused to attend. As one such veteran so aptly phrased it, "I don't do people."

Consequently, reducing resistance to group therapy becomes a critical early goal for therapists working with PTSD veterans. One effective tactic is to educate veterans about the numerous advantages of psychotherapeutic treatment in a group format. Increasing their belief and confidence in the power of group therapy weakens resistance. The primary advantage of group over individual psychotherapy is that group, by its very nature, reduces the extreme social isolation of PTSD veterans. As they participate in a therapy group among other combat veterans, they begin to learn that their adjustment problems are not as unique or as strange as they feared. They learn that they are not the only veteran haunted by nightmares, nor the only one who fears losing their mind. The veterans learn that others also hide shameful secrets, such as the time they froze in fright during a firefight. These lessons provide immense relief as they come to realize that they are not alone with their pain. The group comrades are not repulsed by the gruesome story of how a buddy's brains were blown all over the veteran's uniform by an artillery shell. Veterans receive, perhaps for the first time since the war, acceptance and approval rather than scorn and contempt. The group's support forces them to question their view of themselves as inadequate, as soldiers who could not tolerate combat stress, while everyone else successfully handled it. The group's support undermines their image of themselves as outcasts who are useless burdens on others.

PTSD veterans' delight at finally feeling validated is such a positive and liberating feeling that they begin to value the group members who provide the comfort. They like each other because they respect and appreciate what each member has to say. The acceptance of a new member by the other veterans in a group also leads to a sense of security. A veteran suffering with the hypervigilance of PTSD finds, perhaps for the first time since the war, a place that feels safe enough to let down his or her guard. Here is a place where veterans can relax because they knows the others would not allow harm. Since sleep deprivation is a serious problem with veterans diagnosed with PTSD, it was not unusual for a member to fall asleep during our PTSD group sessions. Instead of viewing this behavior as a negative lack of engagement, we realized that this was a sign of trust. The sleeping veteran felt safe with us. We would never awaken a group member unless the snoring was disruptive. Eventually recovering veterans reciprocate the healing concern they enjoy; they learn to care for others once again. The established members open their arms to the new member, repeating the welcome that was given them. This is a pivotal shift in the veteran's inner world, from avoiding others to establishing positive interpersonal relationships. Contrary to the standard group therapy rules, veterans were encouraged to exchange phone numbers so that they could socialize outside the confines of the group meetings. Rewarding friendships can thus be established. As PTSD combat veterans resurrect their need for the human connection, their dehumanization from the war begins to heal.

Dr. Irvin D. Yalom, a renowned Stanford University psychiatrist, writes in his influential book, *The Theory and Practice of Group Psychotherapy,* that one of the essential healing components of group therapy is altruism.[53] Group members help themselves as they help other members. Membership in a PTSD group provides veterans an opportunity to learn how personally rewarding helping others can be. Developing an interest in the group members forces the veteran out of his or her unhealthy self-absorption into something healthier. Combat veterans suffering from PTSD possess exceptionally low self-esteem; they think that they have little to offer to anyone. But once engaged in the group therapy process, veterans often discover that they contributed an observation or a comment that benefited another member. They learn that they can provide reassurance and offer advice to veterans who need it. They learn how even small acts of kindness, like buying the group donuts or making the group coffee, made them feel good and strengthened their growing connection with others. Discovering that they have something valuable to offer others is a powerful lesson that bolsters veterans' self-esteem.

A combat veteran diagnosed with PTSD can integrate into a psychotherapy group because the group is social unit that mimics military reality. A soldier is always part of a military unit. Rarely has a veteran endured the horrors of war completely alone. Most combat traumas were experienced within a military unit, be it a company of approximately eighty soldiers or a squad of six or seven soldiers. Since the traumatizing event was a social one, it stands to reason that recovery would be enhanced if the psychological treatment transpired as a social event. It is fascinating to observe how PTSD veterans, once committed to a group, will tend to reenact military roles. A veteran might assume an unofficial leadership role in the group, mimicking a sergeant's efforts to ensure the platoon's welfare. Because these reenactments are familiar to new members, they facilitate their relating to the other established members. Group members who suffered similar combat traumas can provide an expert's reaction when a new member first discloses traumatic memories. This type of empathetic feedback provides the healing power necessary to reduce the PTSD veteran's sense of social detachment. Insightful reactions provided by a peer can be as powerful and at times more powerful than the insights provided by the therapist. No longer can the veteran be indifferent to the reactions of others.

Group psychotherapy extends the potential for emotionally healing feedback from just the therapist alone, during individual psychotherapy, to the multiple group members. It provides the venue where a greater number of opportunities exist to generate what is known in mental health as the corrective emotional experience, defined as reexperiencing a pathological emotion within the overall healing context of psychotherapy, which repairs the negative effects of that unhealthy emotion. For example, group therapy can provide an opportunity for an angry veteran to express intense rage to a group of people who will not react with the shock and fear most civilians would display. Within this unique social context, angry veterans are more likely to learn more appropriate methods of expressing and regulating their hostility. Viewing themselves as a member of a cohesive, healing group raises PTSD veterans' self-esteem. They develop an esprit de corps similar to the pride felt by members of elite military units such as the Green Berets or Navy Seals.

Another important advantage of group psychotherapy over individual therapy is that it provides an ideal vehicle for presenting important information to multiple veterans simultaneously. The therapist can use the group to educate veterans about the symptoms and dynamics of their Post Traumatic Stress Disorders. Correcting preconceived misconceptions about their post-trauma disorders provides therapeutic benefits. For instance most newly diagnosed veterans are relieved to learn that they are not "going crazy" or "losing their minds." Their anxiety diminishes when they learn that PTSD is not considered a psychosis, which is defined as a major psychiatric disorder that frequently requires inpatient treatment. A psychotic patient may hallucinate and lose touch with reality as in a schizophrenic disorder. Post-trauma stress is considered a treatable anxiety disorder that does not require prolonged inpatient treatment. Or the psychotherapist could also use the group to teach members various effective coping skills. At our clinic the group therapy format was effectively utilized for anger control training, anxiety management and chronic pain management. (Study the specific chapters devoted to these problems for detailed descriptions of the training.) Military veterans have little trouble embracing these types of formalized teaching programs because of their extensive history of receiving formal classroom training while in the service.

However, not all the psychoeducation that occurs in group therapy is the result of formalized instruction by the group's therapist. Much of the learning the veteran acquires while participating in group therapy results from informal exchanges of information between members. They help to heal each other. One veteran can learn of another member's solution for dealing with a PTSD symptom they both suffer from and adopt it. Or a veteran can learn what not to do by listening to another veteran disclosing the negative outcome associated with an ineffective coping strategy, such as drinking alcohol to fall asleep but awakening still fatigued when the alcohol's effects wear off after only a few hours. In a real sense group therapy is a workshop for veterans to acquire and refine socialization skills. An effective psychotherapy group not only affords veterans the opportunity to learn how to assert their own views, but more importantly, how to tolerate different perspectives.

A portion of this social learning involves unconscious imitation of the group leader's behavior. For example, a skilled group psychotherapist can demonstrate defusing direct confrontations from an angry veteran during a meeting. Veterans who observe this demonstration now possess a behavioral model they can imitate when they themselves are confronted during a future group meeting. At first their attempts to defuse a hostile confrontation are crude and relatively ineffective, but after guidance from a skilled therapist and corrective feedback from the group members, veterans can refine their techniques. After learning such a skill within the group context, the veterans now possess an adaptive skill that can be successfully applied in the social world outside of the group.

Group therapy sessions for combat veterans diagnosed with PTSD are sometimes not as calm and smooth as the image portrayed by the previous descriptions. Much of the group's time will be devoted to dealing with the friction and conflicts that develop between various members who have difficulties relating to others. Group therapy becomes a stage where veterans act out their psychopathology. For example, the angry Marine veteran whose only method of influencing others is to intimidate them will behave that way during group sessions. Veterans will compete for center stage and the psychotherapist's attention. Members will disclose distorted beliefs that will offend other members. Veterans with different status and rank, such as officers versus privates, or who come from different branches of the military, all possess different perspectives that can collide. One of the most potentially volatile clashes that ever occurred in our PTSD groups was the heated argument between an angry African American Vietnam Marine veteran and an equally hostile Hispanic Army infantry veteran over which ethic group had suffered the most discrimination throughout American history. The argument deteriorated to the point that they were standing and screaming into each other's face. Only the forceful but empathetic interventions of the group members prevented the argument from exploding into violence. Yet it is exactly this type of drama that provides veterans an opportunity for personal growth as they are forced by the group's reactions to examine and rethink the distorted assumptions and warped beliefs that lead to such heated exchanges. Contrary to what many psychotherapists believe, expressing strong feelings is not enough; patients must make an effort to think about and understand their emotions for real personality change to occur.

The renowned group therapy expert, Dr. Irvin Yalom, studied the therapeutic effectiveness of what are known as encounter groups, which are group therapies that focus primarily upon their members' emotional communications. He concluded that the factor that differentiated successful groups from the unsuccessful ones was that the successful groups reflected upon the displayed emotions in an effort to understand them and their implications. "There was clear evidence that a cognitive component was essential; some type of cognitive map was needed, some intellectual system that framed the experience and made sense of the emotions evoked in the group."[54]

Because of the current emphasis in psychiatry on evidence-based medicine, contemporary therapists consider the following advantage of group psychotherapy as the most important advantage. Well-designed scientific research studies have repeatedly demonstrated that group psychotherapy is an effective treatment for PTSD. For example, in 2003 a Department of Veterans Affairs clinical study of 360 Vietnam War veterans diagnosed with PTSD found that group therapy reduced PTSD symptoms. Groups of six men received weekly trauma-based cognitive–behavioral group treatments for 30 weeks followed by five monthly booster sessions. The results of this study indicated that PTSD symptom severity, especially social avoidance, decreased significantly from the initial assessment to the one-year follow-up assessment. Forty percent of the study's participants demonstrated clinically significant symptom reductions.[55] Another Department of Veterans Affairs field trial in 2008 studied 102 veterans diagnosed with combat related PTSD. Groups composed of nine to eleven men received biweekly exposure-based treatment for 16 to 18 weeks. Analysis of the treatment results found "clinically significant and lasting reductions in PTSD symptoms for most patients on both clinician symptoms ratings ... and self-report measures with only three dropouts."[56] After extensive study the task force for PTSD treatment guidelines of the International Society for Traumatic Stress Studies concluded, "Group treatment for PTSD is recommended ... based upon consistent positive evidence from 14 recent studies."[57]

Unfortunately even after extensive explanations of all the advantages of group psychotherapy, there remained a small contingent of PTSD veterans who continued to resist. After repeated attempts failed, the only option left was to insist upon group attendance. A rule evolved that to continue in individual PTSD psychotherapy, the combat veteran had to attend not just one, but at least three group therapy sessions. Most grumbled, but then agreed to attend the required sessions. Fortunately many changed their minds about group therapy within the three required sessions. Later a few of the previously resistant veterans returned to thank the therapist for insisting upon their attendance at group psychotherapy sessions. Each veteran announced that because of the group therapy treatments he was more social and less depressed. Each veteran considered group therapy as the critical element in his individual recovery from chronic PTSD. It was quite evident that they had significantly benefited from the trauma-based cognitive-behavioral group treatments of their combat-related PTSD. A few even developed enduring friendships with other members of their therapy groups. A psychotherapist does not have to have many such positive feedback experiences from veterans to appreciate how group psychotherapy provides healing benefits that simply cannot be duplicated by individual psychotherapy.

However, it is important to note that treatment planning for a combat veteran diagnosed with PTSD does require a decision on one type of psychotherapeutic treatment over the other. Both group and individual psychotherapy have their place in a comprehensive PTSD treatment plan.

Each approach has particular advantages. The ideal psychotherapy treatment plan would offer the combat veteran diagnosed with PTSD both types of psychotherapies. Individual psychotherapy would be used during the initial assessment phase and while establishing the therapeutic alliance. After the basics of cognitive psychotherapy are taught, the combat PTSD veteran would be assigned to weekly PTSD group psychotherapy sessions. The patient would still periodically meet with the individual psychotherapist, but now the individual therapy session would include processing problems, such as interpersonal conflicts, that occur because of group therapy attendance.

15

GUILT

In the 1980 *Diagnostic and Statistical Manual of Mental Disorders, Third Edition (DSM-III)*, guilt was listed as one of the diagnostic criterion symptoms of PTSD. It remains unclear why in the revised 1994 DSM-IV edition, guilt was demoted from the list of defining symptoms and mentioned only as an associated descriptive feature.[58] Nevertheless, excessive guilt remains a serious emotional difficulty for many PTSD veterans, even though few combat veterans complain directly of "feeling guilty." Guilt can be defined as a feeling of self-blame for violating an inner standard of acceptable behavior. It arises from the veteran's own internal evaluations of his or her behavior and is usually accompanied by self-anger and even self-punishment.

The following section defines and examines the major types of PTSD guilt found in combat veterans. Behavioral guilt is the painful emotion that results from either acting out unacceptable behaviors, such as shooting a civilian, or failing to perform positive behaviors, such as saving a friend. A particularly debilitating type of guilt is a second type: survival guilt. It is a feeling of shame for having survived a traumatic event in which others died. Survival guilt was first officially named and documented in German concentration camp survivors, who felt an enduring sense of shame at surviving the Holocaust while so many of their family and friends perished. For combat veterans it may include the shame associated with that first sharp feeling of joy associated with being alive after a battle in which your comrades died. It happens after that intense period when the survivor thinks "Better him than me." Along with the guilt, the survivor suffers later from chronic, impacted grief over those who died. Realistic guilt is defined as the anxiety that an individual feels when expecting punishment for a transgression of his or her internal moral compass, the conscience.

During graduate training, my child psychology professor shared a film of a psychology experiment that could be called "The Birth of Guilt."

Behind a one-way mirror the cameraman focused upon a three-year-old boy playing in a room with his mother. On the wall behind the boy and his toys was a conspicuous electrical wall socket. As young boys will do, he repeatedly attempted to stick his finger or some toy into the socket. His mother would then consistently but gently slap his hand while saying "No!" When the mother left the room, the camera recorded the boy playing alone. As expected, he again attempted to put his finger into the socket. But then anxiously looking around, he became more and more nervous, appearing to anticipate his mother's slap. Finally after a minute or two of anxious anticipation, he slapped his own hand. This was the birth of guilt; the boy had internalized his mother's prohibition. When he broke the weakly internalized rule, the anticipation of external punishment was too uncomfortable for the boy to endure, so he punished himself to end the anxiety. Like this young boy, civilized human beings punish themselves with blame and anger after they have done something that violates their moral code. This movie illustrates how guilt is closely associated with the early development of our internalized moral code, our human conscience.

In the violent world of war a soldier may become caught up in gruesomely horrific dilemmas, forcing him to behave in ways that he will later regret. Moral ambiguity and confusion run rampant in war. One Vietnam War veteran's armored personnel carrier (APC) platoon was in a vicious firefight with the Vietcong, when one of his friend's APC took a direct hit from a rocket-propelled grenade (RPG). The RPG exploded violently into the APC, which then caught fire. His friend became trapped in the burning APC by the twisted metal. The PTSD veteran severely burned his arms while failing to pull his friend out of the APC's burning hot aluminum. His friend's screams of agony as the flames consumed him so unnerved the veteran that he shot his dying friend in the head to end his agony. Another Vietnam War veteran was ordered to gather vital intelligence behind enemy lines. Unfortunately both he and his partner were captured and tortured. The veteran was able to escape, but he could see that his partner was still being brutally tortured. At great risk, the veteran stole an enemy rifle and then shot to kill his friend. Both of these men displayed the PTSD symptoms of guilt, major depression, repetitive traumatic nightmares, social withdrawal and rage. Their severe guilt festered out of the combination of their rage at being engulfed in such terrible dilemmas, grief over their friends' deaths and self-hatred over their mercy killings. Both of the men felt that they had broken society's moral code against the killing of friends.

A psychotherapist working with veterans burdened with such guilt must first of all build a trusting therapeutic relationship. The therapist empathizes with the PTSD veteran's emotional pain, but then must also challenge the veteran's dysfunctional interpretations of his or her behaviors, especially the self-blame. One cognitive therapy tactic is to have the veteran consider the use of civilian standards to judge military behaviors. To measure military behaviors by civilian standards is incorrect because it is the application of an inappropriate measuring instrument. It is like taking measurements with a rubber ruler that expands and contracts; measurements made with such a distorting instrument can never be accurate. Civilian values based upon a civilian worldview are not the correct standard to be used for judging behavior within the military world of war. Guilt-ridden PTSD veterans suffering from such memories need to reconsider how much of the tragic situation was truly their responsibility. They need to reevaluate the kinds of military brainwashing they had endured in boot camp where they were forced to pray for war and shout out "Kill! Kill!" while training in bayonet use or hand-to-hand combat. They must give a thorough consideration to the difficulty of fighting a guerrilla war in a foreign land like Vietnam, where standard military conventions were not followed. For example, the Vietnamese enemy deliberately shot to kill American medical personnel, including female nurses, whereas, the German Nazis in World War II spared medics and nurses. The skilled cognitive therapist asks, "What would be the best outcome in such a warped situation? Is it better for your friend to die slowly in intense agony or to limit his dying pain?" A civilian judge might condemn the veteran's actions as a type of murder, but such a condemnation ignores the courage and the affection the veteran felt for his friend — affection that was strong enough to motivate the veteran to carry out such a difficult obligation as a mercy killing. Session after session of these types of cognitive challenges slowly lead veterans to begin to question their automatic guilt-ridden interpretations of the tragic events. As they learn to limit their self-condemnations and began to redefine their gruesome experiences, their traumatic nightmares decrease in frequency and severity.

Another case involved a Vietnam veteran who was out on combat patrol when his unit received rocket propelled grenade (RPG) fire from a reedy area. In reaction to the deadly rocket barrage, the veteran quickly set up his mortar and suppressed the enemy's rocket fire with his return mortar fire. After the firefight he searched through the reeds and was shocked to find the body of a dead Vietnamese adolescent, no older than

16, who had been one of the enemy soldiers firing the rockets. His violation of an internalized cultural code that "Americans do not kill children" caused the veteran significant depression and intense guilt. Establishing a therapeutic alliance with him was difficult, but once established, the treatment plan was to empathize with his emotional turmoil but also to challenge his self-condemnation. Cognitive therapy provided the theoretical foundation for the therapeutic questioning: Was it not true that he had been caught up in a dangerous situation where he had only a few seconds to make monumental life-or-death decisions based upon incomplete information? Was his reaction to the deadly RPG fire a reasonable one given his military training and the realities of the combat situation? Wasn't he 19 years old at that time, an adolescent himself, not much older than the Vietnamese soldier? Was Vietnam an ugly war where teenagers found themselves fighting teenagers? Is it not true that he could blame himself now only because he now had the clarity of hindsight and the time to consider all options? At that time wasn't he doing what he thought was the right thing to do, firing on the enemy, in an attempt to save his own life and the lives of the men in his unit?

Guilt caused by the cruel fate of having to live with the results of a split-second, life-or-death decisions may be challenged by having soldiers rethink their behavior by applying the following thought experiment: Consider a losing quarterback who is hounded by the sports reporter as to why he threw the pass that was intercepted and ran back for the winning touchdown. Here too the sports reporter has the benefit of hindsight, he already knows the result of the quarterback's throw. A smart quarterback would smile and reply that when the football left his hands, it was going to be the touchdown throw that would win the game. The quarterback had not expected that his pass would be intercepted, just as this Vietnam veteran had not expected the results of his behavior. Guilt grows only within a perspective that ignores the realities at the moment of decision.

Further cognitive challenges focused upon the present: How did the PTSD veteran's continued depression, due to his self-condemnation, change things? Was it not true that it did nothing but torture him and infect his entire family with his depressed mood? Do two wrongs make a right? Does his guilt bring the Vietnamese teenager back to life? It was only after he had learned to restructure his previous interpretation of the battle that this Vietnam veteran began to forgive himself and smile again.

Not all guilt ridden PTSD veterans responded as well to cognitive psychotherapy. One soldier disclosed that he was in a trench line defense during a major ground attack on his base. The North Vietnamese Army (NVA) had already hit his unit's ammunition dump: the exploding American shells were wounding some of the defenders. The NVA then mounted a determined ground assault on the front gate and breeched it, but he and the other soldiers fought furiously to beat back the assault. He, like everyone else, had been shooting at the uniformed NVA soldiers storming through the gate. He saw one enemy soldier cut down by his rifle fire. The morning after the battle soldiers policed the battlefield, which means they searched the enemy bodies for intelligence and then buried them in mass graves. When he came to the enemy he had shot, the veteran flipped over the body, causing a breast to fall out of her uniform; he recoiled with shock at discovering that the dead enemy soldier was a female.

Years later he complained of severe flashbacks, significant depression and family problems. During the course of individual psychotherapy his guilt over this battle was revealed; he had internalized the moral code that "American soldiers do not kill women." His behavioral guilt over shooting a female enemy soldier was so deep that it infected his relationships with his wife and his adolescent daughter, whom he was incapable of disciplining. During ongoing cognitive psychotherapy his disordered interpretations were repeatedly challenged: Was it not true that the woman was uniformed and shooting an AK-47 assault rifle at him and his fellow Americans? Was it not true that the bullets from her rifle could have killed him just as dead as any man's bullets could? Was it not true that he did not realize that the NVA soldier was a woman until he saw her breast? Again the cognitive therapy emphasis was not on the power of positive thinking, but rather upon the healing power of reality-oriented thinking. Sadly, his guilt was too entrenched. He could not forgive himself, which resulted in a chronically deteriorating condition of PTSD with severe depression.

As mentioned, the term survival guilt was used to describe the extreme shame Nazi concentration camp survivors felt because they lived when so many had died. There are cases of Jewish survivors who lost their entire families: mothers, fathers, and siblings in the immediate family, and also their extended family of uncles, grandparents and cousins. The living reacted emotionally as if their survival was a cruel mistake of fate. They felt that they had somehow deserted their families by surviving. Thus survival guilt can be defined as a pathological type of chronic grief. Similarly, the survival guilt suffered by PTSD combat veterans is connected to their grief over the death of friends and fellow soldiers.

At times survival guilt is complicated by the random nature of combat survival, as illustrated by the following case report. One veteran had been a Marine whose unit was building a new base far north in South Vietnam. The location was so close to the Demilitarized Zone (DMZ), which separated North and South Vietnam, that it was vulnerable to artillery attacks from NVA units stationed near the DMZ in North Vietnam. This veteran and a squad of six fellow Marines were digging fortifications. They had finished digging a trench, but they had not had time to build any overhead cover for the trench, when an artillery attack from NVA long-range guns hit the base. He and his squad had just dived into their trench for protection, when an artillery shell exploded in front of their trench line. After the massive shock wave passed and the falling dirt had settled, the Marine dusted himself off and looked around. One squad member lying to the right of him was dead and the man lying on the other side of him was also dead. The next man in line had survived but the man next to him was dead. Every other Marine in that trench was killed by the shell's explosion. Decades later he still felt that he had somehow betrayed his dead comrades by surviving; yet at the same time, he was tortured by the recognition that initially he had felt some happiness at having survived the attack. This Marine was burdened not only by his survival guilt but also his puzzlement over the apparent random nature of the deaths. He, like many other combat survivors, had trouble accepting the idea that mere chance could have so much to do with their survival. It was as if God had rolled dice to determine who lived. He would not believe that death could be due to random chance. Consequently he continued to question why he had lived, when the others had died. They had all jumped into the same trench avoiding the same artillery rounds; yet, every other man in the trench had died. He felt that he should have died there, that his survival was a cruel mistake of fate. He continued to struggle with developing some meaning for his survival.

As always the first step in psychotherapy with veterans suffering this type of survival guilt is to establish the therapeutic alliance. Then they are taught the basic philosophy of a cognitive therapy. Only then does the questioning begin over their distorted and pathological interpretation of their survival: What exactly did you do wrong? How would it be better if you had died in the attack? Your situation is like the concentration camp survivors who lost their entire family. How would it better if the sole survivor of an entire family died? Is it not correct that to be truly dead is to be forgotten? Who will remember your dead comrades? Who else can communicate to their families and the world the tragic story of their deaths?

Many PTSD veterans who have lost comrades in battle are confused, like the aforementioned Marine, about how to live out their lives in a manner that honors their fallen brothers. Most of them think that their lives are somehow counterfeit; all too often they deteriorate into a painful self-loathing that can decay into suicidal thoughts. At this point in their psychotherapy an effective strategy is to share the moving true story described in Terry Wallace's book *Bloods: An Oral History of the Vietnam War by Black Veterans*. Mr. Wallace is a journalist who interviewed twenty African American Vietnam veterans and then transcribed their individual experiences into his book. One story concerns Specialist Arthur E. Woodley Jr., an Airborne Ranger with the 173rd Airborne Division. In February 1969 his squad was ordered to find and search the wreckage of a helicopter that was shot down three days prior. After ten hours of searching through very heavy foliage, they found the bullet-ridden wreck; but as they searched the area for survivors, they make a grim discovery. They found a Caucasian soldier who had been staked to the ground and gruesomely tortured by the Vietcong. The skin of his chest was peeled off down to his waist. Miraculously he was still alive. As Specialist Woodley bent to give him water, he saw that the poor fellow was trying to say something. After he placed his ear next to the victim's mouth, he heard the poor man whisper "Kill me ... kill me." During a Public Broadcasting System documentary about the book broadcast on May 20, 1986, the muscular Mr. Woodley, who was then a Baltimore inner city gang leader, openly cried as he continued the story. He did not personally know the tortured soldier, yet he recoiled in horror from the soldier's request. Yet Specialist Woodley knew that they could not call in a medical evacuation helicopter in time to save him and that the poor fellow's suffering was monstrous. The tortured and dying soldier then communicated to Specialist Woodley a persuasive existential argument: "Kill me! I'll die for you.... You live for me."[59] After accepting the stranger's existential deal, Mr. Woodley, a tough Airborne Ranger, explained on television with tears in his eyes how he ended the victim's horrific ordeal by shooting him.

There are those who are skeptical about Mr. Woodley and his story,[60] but no matter. As a Vietnam War combat veteran I was profoundly moved by the victim's dying bargain in Mr. Woodley's story. Since learning of the story, I have shared it with many combat PTSD veterans, especially those like the survivor of the artillery attack, who wonder why they were spared when so many perished. It is my firm belief that the tortured soldier's existential exchange provides for Vietnam War survivors, as well as the survivors of all wars, a powerful strategy for honoring our fallen brothers and sisters. It may also provide a sense of meaning to our lives. *They died for us; in exchange we live for them!* We who are the fortunate ones must live in a manner that truly honors our dead, by living well. We must honor their sacrifice by living a good life ... passionately. It is my heartfelt belief that this is what they would have wanted us to do. Combat veterans that commit suicide, either quickly by shooting themselves or slowly through addictions to alcohol, illicit drugs or food, do not honor the sacrifices of their dead comrades. By following this philosophy of living an honorable life, we earn our right to peace and perhaps even a bit of joy. Every new day is a gift; since our dead cannot, we the living must squeeze as much life as possible out of every precious second. Living a good life in their honor is better than a memorial wall in Washington, D.C.; it is the ultimate monument to the sacrifices of our dead.

Behavioral guilt may have a delayed onset. Combat veterans who had made a reasonable adjustment to civilian life would present at our clinic. They were married men, working full-time and raising a family. However when they would look back at their behavior while fighting in the terror war of Vietnam, they would feel guilty. They complained of a serious depression because they had to kill in the war. Most would call themselves murderers. Their central question was: "Doc, don't the ten commandments say thou shall not kill?" After establishing the therapeutic alliance, I would apply the principles of cognitive psychotherapy by questioning their unrealistically guilty interpretation of their behavior in the war. A major therapeutic goal was to have them restructure their negative self-image. The foundation of the psychoeducational effort was based on the fact that killing in the context of a war is morally acceptable within our Judeo-Christian tradition; it is not murder, which is condemned. Many present day rabbis and professors of ancient Hebrew, such as those teaching at Jerusalem University, insist that the fourth of the ten commandments is mistranslated when it is translated as "thou shall not kill." These Hebrew language experts argue that the fourth commandment is more accurately translated as "thou shall not murder."[61] They report that in ancient Western societies wise religious leaders understood that in certain specific situations killing was considered lawful behavior, therefore acceptable. These special circumstances include when someone kills in self-defense, capital punishment and *the soldier in battle*. All guilt-ridden combat veterans need to understand that killing and murder are not synonymous behaviors. There is a vast moral difference between taking of a life unlawfully, as in murder, and the taking of a life lawfully, as in military battle. A soldier killing in battle is a socially approved, special case; it is a justified type of killing. No courts in Western society charge regular enemy soldiers with murder, let alone their own soldiers, who have killed the enemy during the usual course of battle.

In the United States both military and civilian courts make a clear distinction between different types of killing. For example if a driver accidentally killed a pedestrian by hitting the person with his or her truck, in a civilian court the driver would most likely be charged with manslaughter, not murder. For the charge to be murder there has to exist responsibility, but also a cold-blooded premeditation to harm. A skilled defense attorney would point out that the driver did not awaken that morning with a thought or intent to kill that particular pedestrian. The driver probably did not even know the individual. The charge would be manslaughter because, yes, the driver is responsible for the pedestrian's death, but there was no prior intent to harm this stranger. Consider another example: if a civilian were to kill an armed attacker in self-defense, the civilian would probably not be charged at all. The police would most likely recognize that the attacker's death was a result of the civilian's self-defense against a potentially fatal attack, and therefore, justified. Or consider the harsh reality that the United States military thoroughly trains its soldiers in how to kill and then orders them into a kill-or-be-killed war zone like the Mideast. If a soldier then kills in combat, is it justified? A convincing argument can be made that to kill in a kill-or-be-killed situation, such as in the current war on terror, is one form of self-defense and is thus justified.

All guilt-ridden combat veterans, not just those suffering from PTSD, need to understand that in our society's legal system not all killing is defined as murder. The same reasoning holds true within our Judeo-Christian religious tradition, where murder is condemned, but not all killing is murder. How it is defined depends upon the specific circumstances surrounding the death. A soldier killing in battle is one of those special acceptable circumstances within our Western religious and legal traditions. Those combat veterans who used the above factual information to reconsider and restructure their "murderer" self-definition were then able to report that they felt less guilt and a greater peace of mind.

The most difficult combat veterans to treat were the ones whose guilt had a realistic base. One Marine veteran, who was a sergeant in Vietnam, tearfully recounted how in the middle of a fierce battle with the North Vietnamese Army (NVA), he was ordered by an officer to have a squad of his Marines move to another position. He knew that it was a highly dangerous maneuver, and that anyone sent to that exposed position would probably be killed. Instead of leading the squad, he ordered four other men to the new position, where in due course the NVA killed them all.

Combat PTSD veterans who suffered from realistic guilt, like the above Marine sergeant, benefited from learning and applying Dr. Robert Jay Lifton's concept of animating guilt. Dr. Lifton, a New York City psychiatrist, explains the concept in his book *Home from the War*. In 1970 Dr. Lifton became involved with the veteran advocacy group Vietnam Veterans Against the War (VVAW), which led to his establishing the pioneering Vietnam War combat veteran "rap group." *Home from the War* is his account of these psychotherapy groups and the lessons he learned from them. A clinically significant part of what he learned was a psychotherapeutic method for the healing of realistic guilt. Dr. Lifton defines two types of guilt: static guilt is defined as the veteran's feeling either a sustained "deadening" of numbness or a perpetual "*mea culpa* of self-condemnation.... Animating guilt, in contrast, is characterized by bringing oneself to life around one's guilt."[62] Animating guilt is the healing process for guilt-ridden veterans' acceptance of responsibility for their behavior in a war and then liberating their guilty energy to do good deeds. It is, in one sense, the troubled veteran's balancing of karma through present-day good works. Animating guilt is the healing process of making amends for your regretted behaviors; it can be considered a secular form of Christians performing penance for their sins. For example, a combat veteran who killed a child in order to survive could animate his or her guilt by working in civilian life with children as a teacher or coach. A few Vietnam War PTSD veterans animated their guilt through antiwar political activity; others worked as veteran advocates. The aforementioned Marine sergeant animated his guilt by being elected to a national office of a veterans' service organization and then effectively advocating for veterans in Washington, D.C. His case clearly demonstrates how animating realistic guilt can be adaptive and beneficial for others.

In summary a cognitive psychotherapist treating PTSD guilt challenges and questions the veteran's dysfunctional attitudes and interpretations of guilty behaviors. For example, another effective cognitive tactic is to dispute veterans' dysfunctional thinking with the explanation that the guilt feelings themselves argue against their being the monster they think they are. The true psychopathic monster has not developed an internal guidance system of cultural values. Because they do not possess a conscience, these real monsters are incapable of feeling guilt. Only nonmonstrous, civilized human beings who have a conscience are capable of feeling the emotion of guilt. The following is a list of other challenging questions that a cognitive psychotherapist could use to help combat PTSD veterans rethink their guilt. This list is an adaptation of one found in Dr. Glenn R. Schiraldi's *The Post-traumatic Disorder Source Book*.[63]

1. Is it not true that you were in a life-or-death combat situation within a hostile foreign land, where you were not sure of what was the best course of action?

2. Did you possess, at that time of extreme combat stress, all of the relevant information you needed to make the best decision or were you engulfed in the "fog of war?"

3. Did you have the necessary time to consider all of the many possible options, or were you risking death if you did not make a split second decision?

4. Did you possess any method for figuring out what was clearly the correct choice?

5. Are you sure that there was a clear cut, correct choice or were you in a confusing situation where all your options were less than perfect ones?

6. Are you a perfect human being, intelligent and calm enough to always make the correct decision, even under the extreme conditions of combat stress?

7. What exactly was your thinking at the time of extreme combat stress that caused you to do what you did?

8. Given your horrible situation within the terrible circumstances of that ugly war, did you make a reasonable choice?

16

ANGER AND VIOLENCE

In direct contrast to guilt, PTSD-associated anger has been promoted by the psychiatric establishment from an associated feature to a criterion symptom. In the 1980 DSM-III, anger was listed only as an associated feature. It was described as "Increased irritability that may be associated with sporadic and unpredictable explosions of aggressive behavior, upon even minimal or no provocation."[64] The DSM-III goes on to state that this associated feature is characteristic of war veterans.

Puzzled by this lack of official emphasis after frequently observing anger in PTSD combat veterans, I decided to formally study the personality characteristics of Vietnam veterans. My research compared the personalities of Vietnam War veterans diagnosed with PTSD to the personalities of a control group of Vietnam veterans diagnosed with other psychiatric disorders. This comparison was accomplished by testing both groups with the *Million Clinical Multiaxial Inventory* (MCMI), a well-respected personality assessment instrument. The test results demonstrated that the PTSD veterans scored significantly higher than the control group veterans on the MCMI's two aggression scales; in fact, the two aggression scales were the PSTD veterans' highest scores. The results demonstrate that anger played a central role in the post-war personalities of Vietnam PTSD veterans. The study was presented at the 1981 Annual Convention of the American Psychological Association. The findings were later cited by trauma experts, such as Dr. Charles Figley in his book *Trauma and Its Wake*[65] and Dr. James Choca and his associates in the *Interpretative Guide to the Million Clinical Multiaxial Inventory.*[66] When the American Psychiatric Association published the revised Fourth Edition of their Diagnostic and Statistical Manual in 1994, anger had been promoted from an associated feature to the status of a diagnostic symptom of PTSD.

One basic weakness in the mental health books and articles dealing with anger is concept and word confusion. Different terms, such as hostility, temper, anger, aggression, rage, and violence are used almost interchangeably. Even in the professional literature the terms are ill defined and used as synonyms, but they are not the same exact concept. Using them synonymously leads to fuzzy thinking and illogical arguments. Specific definitions are required to indicate exactly what is being considered. Therefore for this volume, anger is defined as a negative feeling, the intense internal arousal of emotional displeasure, usually accompanied by a sense of antagonism towards someone or something. Many leaders in the religious and the psychological communities condemn anger as something to be avoided at all cost. Their self-help book titles such as "How to Control Your Anger" or "How to Calm Your Temper" demonstrates this condemnation. Theses authors routinely fail to recognize the fact that anger, like any human emotion, is morally neutral, that it is not in itself morally good or evil. What determines morality is behavior, not feelings. It is what you do with your anger that really matters. The anger-avoidance argument fails to acknowledge the undeniable existence of righteous indignation. Consider for a moment Martin Luther King, Jr. or Mahatma Gandhi; they were angry men, but they had a right to be angry over the plight of their people. Yet they were noble men, able to channel the energy of their righteous anger into the nonviolent resistance of boycotts and mass marches, tactics that were more effective in advancing their causes than violence.

Violence is hereby defined not as an emotion, but as destructive behavior. It occurs when an individual's anger is so intense that it explodes into furious acting-out. The only aim of violence is to destroy, hurt or kill. Like Dr. King, Malcolm X was angry at the status of African Americans in America; however, unlike Dr. King, he channeled his angry energy at first into violence. It is ironic that after Malcolm X changed his strategy to one of nonviolence, his followers, to whom he had taught violence, assassinated him. Our popular culture glamorizes violence in media outlets such as movies, television and video games. By removing authentic depictions of the painful consequences of violence, the mass media make it appear exciting and glamorous. Hollywood gives violence a macho appeal. Yet the stark reality is that interpersonal violence is primitive, grotesque, and morally reprehensible. It is a base regression to our savage past that must be condemned and restrained. No soldier who has survived the gruesome horrors of combat would ever consider violence glamorous.

It is popularly thought that violence is unalterably linked to and caused by anger. As one veteran expressed the connection, "When I get angry, I get violent, and then I am not the last guy in the room to get hurt." Because of this concept of a strong causal link between anger and violence, when someone condemns violence, it tends to automatically spill back into a condemnation of anger. Even though we live in a violent society, refined people in polite circles are not allowed to be angry. Just as Victorian Europeans denied and repressed their natural sexuality, upper and middle class Americans tend to deny and repress a core part of their human nature, feeling angry. It becomes an embarrassment to be avoided. Observe the reaction in a busy restaurant when a customer becomes angry and loud with the waiter. As the other diners hear the angry words, the ripples of embarrassment spread out from that table to overwhelm the entire room.

But the concept of an unalterable causal link between anger and violence is an inaccurate one. Anger does not invariably lead to violence, as evidenced by the previous examples of Gandhi or Dr. King. Not that we could all become such saintly men; however, their examples do prove that humans do possess the capacity to be angry, even justifiably so, without inevitably deteriorating into violence. It is important to recognize that anger can be acceptable, even useful. Anger possesses positive attributes, such as its energizing or communicative characteristics. Anger can increase an individual's psychic energy to the point that she or he will then confront and proactively deal with a problem. An individual's anger communicates to others in a problematic social situation messages of determination and potency. Finally, acknowledging one's anger can enhance one's self-concept, leading to a personal sense of competency and control.

It is essential at this point to acknowledge that my conceptualization of anger and its regulation has been influenced by the research of Dr. Raymond W. Novaco, professor of social ecology at the University of California. I first learned of his innovative work in the early 1970s when we were both graduate students in Indiana University's clinical psychology program, Dr. Novaco has not only produced influential research in the field of anger regulation, but also successfully applied his ideas clinically to both active duty military and combat veterans at Department of Veteran Affairs hospitals.[67]

People think that anger inevitably causes violence because few of them have learned how to break the connection. Breaking that link requires training and social maturity. Try this experiment: ask a three year old girl if she would like a candy bar, but also promise her that if she were to wait five minutes, she could have two candy bars. What is the most likely outcome? The three year old child will choose the immediate reward of one candy bar. Good parents strive to teach their children how to delay the gratification of such childish impulses. Even throughout adolescence, good parents have to teach their immature offspring that lengthening the interval between desire and gratification usually leads, as in our experiment, to the greater reward.

Unfortunately military training for war causes regressive effects on a soldier's mature ability to delay angry impulses towards violence. During the Vietnam era the United States Army initiated quick kill training, which is basically teaching recruits to fire their rifles on impulse, striving to make rifle firing a type of reflex. At first the trainee was taught how to fire his rifle on a standard firing range. On the range the soldier had enough time to recognize the bulls-eye target, to align the rifle's sites on the target and then, as taught, to slowly squeeze the trigger. It takes time to consciously aim and fire the rifle. But the U.S. army leaders knew that in the Vietnam War the most frequent combat engagement was the enemy's ambush, a fast attack when the soldier does not have the luxury of time. Consequently quick kill training was developed to teach soldiers an effective technique for quickly countering deadly ambushes.

Basically in quick kill training recruits were taught to simply point their rifles and fire without consciously aiming. Training started with BB gun rifles and large cardboard circle targets, which were initially thrown up directly in front of the trainee. The idea was to be able to rapidly point the rifle up and shoot the flying cardboard circle. After the recruit mastered close range firing, the cardboard disks became progressively smaller and the distance to the target was gradually increased. In a surprisingly short time trainees were shooting small half-dollar size moving targets out of the air many meters away. Then the future infantryman was given an M-16 rifle loaded with live ammunition and sent down a heavily wooded path, where human silhouette targets would randomly spring up on him. The trainees were ordered to apply their quick kill skills, to reflexively point and fire, in these simulated ambushes. Again the training proved to be quite effective. Many of these same infantrymen successively applied their quick kill firing skills later in Vietnam firefights against Vietcong and NVA ambushes.

An extremely effective measure for countering ambushes, quick kill reflexive firing, once mastered, lead to difficulties for returning veterans in controlling their impulses towards violence. Because of the quick kill training, Vietnam combat veterans had learned, when threatened, to literally shoot first and ask questions later. Application of the reflexive firing resulted in a shortening of the veteran's processing interval between perceiving a threat and acting out in violence. Its application caused a regression in social maturity; any previously learned inhibitions against immediate gratification of impulses were overruled. Once a combat soldier had learned to act out reflexively and had been dynamically rewarded with survival, it then became an overlearned habit that was extremely difficult to break.

Yet breaking the habit of impulsive acting out is exactly the goal which cognitive psychotherapy for anger regulation strives to reach. My anger management training program attempted to reestablish within the combat PTSD veteran a mature self-control, relearning how to delay acting out on hostile impulses. The first step was to have the angry veteran understand the basics of cognitive therapy, such the A-B-C analysis. Veterans were taught how automatic interpretations of situations determine emotional reactions. One example provided was how individuals respond with different emotions to a threatening person. The process that determines whether an individual's emotional reaction would be anger or fear was the automatic appraisal of the threatening person's potential for harm in relationship to the individual's own self-defense skills. If the veteran was physically fit from years of martial arts training and the aggressor appeared to be out of shape, then the resulting emotion would be anger. On the other hand if the veteran was weakened by physical disabilities and the aggressor appeared to be large and muscular, then the resulting emotion would be fear. Thus the veteran's emotional response to an interpersonal provocation was the result of rapid automatic comparisons of their mutual fighting powers, an evaluation that occurred outside of awareness of the veteran's unconscious mind.

The next major step focused on helping combat PTSD veterans identify and reality test their distorted conceptualization of threats. For example one veteran disclosed in individual therapy that most of the time he illegally carried a concealed handgun. When this behavior was challenged, the veteran answered, "Doc, you don't understand, there is a war out there in the streets of my 'hood.'" The accuracy of his evaluation of the dangerousness of his neighborhood was then questioned with an emphasis on his distortion of reality: "You say there is a war going on in your neighborhood, well where are the heavy machine guns? Where are the mortars and artillery? Isn't it true that what you are really dealing with are untrained young punks, who hold and fire their Saturday night specials sideways because they saw it in a Hollywood gangster movie?"

In group sessions the cognitive therapy interventions were also directed at helping the combat PTSD veterans recognize that emotions felt after a perceived personal threat were the direct result of unconscious and automatic thinking. They were taught that past appraisals of threats may have been distorted and illogical. Discussion often centered on what the veteran thought after being confronted with direct interpersonal provocations. One common answer was that these confrontations were "challenges to my manhood." Again the accuracy of this dysfunctional interpretation were questioned: "Didn't you fight in and survive the horrors of that nasty Vietnam War? Doesn't that already prove that you are a real man? Why do you have to prove your manhood to anyone again?" Another factor related to the manhood issue for Vietnam War veterans was their poor self-image. Many had bought into the lie fostered by the mass media that they were losers because of America's inability to win the Vietnam War. (See the chapter on low self-esteem for more details.)

The critical step in cognitive anger management was to help angry PTSD veterans learn a set of specific cognitive coping skills designed to deal with direct personal provocations. Once they had acquired some understanding of their prior dysfunctional interpretations, which can be considered as a type of private speech, they were taught a couple of simple self-directed questions that would help them regulate their anger. These self-control questions were designed to make the veteran's threat appraisals more accurate, reasonable and deliberate. The aim of the first question was to help in discriminating when physically acting out anger was justified from the many situations when it was not. When angry veterans felt their bodies energizing towards violence by, perhaps, fists clenching, they were taught to first ask themselves "What is the threat?" This private question was designed to trigger considerations of where and what exactly was the danger in the situation and how severe it was. They were taught to spend a few seconds appraising if the adversary was armed or not, whether there was more than one adversary, whether there was an escape route, whether the adversary was chemically altered by drugs or alcohol, whether the adversary was bluffing or truly menacing, what were their own capabilities for self-defense and so on. Like the standard advice of counting to ten, asking oneself "What is the threat?" lengthens the time interval between recognizing a threat and responding to it. But the advantage here is that the veteran is filling this vital interval with a task-oriented cognitive analysis that will increase the probability of a favorable outcome. Angry veterans were taught that even if violence were justified, without a thorough threat analysis the chances of reaching a successful outcome were limited. It was pointed out that more than one combat veteran has been beaten and severely injured because of failing to notice that an opponent was armed or that the opponent had friends there who would join the fight.

To aid in discriminating when violence may be justified, two legal principles were introduced into the psychotherapeutic training discussions. The primary one is the inalienable right of self-defense. Judges and defense lawyers all acknowledge that human beings have a legal right to defend themselves against being physically harmed or killed. Usually veterans would then ask what they were allowed to do in defending themselves. But there is no one simple answer to that question. The right answer always was "It depends." What actions are legally acceptable always depends upon the particular details involved in each particular situation. This answer leads directly into the second important legal principle of proportionality. Even in self-defense, the level of violence must always be in proportion to the level of the threat. Veterans were taught to realize that if they were violent and harmed another human being, they most likely would find themselves in a court explaining their behavior to a judge and jury. Judges and juries are more likely to accept and view violent behavior that was proportional to the threat more favorably than otherwise. For example, consider an aggressor who pushed or bumped a veteran while cutting in front of the veteran who was standing in line for a movie. If the veteran were to break the aggressor's arm in a subsequent scuffle, a jury will most likely deem this response disproportional to the threat. The veteran would have harmed the attacker more than the attacker harmed the veteran. Pushing the aggressor back out of line or complaining to the manager would be a more proportional and thus more legally acceptable response. However, if an aggressor were to then pull a knife and attack the veteran, then the veteran's breaking the attacker's arm in self-defense would be viewed as an acceptable response. The veteran's violent behavior was proportional to the potential violence of the attack. Exactly the same injury to the aggressor would be judged as appropriate in one scenario and not in the other. This concept of a proportional response to threat dictates that killing or seriously injuring an attacker would be justified, if and only if the veteran's very life were realistically threatened by a direct potentially murderous attack.

The second private self-control question taught angry PTSD veterans was "What is my goal?" The idea was to think in terms of "What am I looking for here? What do I want out of this situation?" This one is the more important of the two questions because it places veterans squarely in charge of their response to the provocation, rather than reflexively reacting to every provocation. A minnow does not grow into a big fish by biting at every piece of bait. This question reflects an acceptance of one's self-responsibility in threatening situations and a recognition that one's actions here could result in standing before a judge and jury defending one's behavior. The second question also reflects a personal philosophy on fighting adopted by some Vietnam War veterans. During the Vietnam era politicians made decisions that resulted in their having to fight in that war. Since then, they promised themselves that they would never again allow others to dictate when, where or if they were going to fight. Their next fight, if it ever happened, would be one of their own choosing. The philosophy was summed up in the phrase "Choose your wars."

To illustrate an application of the self-control questions, veterans were given a common example as a model for discussion. Every working day local combat veteran commuters had to cope with long drives over major highways in crowded rush hour traffic to reach their places of employment. Consequently twice a day they were realistically in a dangerous, potentially deadly, situation. Episodes of road rage were occurring in our community, as well as all-too-regular fatal motor vehicle accidents during rush hours. "What is the threat?" In the case of a veteran's commute, it was the possibility of serious injury or even death from road rage or reckless driving. So the threat was a real danger. Now apply the second self-control question, "What is my goal?" The only reasonable goal for the veteran was to arrive both at work and back home safely. It was not to cross horns with every inconsiderate driver stressed out for whatever reason or, even worse, to crash into them. With this goal in mind the veteran would be better able to tolerate unsafe aggressive drivers and even at times personal insults from other men and women commuters.

Another example used for mental rehearsal was the situation in which an unmarried male combat veteran dresses up to go out to a nightclub to meet and dance with women. But in a crowded nightclub the chances are high that the veteran might bump into another man and a drink could be spilled, potentially leading to a personal confrontation. Again the two self-control questions were applied. First the specific threat should be evaluated: How hostile is the opponent? Is he alone? Is he drunk? Does he have a weapon? Then the veteran should ask himself the second and more important question: "What is my goal?" In group psychotherapy veterans were encouraged to think along these rational lines: "Did I dress up in these expensive clothes and put on aftershave to fight this idiot? No. Will fighting him help me reach my goal of meeting an attractive woman? No. Do I have to prove how rough and tough I am? No. Am I less of a man if I walk away? No. My goal tonight was to meet and dance with women, not to fight this drunk." One of my PTSD veterans disclosed at a later group therapy session that a situation similar to this model scenario happened to him one night at a club. He was justifiably proud of the fact that he had applied his anger-regulation private speech training successfully and decided to walk away from the belligerent drunk. The rest of the group members responded with a round of applause.

The final component of the combat veteran group's anger regulation training was teaching the basics of the emergency alarm response and then the application of relaxation therapies to calm their anger-related physiological arousal. (Review the chapter on anxiety and fear for details of relaxation training.)

17

DEPRESSION AND
SUICIDAL THOUGHTS

People tend to consider someone who is in a sad mood as depressed. But being sad or having the blues is a normal emotion, especially during times of increased stress. The sadness felt after the death of a loved one is not depression, but rather normal grief. Feeling blue after being laid off from a job is normal. When psychologists and other mental health professionals discuss depression, they are not talking about feeling blue, but rather an abnormal emotional state that significantly interferes with the individual's life. They are discussing clinical depression, a serious psychiatric condition defined as a significantly sad mood that persists. Mood is defined here as the predominant emotion state of an individual over a lengthy period. The difference between common sadness and clinical depression is like the difference between breathing hard after a fast sprint and being chronically short-of-breath. The former is expected and normal, given the stress of the sprint; the latter is an abnormal condition. The characteristics that separate normal sadness from clinical depression are its intensity, persistence and interference in a patient's life functioning. Usually clinical depression requires psychiatric and psychological treatment.

Although depression is not listed in the DSM-IV as a diagnostic symptom for Post Traumatic Stress Disorder, it is the psychiatric diagnosis that is most often listed as a codisorder in those patients with a PTSD diagnosis. Estimates of the percentage of patients who are dually diagnosed with PTSD and depression are as high as 80 percent.[68] Combat veterans suffering from PTSD have an increased risk for the development of depression. The stress of dealing with the various symptoms of their PTSD drains the veteran's psychological energy, establishing the perfect conditions for the development of depression. There are a number of symptoms, such as insomnia and irritability, that overlap the two disorders. If the depressive symptoms are numerous enough in a traumatized veteran to meet the diagnostic criterion, then a separate depression diagnosis is given along with the PTSD diagnosis. The DSM-IV lists two different types of depression; the first is termed *dysthymic disorder*, a technical term for mild depression; the second is called *major depressive disorder*. Besides the obvious severity of symptoms, the two disorders are distinguished by their onset and duration.

Major depression consists of time-limited episodes of depression that can usually be distinguished from the individual's normal level of functioning at both work and home. In contrast, dysthymia is characterized by a daily display of milder depressive symptoms that persist for at least two years. The mild symptoms become the individual's usual pattern of daily behavior. Because dysthymic symptoms can appear to be typical and almost normal, it can be problematic for troubled individuals or their families to recognize the disorder and to seek treatment.

Major depressive disorder is characterized by a mixed pattern of possible symptoms, including physical, emotional, psychological and social symptoms. To meet the diagnostic criteria a veteran must exhibit one of these two symptoms: sad mood or diminished interest in life's activities. A depressive mood is the most common complaint of veterans, who may describe it as feeling "down in the dumps" or "gloomy." At times the lowered mood may be reported as increased irritability and/or frustration over minor irritants. A few veterans may not recognize their depression, but usually family members will identify it. The other required symptom is a reduction in the pleasure derived from daily living. Veterans may complain that they have lost their zest for life. Frequently there is a reduction in sexual desire and sexual behaviors. Often there is a corresponding loss of interest in other behaviors that used to provide pleasure. The depressed veteran may report that for fun he or she likes to go bowling, but when asked, is surprised to realize that the last time was over two years ago. Families often complain that veterans no longer participate in family social gatherings.

A characteristic of major depressive disorder that distinguishes it from normal sadness is the varied biological symptoms displayed in the clinical picture. There may be appetite changes within the veteran. A common milder symptom is weight gain associated with the veteran consuming more highly caloric, sugary comfort foods like cakes and candies. A more serious symptom is a loss of appetite that reflects a loss of pleasure in eating. Veterans may report that they have to force themselves to eat, evidenced by loose clothes. The most common physical symptom is an overall loss of energy. The veteran complains of fatigue; even the easiest tasks seem to require maximum effort. There is a generalized slowing down of all behaviors. The veteran may complain that a simple chore like washing dishes is exhausting and takes much longer to complete. Another symptom of this depressive weariness may be chronic excessive sleeping; sleeping becomes an escape from unhappiness. Most seriously depressed veterans do develop a sleep disturbance, but its predominant form is insomnia. The veteran may experience difficulty falling asleep or experience interrupted sleep with problems returning to sleep. For depressed veterans suffering from PTSD, the insomnia is frequently caused by recurrent nightmares that are frightening enough to awaken them. Then they may have trouble returning to sleep because of their anxious anticipation that the nightmares may reoccur.

However for a minority of depressed veterans, the clinical picture in terms of personal energy is the exact opposite. They appear agitated and hyperactive, but their agitation is nonproductive. This agitation is displayed by behaviors such as pacing nervously, nail biting, foot tapping, or compulsively smoking. These veterans will also complain of having trouble falling asleep or relaxing. They have difficulties sitting still and complain of being easily distracted and an inability to concentrate. Inattention is just one of the many cognitive symptoms of major depressive disorder. Depressed veterans may complain of memory lapses, trouble making decisions, and a general inability to think clearly. Frequently their minds are preoccupied by obsessive worries and self-doubts. They may experience frequent thoughts of death and possibly ominous thoughts of suicide. They may think that their families would be better off without them. With older depressed veterans psychological testing can be quite useful in ascertaining whether their cognitive problems are purely emotionally based or a sign of a neurological disorder like dementia.

The final set of symptoms included in the DSM-IV criteria for major depression involves the individual's sense of worthlessness. Depressed veterans exhibit feelings of inadequacy and low self-esteem out of proportion to their personal reality. They may consider themselves complete failures or completely incompetent even though they had held positions of authority in the military or in the civilian world. Depressed combat veterans often feel inappropriate guilt associated with sins of commission or omission. When evaluating their performance in combat, they apply unrealistic perfectionistic standards. For example, medics who obsessively criticize themselves for the few soldiers they did not save, completely ignoring the soldiers whose lives they did save. Many depressed veterans possess an exaggerated sense of responsibility, which leaves them feeling guilty over events and situations that realistically they had no control over. One Vietnam Marine felt extremely guilty for his firing on some hidden figures, who later turned out to be fellow Marines. He blamed himself totally for their wounds, ignoring completely the sad fact that he was directly ordered by a Marine officer to shoot. He did not take into consideration that there were other squad members who were also shooting and who could have caused the unfortunate wounds.

The depressed PTSD veteran's sense of worthlessness can deteriorate into suicidal thoughts and, tragically, even suicide attempts. Statistical studies demonstrate that "up to 15 percent of individuals with severe major depressive disorder die by suicide."[69] Suicide will be thoroughly examined in a later section of this chapter. Thus major depression includes numerous physical and psychological symptoms that infect the PTSD veteran's entire life, even at times threatening his or her very existence.

One peculiar symptom that is presented by a few seriously depressed male veterans is their inability to cry. They buy into the military's macho brainwashing, which states that real men do not cry. In the military a macho man is never allowed to be depressed or even sad. The one and only negative emotion that male soldiers are allowed to express is anger. So through a strange psycho-physiological metamorphosis, any inner sadness is externalized, not through a healthy release like crying, but rather through an inappropriate expression of anger. Considerable psychotherapeutic efforts must be devoted to educating these men that crying is a normal, psychologically healthy, human expression of emotion. If and when tears water their eyes, they should be given permission to express their painful sadness. They need to be reassured that if they were to express their sorrow through tears, they would not be any less of a man. Have they not already proven through combat that they were real men? That proof does not dissolve with tears. Those veterans who are able to allow themselves to cry enjoy the ensuing relief. For those unable to allow themselves to cry, there are further questions.

PSYCHOLOGIST: "Forced choice. Who cries more in America, men or women?"

VETERAN: "Women."

PSYCHOLOGIST: "Correct. Forced choice, who lives longer in America, men or women?"

VETERAN: "Women."

PSYCHOLOGIST: "Correct. There is a strong connection here. Part of the reason American women live longer than men is because they take advantage of a healthy way of expressing sorrow, crying. Do you realize that scientists recently discovered stress chemicals in human tears? Crying, and thereby dumping those harmful stress chemicals, is one of the mechanisms your body uses to reduce stress. Try it and experience the relief."

These men must be reassured that a combat veteran does not change into a sissy boy just because he cried, especially when there is a perfectly legitimate reason to do so. Yet there are combat veterans who are incapable of permitting themselves this healthy release. One PTSD veteran, while disclosing a significant loss, filled his eyes with tears. Finally a teardrop formed and began to flow down his face. When he became aware of this teardrop, he completely tensed up; no way in hell was he going to allow another man to see him cry. He then performed an astonishing feat, literally sucking the tear back up into his eye. By maintaining his macho image he had placed himself at higher risk for future psychological problems.

Psychological Theories of Depression

Psychologists have generated a number of theories in an attempt to explain the inner workings of depression. The first of these is loss theory. The theory's basic principle is that depression occurs when the individual suffers a significant psychological loss. A secondary axiom is that the intensity of the subsequent depression is directly proportional to the personal value invested in the lost object. Combat veterans are at risk for many types of losses. Some are tangible like the loss of limbs or the loss of a friend. Other losses are intangible such as the loss of innocence or as grim as the loss of human compassion. Veterans may become depressed when they realize that they have lost the ability to empathize with fellow human beings. At times this insight occurs when veterans react to the death of a comrade with only the thought "better him than me." Veterans then recognize that they no longer view death in the same way that others do; their human connection with others is broken. Some other intangible and equally painful losses for veterans because of combat traumas include the possible loss of a sense of security, personal freedom, friendliness or a sense of humor.

A history of prior losses will sensitize an individual to loss, insuring that any further losses will be especially damaging. Humans possess only a finite amount of psychological energy for coping with significant losses. Multiple losses deplete that store of coping energy. For example, deaths of loved ones in veterans' prewar lives or earlier in the war place them at significantly higher risk for depression following any future deaths of people close to them.

One Vietnam veteran had been the only child of loving parents. Tragically both parents were killed in an automobile accident during the veteran's senior year in high school. Reeling and confused from the blow, he volunteered for the army. He was trained as a combat engineer and sent to Vietnam, where he was assigned to a squad whose job was to clear roads of land mines. Because of his loneliness, he developed a strong bond with his fellow squad members, who became like brothers to him. One day for a legitimate reason, he did not patrol with his squad. Then tragedy struck him again. An awful explosion of a land mine killed his entire squad. Not fully recovered from the deaths of his parents, this young man was completely overwhelmed by the deaths of his new family, his combat engineer squad. His personal resources for recovering from the deaths of people he cared for was totally depleted. His legitimate grief deteriorated into a chronic major depression that was so severe he could no longer function as a soldier. Years later, he still required psychiatric and psychological treatment for the depression caused by the one-two punch of his losses of people he loved.

Major depression caused by the deaths of loved ones is differentiated from normal bereavement by the severity and persistence of the symptoms. One veteran, whose adolescent son was killed in a robbery, disclosed during the initial interview that he had been wearing his son's clothes and sleeping in his son's bed since the death. The first impression was that he was displaying a peculiar and intense form of short-term grief, but later in the interview the veteran reported that the tragic shoot-out had occurred three years prior. The persistence and severity of his unusual symptoms were above and beyond the level of normal grief; therefore, his condition was diagnosed as major depression.

A second influential theory of depression can be termed the self-directed anger theory. It is an outgrowth of Dr. Sigmund Freud's psychoanalytic theories. A basic tenet of this psychodynamic theory is that the depressed patient feels angry towards someone or something, but for some reason he or she is unable to outwardly express this anger.[70] The individual may believe that to act out of anger would lead to even further rejection and loss of affection from others. Or the patient may think that the hated object is so big and powerful, such as the Veterans Administration or the Federal Government, that any expression of anger would be ineffective. Or the person he or she is angry with is already dead. This inability to discharge passionate anger generates a crippling sense of helplessness. Instead of the anger being expressed outwardly, it is displaced inwardly. Some depressed patients mutilate themselves. Others are so angry they want to kill, however, the gun is pointed towards themselves. Attempts are made and some actually do kill themselves. What is true in the extreme is also somewhat true at the more normal levels. Most depressed individuals do appear to be mad at themselves at some level. For example they tend to be extremely self-critical and guilt ridden. When things do not work out well for them in social situations, they immediately blame themselves and no one else. They are harsh in their self-criticisms because their self-evaluation standards are perfectionistic. It is as if their self-esteem is so low that the only way they can prove that they behaved adequately is to be perfect. Then there can be no doubt about the acceptability of their performance. Of course the desired level of perfection is never achieved, ensuring for the individual constant failure and continual feelings of worthlessness.

The two previously reviewed theories of depression regard the problem as primarily an emotional disorder and thus disregard its cognitive components. In contrast, the third theory examined is one that emphasizes the distorted thinking of the depressed patient. Dr. Aaron Beck, a pioneering American psychiatrist in the field, originated the cognitive theory of depression while at the University of Pennsylvania. He based the theory upon his extensive clinical observations and experimental research on depression. The theory's fundamental concepts are called the cognitive triad, which describes the three characteristic patterns of faulty thinking central to depression.

1. The depressed patient has a negative view of self. Patients consider themselves as incompetent and flawed. They think that they do not posses the skills or talent necessary for success.

2. The depressed patient has a negative view of life. Patients categorize everything that happens to them as unfavorable.

3. The depressed patient has a negative view of the future. Patients think their current problems will continue indefinitely. They expect nothing but failures in their future.[71]

This triad of depressive cognitions can dominate the patient's conscious experience. At first some objectivity may exist in the depressed person's thinking; but, as the depression intensifies, the patient's thinking becomes more and more irrationally distorted. All of life's situations are deformed to fit into this dominant, but pathological, model of self, life and future. The depressed person's life map does not fit the territory, but in response he or she does not redraw the map. Instead the patient deforms the territory to fit the map. This type of perverted thinking is reminiscent of the American generals who could not adapt to the enemy's jungle fighting style during the Vietnam War. Instead of developing new fighting strategies (redrawing their cognitive maps of the war), the generals used huge Rome plows to bulldoze much of the Vietnamese jungle out of existence.

Cognitive Therapy for Depression

Dr. Beck's cognitive theory of depression seamlessly became the foundation for a cognitive therapy of depression. Remember the first principle of cognitive therapy is that events do not cause human emotions; instead it is the meaning the individual gives to an event that determines his or her emotional reaction. It is not what happens to someone, but rather how a person interprets what happened that determines how the person feels about the event. This basic concept of thinking causing emotions can be effectively applied to a veteran suffering the torments of depression. Cognitive therapy asserts that the veteran is maintaining a dysfunctional mental map through errors in informational processing. The veteran is convinced that his or her negative self-evaluation is accurate and that his or her terrible feelings are realistic and inevitable. The initial goal of the cognitive therapist is to have the depressed veteran at least consider the possibility that this evaluation may be in error. At first the therapist points out the dysfunctional thoughts and demonstrates how they have not been working for the veteran. Then the therapeutic strategy shifts to teaching the veteran how to recognize his or her own cognitive distortions and then reevaluate them. The ultimate therapeutic goal is for the depressed veteran to learn how to talk back and argue with his or her internal critic.

Influenced by the persuasive pharmaceutical advertisements, many people think that medications are the only treatment available for depression. However, cognitive therapy for depression has evolved into one of the most widely practiced forms of psychotherapy. A principal reason for its popularity among clinical professionals is the extensive scientific evidence that cognitive therapy is effective in reducing the symptoms of depression. In 1977 Dr. Beck and his research team at the University of Pennsylvania studied 40 moderately to severely depressed patients. Half of them received 12 weeks of cognitive therapy; the other half received standard antidepressant medications. The study's results demonstrated that cognitive therapy was at least as effective as medication in reducing depressive symptoms and that for some patients it was even more effective than antidepressant drugs.[72]

More recently academic and clinical experts reviewed the most scientifically rigorous studies comparing cognitive therapy with medications. Again the results indicated that cognitive therapy was at least as effective as medications, but also that cognitive therapy patients were less likely to relapse than those treated with antidepressant drugs.[73] One University of Amsterdam study in 2005 found that cognitive therapy reduced the occurrence of relapse from 72 percent to 46 percent for over 100 patients diagnosed with recurrent depression.[74] Another study out of UCLA compared sophisticated brain scans of patients successfully treated with cognitive therapy to those of patients who had responded well to medications alone. This study's results indicated that there were brain chemistry changes in all the post-treatment patients, whose scans revealed the favorable sign that their brain metabolism had slowed down. The study also demonstrated that there were no differences between the two treatment groups in the extent of metabolic reductions. Cognitive therapy improved the brain chemistry of depressed patients just as well as the medications did.[75]

The positive results generated by these scientific studies offer hope to those depressed veterans who have not responded well to antidepressant medications as well as to those veterans who chose not to be treated with antidepressant medications. The results provide compelling evidence that cognitive therapy must be considered a first-class treatment for clinical depression. Psychotherapists can apply cognitive therapy to depression with the confidence that they are utilizing a psychotherapy that routinely delivers successful outcomes.

Once engaged in psychotherapy, the cognitive therapist challenges the depressed veteran's cognitive triad of distorted thinking. The first distortion of the cognitive triad is the veteran's negative view of self. An utterly negative self-image may become so solidly entrenched that it distorts accomplishments. For example one World War II veteran had serious doubts about his ruggedness as a soldier. In an attempt to prove to himself that he was tough, he decided to undergo the grueling training required to become a member of an airborne parachute division. As expected, the weeks-long airborne training was exhausting; however, he was able to complete the course and consequently was awarded his parachutist pin. But he interpreted the award in a distorted way, devaluating his true accomplishment. His conclusion was that because he successfully passed the airborne course, it could not have been that formidable. A cognitive therapist would challenge the veteran's discounting the grueling training successfully completed. The cognitive strategy would be to analyze the basis of the veteran's previous evaluation of the airborne course as one that demanded toughness or to examine the veteran's explanation why some strong soldiers had failed the course.

The second element in the cognitive triad of a depressed veteran is his or her pessimistic view of the future being filled with nothing but hardship and failure. A depressed combat veteran who is also diagnosed with PTSD might tell a therapist, "I will always have nightmares forever, so why try to fight it?" A skilled cognitive therapist would challenge this negative expectation as an irrational prediction of the future. Who can accurately predict the future? The gypsy fortune-teller's claim of knowing the future is nothing but a money-making scam. The absolute reality is that no one, not even a gypsy, can forecast what the future will hold. The depressed veteran's reasoning is that what has been true in the past will always be true. But where is the evidence supporting this assertion? In reality things change all the time. The depressed veteran's gloomy prediction is nothing but an arbitrary conclusion. The veteran has imagined a dark future and then emotionally reacts to the self-generated image as if it were a solid fact.

The third pillar in the depressed veteran's cognitive triad is the negative view of his or her life. The veteran may complain, "My life is filled with nothing but pain and sorrow." In response a cognitive therapist would point out that the veteran's evaluation of his or her life is irrationally based upon a limited perspective. The reality is that everyone's life is lavishly complex, filled with numerous developments, different situations and unexpected events. Yet the depressed veteran's crude perception attends only to the negative factors. The complexities of the depressed veteran's life could logically lead to positive alternatives, yet the veteran continually construes life in only one manner, totally defeatist. It is as if the veteran is wearing an exceptionally thick pair of warped goggles that filter out everything but the negative.

Similar to the inaccurate beliefs inherent in PTSD are the fundamental thinking errors inherent in major depression. The turmoil of the depression weakens the veteran's ability to think accurately and to hold the proper perspective. The following list evaluates a few of the dysfunctional thinking habits associated with depression.

1. *Emotional reasoning* is the belief that if the veteran feels a certain way, then it must be true. The corollary is that the stronger the feeling the more accurate the belief. Examples of this illogic are "I feel like a loser, so I must be incompetent" or "I feel overwhelmed, so my life is hopeless." But feelings are not facts; they are an inaccurate and ineffective way to judge reality. One may feel secure but see the danger hiding around the next corner.

2. *Absolute thinking* is interpreting the world with only two categories. It is thinking only in terms of a dichotomy, such as right or wrong, good or bad, with nothing in-between. An example of this depressive illogic is "I failed this time, so I must be a total loser." However the truth is that life in the real world is more complex and more nuanced than simply black or white. Accurate and mature thinking recognizes that life involves many shades of grey, involving numerous dimensions across a wide continuum. Not achieving complete success does not automatically mean that one is a total failure.

3. *Excessive self-criticism* is the disastrous consequence of the dichotomous thinking error previously analyzed. Depressed veterans apply an all-or-none standard to their every effort, resulting in harsh self-evaluations such as " I failed, it wasn't perfect; I can never do anything right." A cognitive therapist might challenge such illogic with this these questions: "How can anyone perform well under such a harsh critic? Did you perform well under the screaming drill sergeant in basic training? Of course not, the sergeant only increased your anxiety, making you perform even worse. Instead of being your own drill sergeant, why not try to be your own best friend?"

4. *Personalization* is the term used to describe a veteran's assuming complete responsibility for events over which she or he had little control. It is a major source of guilt, an emotion tightly intertwined with depression. "You arbitrarily conclude that what happened was your fault or

reflects your inadequacy, even when your were not responsible for it."[76] A depressed veteran may lament, "It is my fault that my buddy died; I was not able to drag him out of the killing zone." A cognitive therapist would challenge the needless self-condemnation by pointing out that the veteran is completely ignoring the harsh reality of war. The true cause of the friend's death was the Vietcong shooting him in the head. The therapist would then help the veteran articulate the most accurate statement about the tragedy: "I really wish I could have dragged my buddy out of the killing zone to safety."

Grief

One of the most devastating losses for combat veterans is the violent death of a close friend from within their squad. Usually the friend had shared the stress and horror of life in a combat zone. They may have even shared the terror of combat assaults and ambushes. Surviving battle together produces a passionate bond between soldiers; it is not just a phrase when soldiers refer to the men in their squad as their "brothers." Thus the death of a member of such a family is especially depressing.

A critical early step in providing cognitive therapy for veterans suffering pathological grief caused by the death of a fellow soldier is resurrecting the spirit of the dead soldier. Veterans are encouraged to share their memories of their dead friend. They are asked to share not only their friend's name and other basic facts, but also as many details as they could recall about the friend's personality and background. To help guide a veteran's memory, the therapist may ask the following types of questions: What were the friend's likes and interests? What were his or her future plans? Did the friend have a partner? If so, how was the partner described? What was it about this person that made you want to be friends? What kind of fun activities did you do together? After the memories are recalled, the therapist points out how in a sense the veteran had resurrected the friend's spirit that day. The veteran should be complimented for not forgetting his or her dead buddy because "To be truly dead is to be forgotten." The most remarkable fact was not that this friend had died, but rather that he or she had lived. In my clinical practice I would then state how sincerely honored I was to be part of this spiritual resurrection. Using the friend's name, I would share with the veteran how the detailed description made me feel like I knew the person. Since the dead person's spirit was with us in the room, the veteran would be encouraged to express his or her grief by communicating what he or she needed to say to the friend. Some veterans would disclose how they missed their friend, others how ashamed they were at not being able to save their friend, and some would use the opportunity to simply say good-bye to their dead brother or sister.

The job of a cognitive therapist working with combat veterans requires challenging any dysfunctional beliefs that veterans may have on how to best demonstrate their grief over a friend's death. For many veterans the only answer is the painful one of chronic mourning. Cognitive therapy for grief works on developing a meaningful alternative. One helpful cognitive technique includes the use of imagination. Veterans are asked to imagine changing places with their dead friend. The friend is now alive here on earth, while the veteran is now floating in heaven, observing the friend's life from above. After this exchange of fates, the grieving veteran would be asked the following types of questions: "How would you want your friend to live life? Would you want your friend to live out life totally depressed every day because you died? Would you want your friend to kick herself or himself in the butt constantly for not saving your life? Would you want your friend to poison his or her liver through excessive drinking to forget your death? Or would you want your friend to live a peaceful and contented life, remembering you with affection? How would you want your friend to honor you?

An important concept at this juncture in cognitive grief therapy involves the sharing of Specialist Woodley's story from Mr. Wallace's book *Bloods*. The therapist emphasizes the philosophic conclusion of the tale: *"They died for us, we live for them."* Unhealthy grieving can be challenged with this perspective through the following types of reality-oriented questions: "Does your ruining your life with depression (or booze or drugs or whatever) bring your friend back to life? Isn't it true that two wrongs don't make a right? How does wasting your life honor your friend? Or bring honor to you? It only doubles the tragedy. Making the most of your life in memory of his or her life is the most valuable monument you can build to honor your dead friend. Remember, they died for us, so we live for them. Healing your sorrow over this death comes not from trying to forget, but from remembering your friend in a special way. Truly honor your friend by living a good life."

In summary cognitive therapy for a depressed combat veteran focuses upon correcting faulty concepts and self-defeating thoughts. Therapy helps the veteran become aware of dysfunctional beliefs and their destructive power. Usually veterans resist change because they have practiced depressive thinking for so long that they become skilled in its application. Depressive thinking just feels right. But feelings are not facts. The therapist may respond by questioning the reality of the veteran's symptoms and complaints: "If your current ideas and thinking patterns are working so well for you, why are you in a therapist's office complaining about uncomfortable symptoms?" The next step is to develop an arsenal of rational arguments against the depressed veteran's self-defeating thoughts. Veterans must then practice these new functional arguments in their daily lives in order to fully correct their faulty thinking. The main therapeutic goal is to teach depressed veterans how to rationally talk back to their mean internal drill sergeant.

Suicide

Major depression is a troubling concern for mental health professionals because it is one of the few psychiatric disorders that can prove to be fatal. Major depression may deteriorate into suicide. Currently the problem of suicide has grown to epidemic proportions in both the U.S. military and in veteran communities. Death is less terrifying and more of an option to veterans who have in a sense lived with the grim reaper in a war zone. Recently published research reported that in the years between 1993 and 1998 over 10,000 veterans were hospitalized in the Department of Veteran Affairs medical centers because of suicide attempts. During those years, suicide was the second leading cause of veterans' deaths within the VA, accounting for a full 13.1 percent of all veteran deaths. Only heart disease, at 20.2 percent accounted for more veteran deaths. In contrast suicide was the ninth leading cause of death for the entire population of the United States during the study period, accounting for only 1.8 percent of the deaths. This comprehensive research also revealed that PTSD veterans and veterans who had served in Iraq or Afghanistan had a 33 percent greater risk for suicide. Recently the VA reported that between 2005 and 2007 the rate of suicide among younger veterans increased 26 percent.[77] Suicide is also a serious problem for the U.S. military, as demonstrated by recent Army statistics. "During the first seven months of 2011, about 160 active-duty and reserve soldiers have committed suicide, which is about on par with the number of troops taking their own lives during the same months in 2009 and 2010." Deplorably, the U.S. Army recorded 32 suicide deaths during the month of July 2011, the highest total since the Army began publishing monthly rates in 2009.[78]

Fortunately there is hope that suicidal intentions can be successfully treated. Scientists have compiled compelling scientific evidence that supports cognitive psychotherapy in the treatment of suicidal patients. Dr. Aaron Beck and his research team at the University of Pennsylvania have demonstrated successful applications of cognitive therapy to reduce depression in suicidal patients and to actually decrease the number of suicide attempts. In the 1970s Dr. Beck's team conducted a series of studies to test the effectiveness of cognitive therapy with depressed suicidal outpatients versus the standard antidepressant medications of the era. The results indicated that the cognitive therapy group decreased their level of hopelessness, a strong indicator of suicidal risk, faster than the patients treated with mediations. At a six-month follow-up evaluation, the cognitive therapy group had maintained their improvement; their clinical progress was significantly better than the drug treated group.[79] In 2005 Dr. Beck and his research team conducted a large-scale randomized controlled trial of cognitive therapy versus the standard care available for psychiatric outpatients, one that included both conventional psychotherapy and antidepressant medications. Their 120 patients had all attempted suicide at least once. Because even one previous suicide attempt increases the risk for further attempts from 38 to 40 times more, it is apparent that Dr. Beck's patients were an extremely high-risk group. They were randomly assigned into two equal treatment groups. At the 18-month follow-up evaluation, Dr. Beck's team found that the cognitive therapy patients experienced less depression and less hopelessness than the standard treatment group. They also found that patients in the cognitive therapy group were 50 percent less likely to have attempted suicide during the follow-up period than those who received standard psychiatric treatment.[80]

Psychotherapeutic Treatments

The following section describes a treatment protocol I developed for treating suicidal veterans within an outpatient setting. The procedures are based upon the fundamental premise of accepting the gravity of the veteran's death wish, but at the same time not agreeing with it. Each psychotherapeutic intervention was designed to challenge the veteran's maladaptive cognitions, taking into account every veteran's distinct personality and social situation. Questioning targeted the veteran's disclosure of suicidal intent. The questions were specifically designed to shock the veteran's dysfunctional belief system because just one breach in the veteran's assumptive model could be enough to bring down the entire house of cards. Of course during the initial interview there were other types of evaluative questions asked, for example, questions to determine the probability of an imminent suicidal attempt and thus the need for immediate hospitalization, but they are not included in this description. The ultimate therapeutic goal was to have the suicidal veteran agree to a no-harm contract and engage in treatment.

If during an interview a severely depressed PTSD veteran revealed suicidal intent, then this deadly threat would immediately be confronted. Was the veteran religious? If so, then the challenges would be to his or her religious beliefs: "How exactly do you think God will respond to your killing yourself? Is it not true that God reserves the right to decide when we die? Many religious leaders believe that suicide is an unforgivable sin, so are you sure that God will forgive you? If you are already dead, your time is done. When are you going to have the time to ask God for forgiveness?" This line of questioning would continue in a direct, but always therapeutically supportive, manner. The goal was to jolt suicidal veterans out of their deadly mind-set. If shocked veterans reacted by questioning even one of their maladaptive beliefs, then the dynamics of their depressive system shifts, thus generating the first spark of hope. The cognitive therapist might ask "What exactly do you think happens after you die? Being dead does not appear to be much fun. All they do is lie there, eventually starting to stink. You are convinced that your current life is dreadful and unbearable, but what if death is worse? Do you believe in Hell? Do you really want to suffer the fires of eternal damnation?"

If the suicidal veteran is not religious, then is he or she a parent? If so, then the therapist would educate the veteran about the pathetic world of children whose parents have committed suicide. The reality is that these traumatized children are three times more likely to kill themselves than other children. Many people know that the writer Ernest Hemingway killed himself at age 62, but few realize that his own father had killed himself when Ernest was a youth. A few years ago Ernest Hemingway's granddaughter Mariel killed herself with a drug overdose. This is but one celebrity example of how a parent's suicide becomes a model for the children to imitate. For the rest of their lives, whenever they are severely stressed or depressed, these burdened children will consider suicide as a genuine option. Suicidal veterans were encouraged to think about what exactly they are teaching their children. "Is this the lesson you want your children to learn: that when things get tough in life, don't try to deal with it, just give up and shoot yourself in the head? Do you really hate your children that much?"

If appropriate, a true suicide story would be shared. Years ago while visiting my brother in Pittsburgh, we traveled to his friend's home for an evening of socializing. After an hour, the host's wife came into the room with a phone call for the host. After finishing the call, he surprised us all with the bad news. His neighbor, who had served as an Army medic during the Vietnam War, had killed himself that evening by hanging himself on the back yard tree. What was even worse was that his ten-year-old son had discovered his father's body dangling from the tree. Of course our social evening was now over, but before we left, the host's wife asked me, as a clinical psychologist, for my reaction to the suicide. Not knowing anything about the neighbor's psychological problems, my response was that he had obviously not thought much about the emotional effect his suicide would have on his wife and children. Exactly who did he think would discover his body, when he hangs himself on a tree in their back yard? My fear was that the poor boy would develop psychological problems due to the discovery of his father's body. Later I learned that at the veteran's funeral, his adolescent daughters had cried normally, but the young son had not. The boy's lack of appropriate emotional expression was a pathological sign. By his suicide, the father had escaped his own psychological demons, but by doing so had cursed his ten-year-old son. The boy could possibly be burdened for the rest of his life by massive guilt. The boy might blame himself for not somehow preventing his father's death. At worst he may blame himself or something he had done as the entire reason why his father killed himself. If and when the son ever truly resolves his guilt, he still will have to deal with the example his father taught him. Whenever he encounters serious stressors in his life, he will have to wrestle with the demon option of what his father taught him about dealing with life's problems.

A few veterans argued that their children had nothing to do with their depression or suicidal thoughts. They claimed that they loved their children and would never hurt them. The therapeutic counter is that even if it were true that their children had nothing to do with their depression, if after suicide, how could a veteran be sure his or children would understand that fact? It is more likely that the veteran's children would agonize over what they could have or should have done to prevent the death. The children would recall and then regret all the little things they did that irritated or upset their parent and blame the suicide on that, even if it were not true. This type of brooding breeds guilt. A few seriously depressed veterans claimed that their children would be better off if they were dead. During family therapy sessions that assertion would be tested. Invariably every child asked would answer that he or she would rather have a living depressed parent than a dead one. Eventually each suicidal parent would be questioned directly: "Are you really going to emotionally burden your children for the rest of their lives just so you can escape your pain? Do you really hate your children that much?"

If a suicidal veteran were not a parent nor religious, then the appeal would be to the universal desire of combat veterans to deny the enemy victory. In these cases veterans would be asked to consider the fact that if they were to commit suicide, they would become just another needless casualty of war. If the veteran had served in Vietnam for example, then the Vietnam War would be blamed for his or her death: "It is as if the Vietcong were issued a special sniper rifle that could shoot into the future. They shot you dead in Vietnam, but you just did not realize it. Your name should be chiseled into the Vietnam Veterans Memorial Wall in Washington, D.C. with all the other casualties but, of course you know, that will not happen." Vietnam veterans hated the Vietcong, so the mere idea of giving the enemy another victory would disrupt the veteran's depressive thinking. It was simply intolerable to have their deaths by suicide considered as just another body count for the Vietcong.

If the depressed veteran's suicidal intentions were not resolute, then the cognitive therapist explored alternative methods of escape. The first step was to provide feedback regarding the veteran's complaints and true intentions. "You do not seem to be the type of person who really wants to die. The nature of your complaints suggest that what you really want to do is escape from your nasty spouse (or job, or in-laws or neighbors, et cetera)." The next step focused upon creative alternatives. "Your thinking appears to be rather narrow. Why does it have to be only the extreme of death? Are there not other less extreme ways of escaping? Why not just divorce your spouse? Why not move your family to another state? ... Why not run away to start a new life in Brazil? If you were to pick a new life, what would it be? Would it be a park ranger in the Alaskan wilderness or a scuba diver in the Florida Keys hunting lobster?" The real therapeutic goal here was not to have the veteran actually move to Brazil, but rather to stimulate the consideration of alternatives. If and when veterans begin to think in terms of constructive alternatives, then they are problem solving, which changes the dynamics of their dysfunctional belief system. There is less concentration on death and more consideration of life and on the possibility of an improved future.

If there were any signs of the veteran's deadly resolve weakening, then the intensity of the questioning was ratcheted up a notch. Veterans would be asked how sure they were that their suicidal plan would actually cause death versus causing serious injury such as total paralysis, a fate many considered worse than death. They would be asked to bear in mind the fates of those veterans who were also convinced that they had a foolproof suicide plan, which then failed with tragic results. They were told of the veteran who had a plan of jumping off of a bridge. To make doubly sure of dying, he planned to jump from a railroad bridge onto the tracks just ahead of an oncoming train, which could then run over him. In fact he did jump, but his body bounced to the side and then the train ran over his legs, traumatically amputating both of them. They were told about the female patient who had squirted lighter fluid all over her head and lit herself afire, only to survive horribly scarred and disfigured. She was forced to endure the pain of multiple surgeries as her surgeons valiantly tried to save her burnt face and neck. She was left living with the agony of chronic, searing burn pain.

If none of the cognitive therapy challenges appeared to be working, then the final appeals questioned the timing of the possible suicide. The cognitive restructuring appeals involved the following lines of reasoning and questioning: "It appears that you may in fact kill yourself, but what is the rush? If you kill yourself now, case closed. You are dead; you have no other options. The only things left to do are to write a chart note of your death and then store your medical file away in a basement warehouse. Then it is simply on to: 'Next patient please.' But think about it, you can always postpone suicide, while receiving treatment and possibly discovering solutions. If you try this strategy and it works out, great, no problem. You will be feeling better. But if it does not work out, then you still have the time to kill yourself. Do you realize that during this interval modern scientific medicine will be searching for a cure? Do you want to be like the early California A.I.D.S. patients, who were so frightened by their disease and had such little hope that they killed themselves in droves? But modern scientific medicine did produce effective treatments for A.I.D.S., which is not the death sentence it once was. There is no total cure, but now with the latest medical treatments, A.I.D.S. patients can live on for decades, as

Magic Johnson has. Do you really want to kill yourself, and then within the next few months, modern medical science achieves the miracle break-through cure for your type of depression?"

If and when the combat veteran's suicidal resolve weakened, then the therapeutic emphasis switched to having the depressed veteran agree to a no-harm contract and continued mental health treatment. Of course all of these severely depressed veterans would be closely monitored during ongoing treatment for any reoccurrence of suicidal thoughts. If there was such a poor response to psychotherapeutic interventions that genuine sui-cidal plans or intent were eventually discovered, then the suicidal veteran would be referred immediately to psychiatry services for an evaluation to determine if inpatient hospitalization was required to ensure the veteran's physical safety.

18

Low Self-Esteem

Even though it is not listed in the DSM-IV as a PTSD symptom, nearly all of the Vietnam veterans presenting at our clinic suffered from low self-esteem. Many of the PTSD veterans from other wars also suffered from the same problem. Their low self-esteem contributed to both their depression and to their social avoidance. Cognitive therapy was applied to provide these combat PTSD veterans an entirely different perspective of themselves based upon their recognition of a warrior spirit. The therapeutic goal was for them to achieve the positive self-image of a warrior who holds a tough-minded attitude towards life — a warrior who does not avoid problems, but rather, directly attacks them. A warrior who accepts the fact that life can be unfair and unjust at times. Psychotherapeutic discussions aimed at these worthy goals were based upon the following types of reasoning: "The most critical question is not: Why are you having problems? The most critical question is: Why aren't you stark raving mad, locked away forever in some back ward of a psychiatric hospital? Believe me, most of the patients stuck in the locked wards have been through less stress than you have. The fact that you survived mortal combat demonstrates your psychological strength, your ability to handle extremely tough situations. You didn't do anything stupid like charge a machine gun nest while acting out a John Wayne fantasy or needlessly expose yourself to enemy fire trying to take pictures of the war. Reconsider not only the firefights you survived, but also the war zone living conditions, the dirt, the heat (or the cold), the mud (or the sand). Those primitive conditions are also stressful. Yet you survived it all. You have been through hell, and sure you are scorched a bit, but you have not been consumed by the flames."

"After the hell of combat in Vietnam (or Afghanistan or Iraq) what else can life throw at you that could be worse? Oh yeah, you had a fender bender accident or the air-conditioning unit failed. You have been through much worse. Combat veterans have proven that they can handle civilian catastrophes. In 1992 after Hurricane Andrew hit Southern Florida, national news services repeatedly broadcast that Vietnam veterans provided heroic rescue operations and security patrols in devastated neighborhoods.

Psychotherapeutic efforts to strengthen the self-esteem of veterans with PTSD included open discussions of the benefits of combat military service. One major benefit is the close personal bond the soldier develops with the other men in his unit. Soldiers learn to depend on each other in combat, developing an emotional connection as strong as any family ties. Many American soldiers have been killed or wounded attempting to aid a wounded friend. This brotherhood in arms lasts years beyond their military service. More than a few combat veterans travel great distances every year to their military units' reunions in order to keep in touch with their combat brothers. PTSD veterans were encouraged to attend their military units' reunions or general reunions such as the annual reunion for Vietnam War veterans in Melbourne, Florida. Socially isolated Vietnam veterans initially resisted the recommendation to attend the Melbourne reunion, but if they attended once, they would be delighted by the comradeship they enjoyed there. For dozens of Vietnam veterans the Melbourne reunion became the highlight of their yearly social calendar; for some isolates, it was their entire social calendar.

Another advantage of military service for the combat veteran is that he has forever proved his masculinity and toughness. Directly facing life or death choices in combat creates in the veteran a fortitude that no one can ever seriously question. Even onto old age, the war veteran's combat history ensures the authenticity of his masculinity.

The examination of self-esteem issues has to this point been broad enough to be applicable to combat veterans from any of America's recent wars. In most respects combat stress across wars is similar. The many stressors and strains of the American combat soldier in twentieth century warfare remain basically the same in the twenty-first century. But America's decade-long Vietnam War during the 1960s and 1970s stands out as being especially difficult for its veterans because in no other American war were its veterans viewed with so much scorn and disdain. The one-two punch of Vietnam veterans having to cope not only with a vicious war, but also with the second war of coming home creates for the Vietnam veteran suffering from PTSD a distinct set of self-esteem issues.

The Korean War veterans' homecoming is the closest to the Vietnam

War veterans' in that its veterans were not greeted by the brass bands and parades given in appreciation to World War II veterans. Korean War veterans were viewed with some suspicion in the United States because of the widely publicized scandal of a few brainwashed prisoners of war, who chose to stay behind in communist countries rather than come home to America. But the Korean War veteran did come home to a thriving 1950s American economy, when good jobs were plentiful. The Korean War combat veteran came home and went to work.

Coming home was not easy for returning Vietnam War veterans, particularly those with PTSD. Anti-war media coverage convinced some citizens that America's involvement in Vietnam was an immoral act. The anti-war movement in the United States attempted to seize the moral high ground by arguing that the moral imperative was for young American men to dodge the draft. The media's immorality rhetoric deceived many Americans into scapegoating the individual soldier for America's involvement in the Vietnam War. The combat veteran became a symbol of the war and an easy target. Some anti-war extremists spat at and attacked returning Vietnam War veterans. One of our PTSD Vietnam veterans had his wounds infected by bags of urine thrown at him upon returning to the Oakland, California, airport. It is shocking and indefensible that American veterans returning from any theater of war would be subjected to this type of disrespect.

A few skeptics questioned the reality of these assaults, claiming they are a type of urban legend. Sociologist Jerry Lembcke wrote a book entitled *The Spitting Image: Myth, Memory and the Legacy of Vietnam,* which is based on the weak evidence of reviewing mass media reports, yet claims that returning Vietnam veterans were not spat upon.[81] Yet there exists ample evidence proving that these assaults did in fact occur. For example in an *Esquire* magazine article entitled *Homecoming*, the author Bob Greene documents, through scores of letters from named Vietnam veterans, many actual dates and places of these vulgar spitting incidents. Mr. Greene also writes, "Some [other letters] came from men who were not physically spat upon but who felt symbolically spat upon by society."[82] These types of vulgarities provoked in Vietnam War veterans an overall feeling of being rejected by their coworkers on the job, by their classmates on the campus and most tragically by their families at home. Being a Vietnam War veteran became a dirty secret that they learned to keep to themselves. This hostile environment exacerbated the self-esteem issues of many veterans struggling with PTSD.

The Iraq or Afghanistan war veteran's homecoming can be problematic as well, since many Americans question the reasoning behind these wars and the need for American soldiers fighting terrorists in these countries. Mass media coverage of Americans' involvement in these conflicts has been mixed; along with positive reports there has been extensive coverage of the isolated instances in which a rogue soldier or a small unit transgressed the rules of war. Mideast veterans with PTSD may internalize negative media coverage of the politics of the Iraq and Afghanistan wars as a judgment against their service during those wars. Psychotherapy interventions like those listed below can help the PTSD veteran of the Mideast wars clarify that distinction and improve lowered self-esteem.

Combat PTSD veterans of all these wars regularly presented at our Department of Veterans Affairs mental health clinic with massive guilt and low self-esteem because they had accepted other people's blaming them for their wars. They frequently complained, "But Doc, I pulled the trigger." Psychotherapeutic efforts utilized the principles of cognitive therapy to help them rethink their negative self-evaluations. One effective therapeutic response that exemplified this strategy was: "But who gave you the gun? Who trained you to kill, paid for your bullets and then sent you into a kill or be killed war? It was the very same people who later turned on you and attacked because you pulled that trigger to save your life." Continued therapeutic discussions focused upon the guerrilla nature of terrorist warfare, where there is not a conventional rear area where the soldier could escape from combat. American soldiers in Vietnam, Iraq and Afghanistan were always surrounded, usually outnumbered and always vulnerable to ambushes and direct frontal assaults. Our enemies in these conflicts considered them as total wars, one in which they were justified in exploiting their entire populations, men, women and even children as combatants. During cognitive psychotherapy the PTSD veteran's guilt was targeted for restructuring: "You need to learn that by accepting society's blame, you relieve them of their responsibility and guilt. You have big strong shoulders, but you are not strong enough to bear the weight of the entire country's guilt over the war. It will crush you."

Another effective psychotherapeutic strategy for improving low self-esteem was to resurrect pride in military service by considering the PTSD veteran's military service in its true historical context. PTSD veterans were taught to recognize that young Americans bearing arms for their country are a direct historical extension of that proud warrior tradition that has been reflected in different times and cultures: the European knights in shining armor, the Japanese samurai, the American Indians who called their young warriors the Braves. These courageous warriors were respected and rewarded throughout the ages by their cultures. Likewise America rewards its warriors with extensive benefits for military service, including the G.I. Bill for education and home loans and health care through the Department of Veterans Services, to name but a few.

Another psychotherapeutic remedy for low self-esteem was to have the combat PTSD veteran reconsider his or her military service from the point of view of their own family's military history and tradition. Many PTSD veterans reported that their families had a proud military tradition that was similar to my own, a typical Middle America one for those of us from the baby boom generation. During World War II, my father served on a Navy destroyer in the North Atlantic; one of my uncles fought as an infantryman in Africa and Europe during that war; another uncle lost an eye fighting the Japanese in the South Pacific. Two of my cousins fought as Marine infantry during the Korean War. The Vietnam War was my generation's turn to fight. Combat PTSD veterans were trained during cognitive psychotherapy to view their own military service as a direct extension and an honoring of their family's patriotic values and major sacrifices in defending this country across generations.

The role of a war's outcome in a combat PTSD veteran's low self-esteem is exemplified by the Vietnam War and its aftermath. During psychotherapy, combat PTSD veterans suffering from low self-esteem were taught not to confuse the war with the warrior, but rather to separate the individual soldier's military duties and combat efforts from the war's unsuccessful outcome. PTSD veterans were trained to recognize that because the Vietnam War ultimately proved to be a failed enterprise does not mean that the men and women who fought in the war failed to fully perform their military duties. Since many of our mental health clinic's PTSD veterans had a background in organized athletics, a sports analogy was used to enhance understanding of this therapeutic concept. The ability to separate an individual's success from the group's outcome is a distinction learned by many athletes who play team sports. During their athletic careers they learned that they could play well in a game, yet their team might still lose. The loss was not due to his or her playing poorly; the lack of team success had more to do with other team members not playing up to their potential. The Vietnam War was similar in this respect. The fact that America's involvement in the Vietnam War was not a success does not mean that the common American soldier lacked courage or fighting ability. In the Vietnam War under extremely adverse conditions, the vast majority of American soldiers, Marines, airmen and sailors performed their military and combat duties with honor and courage. The same is true for American combat veterans of the Iraq and Afghanistan wars.

In addition the PTSD combat veteran's self-esteem is vulnerable to Hollywood's portrayal of American soldiers in their respective wars. Movies like *Platoon, Jarhead* and *The Hurt Locker* are examples of descriptions of a combat veteran's experience that may be misinformed or biased. Such fictional Hollywood renderings of soldiers in a war can lead to complicated self-esteem issues for PTSD veterans of those wars. During the Vietnam era, numerous television programs and movies portrayed the Vietnam combat veteran as a violent, psychologically disturbed misfit. For example, the Oscar winning Hollywood movie *Platoon* portrays American infantrymen assaulting Vietnamese villagers, abusing drugs and even attempting to kill each other. The actual leader of the infantry unit depicted, which was Bravo Company, 3rd. Battalion, 25th Infantry Division, was Army Lieutenant Colonel Robert Hemphill. He was appalled by *Platoon*, regarding its portrayal of American soldiers in Vietnam is nothing but an exercise in misinformation: "The movie was completely distorted and nothing like my own experience or that of anyone I knew."[83]

Contrary to this media portrayal the average Vietnam War veteran is not a disturbed misfit. On November 16, 2000, in a front page article entitled "Dispelling Myths About Vietnam Veterans," *USA Today* reported that "a growing number of researchers, scholars and prominent veterans are attacking the negative stereotype as pure myth.... Their evidence suggests that most veterans are as happy, well adjusted and successful as nonveterans. Many who served in the war went on to become corporate chief executives, famous authors, military leaders and candidates for the presidency."[84] The article goes on to cite the Bureau of Labor Statistics' report that unemployment for Vietnam veterans during October 2000 was 2.7 percent, which was well below the 3.9 percent national unemployment rate at the time. Further Bureau statistics demonstrated that in 1992 Vietnam veterans had a high-school dropout rate that was only one-third the rate for non-veterans and that Vietnam veterans earned a higher weekly salary than non-veterans.[85] The reality that most Vietnam veterans are not disillusioned by their military experience is demonstrated by the results of a 1980 national Harris Poll, which found that "a full 90% of Vietnam vets said they were proud to have served their country."[86]

Times do change. Americans have rethought their prior attitudes towards Vietnam War veterans. A 1990 Gallup Poll documented that 87 percent of the American public held Vietnam veterans in "high esteem."[87] Most Americans currently recognize what an unjust homecoming Vietnam veterans received and have developed a newfound desire to show their appreciation for Vietnam veterans' sacrifices. One such example comes from our local community of Jacksonville Beach, Florida. The city dedicated its 2003 Independence Day celebration to honoring Vietnam veterans. In their honor the city issued an official proclamation which included the following statements: "Whereas, we gratefully acknowledge that we live in freedom today because of the many sacrifices that have been made by the valiant service people in the Armed Forces; Now, therefore, I, Bob D. Marsden, Mayor of the City of Jacksonville Beach, do hereby proclaim July 4th, 2003, as a day to honor those who served in the military and specifically those who served our country in Vietnam." Similar observances have taken place in many other cities and towns.

Thus we see that the veteran's positive self-esteem can be another casualty of combat in any war. The combat PTSD veteran has to struggle to preserve his or her self-esteem while being subjected to the dehumanization that is inherent in any war, where completing a combat mission is valued by the military leaders as much more important than the lives of individual soldiers. As detailed in this chapter, the combat PTSD veteran must also cope with society's potentially negative view of the war, which can sometimes lead the people in a veteran's life to take a negative view of the combat veteran himself. Dealing with such complex challenges is always difficult, and for some PTSD veterans it proves to be overwhelming, leading to drug or alcohol abuse, which is the subject of the next chapter.

19

SUBSTANCE ABUSE

In the Vietnam-era military, the most popular method of unwinding after duty was drinking alcohol. All American military bases had separate enlisted men's, noncommissioned officers' and officers' clubs, where the alcohol was inexpensive. Every change of command ceremony, every training class graduation, every Friday night happy hour provided a good reason to drink. In 1969 at our artillery firebase clubs, a full-size shot of liquor only cost 25 cents. So a soldier could buy eight stiff drinks with two dollars, enough to intoxicate most men. Alcohol's major importance is illustrated by the following short war story. Our firebase was located near Tan Tru village in the Mekong Delta. All supplies were delivered from larger bases down Highway 1. The base was connected to Highway 1 by a three-mile dirt road that included a bridge over a small river. One night the Vietcong blew up this bridge, reducing it to bent metal rubble. This attack resulted in serious supply shortages because trucks delivering all our supplies, including the vital artillery shells, had to cross the bridge. Consequently artillery shells had to be flown in by helicopter; however, their bulk and weight forced the air resupply runs to be limited in number. After about a week without resupply, the beer in the base's clubs ran out. This proved to be a serious problem because the brass would not allow valuable helicopter "blade time" to be used for beer runs. In desperation, a supply sergeant worked out a plan. One large truck was filled with cases of beer at the Tan An supply depot and driven to the south end of the downed bridge. Another truck left our base with a dozen soldiers aboard and drove to the north end of the downed bridge. Once there, the men crawled over the metal rubble and formed a human chain. Cases of beer were then transferred one at a time, hand to hand, from the resupply truck to our truck. The enemy may have blocked ammunition resupply, but the beer got through.

Given this attitude within the military, it is not surprising that Vietnam veterans frequently developed the habit of consuming large quantities of alcohol. After the war, PTSD veterans learned that it could be used as self-medication to treat symptoms like hyperarousal or insomnia. Unfortunately when someone drinks himself unconscious, the slumber is neither healthy nor restful. Typically the drinker develops a tolerance for the substance, requiring more and more drinks to reach the desired altered state of consciousness. After years of alcohol abuse there is an elevated possibility of developing diseases of the liver, such as cirrhosis, and diseases of the brain such as amnesia or dementia. In 1985 the psychiatrist who headed the Gainesville Florida's VA hospital's alcohol treatment program presented an alcohol seminar for mental health professionals. He taught that when evaluating a new patient who was a career soldier from the Vietnam era, it was wise to assume that the veteran was an alcoholic until proven otherwise.

A rarely understood difficulty for the PTSD veteran is that alcoholism complicates Post Traumatic Stress Disorder. It not only makes treatment of the disorder more difficult, it also makes its diagnosis more complex. The coexistence of the disorders in a veteran makes it difficult for psychiatrists to sort out where the PTSD ends and the alcoholism begins. There are only a few specially trained diagnosticians capable of skillfully separating out the two disorders. The general tendency is for psychiatrists to react to the alcoholism first and foremost, even if PTSD symptoms are recognized. The thinking is that the veteran's alcoholism needs to be controlled before effective treatment for the PTSD can begin. Consequently veterans would be referred to VA alcohol treatment programs. Difficulties also occurred when a combat PTSD veteran initially sought treatment from various civilian alcohol treatment programs. PTSD veterans complained that when they would bring up their Vietnam War issues in group therapy, they would be criticized and informed that Vietnam was just a cop-out, a form of denial of their only real problem, alcoholism.

What is the answer to this dual diagnosis dilemma? All combat veterans would do well to limit their alcohol consumption as much as they possibly can before seeking PTSD treatment. Unfortunately this solution works for only a few highly motivated veterans. Probably the best answer for most PTSD veterans would be to seek treatment in what are known in the mental health field as dual diagnosis programs. In these types of treatment programs the staff have been specially trained in diagnosing and treating patients who have drug or alcohol abuse problems accompanied by a psychiatric disorder. Even more specialized dual diagnosis treatment programs are the ones that concentrate upon treating the combat PTSD veteran who has an accompanying alcohol abuse problem. The Department of Veterans Affairs provides this specialized dual diagnosis treatment at a number of medical centers, such as the one located at Bay Pines, Florida.

Similar problems occur when the combat PTSD veteran is abusing other drugs besides alcohol. All the illicit drugs produce harmful effects on the abuser, but in our community, crack cocaine is the worst. Its low cost and addictive power has made it the scourge of most American big cities, including Jacksonville, Florida. One local hospital's inpatient alcohol treatment program occasionally admitted patients who were abusing street drugs such as crack cocaine. By the 1990s the program evolved into, in effect, a crack cocaine treatment facility because of the large number of crack-addicted patients treated. This virulent poison ruined far too many lives and entire families. One shocking case from the hospital substance abuse program demonstrates crack cocaine's evil effects upon entire families. During the intake interview a new patient, who was a tall, muscular man in his twenties, was asked why he was entering the treatment program. His answer was that a court judge had ordered him there. He was then asked what type of legal difficulties caused the court order. He answered that he had been convicted of assault for beating up his grandmother. Apparently he had been so desperate for crack cocaine that he was stealing money from his grandmother's purse, when she walked into her bedroom. Upset by his theft, the grandmother berated him. Enraged by her scolding, he went berserk and attacked his frail grandmother with his fists. His lack of guilt over the attack is another factor that makes the case a memorable one. Other substance-abusing patients in the program were middle class housewives who traded sexual relations with low-class drug dealers for their crack cocaine. Similar types of crack addiction tragedies happened to combat veteran abusers treated at our mental health clinic. Crack cocaine veterans lost well-paying jobs, their homes and sometimes even their families because they could not control their addiction to the poison.

Self-help groups like Alcoholics Anonymous (AA) and Narcotics Anonymous (NA) are another source of effective substance abuse treatment for the PTSD veteran. Their major advantage is that along with outpatient group therapy, these outpatient programs routinely provide the addict with a sponsor, who is a recovered alcoholic or drug addict. Sponsors make themselves available 24 hours a day, 7 days a week for counseling and support, which is an invaluable service that private outpatient programs do not usually provide.

20

MEDICATIONS

This chapter examines the application of pharmacology, which is the use of medicines, in the treatment of PTSD. In the mental health field, a psychiatrist usually prescribes medicines for mental problems. People frequently are confused about the differences between a psychiatrist and a psychologist. There are different kinds of psychologists; the mental health type referred to by this question is a clinical psychologist, who usually earns the Doctor of Philosophy Degree (Ph.D.) by performing research in the field of clinical psychology. He or she then further studies clinical diagnosis and treatment of mental disorders through a year long internship at a psychiatric hospital. Clinical psychologists serve patients by providing psychotherapy and psychological testing services, usually as part of a mental health team. On the other hand, a psychiatrist is a trained Medical Doctor (M.D.), who then receives four years of specialized training as a hospital resident, primarily in the treatment of mental illnesses with medications. The practical difference for the veteran is that the clinical psychologist provides the psychotherapy while the psychiatrist prescribes the medicines. Other types of medical doctors can prescribe psychiatric medications, but they do not have the extensive training in the field that a psychiatrist receives.

Psychiatric medications do provide PTSD symptom relief, at times significant relief, but they do not provide the complete cure that veterans usually desire. Some veterans expect that there exists a magic pill that will make their PTSD disappear. They think that their only responsibility is to convince their psychiatrist to prescribe it for them. Education about medications is needed to lower veterans' expectations about the effectiveness of medicines used in PTSD treatment. They, like all Americans, have been spoiled by modern laboratory medicine's spectacular successes in developing potent medicines. The products of this impressive research effort were chemical compounds that eliminated the viruses and bacteria that were the source of such deadly diseases as tuberculosis and syphilis. Modern laboratory medicine's successes fostered high hopes that new medicines could be developed to cure any disorder. But PTSD is not a germ-based disease; it is a complex behavioral disorder caused by traumatic experiences producing the negative emotions of fear, guilt and depression. "No magic pill can erase the image of a best friend's shattered body or assuage the guilt from having traded duty with him that day."[88] There exists no quick and easy solution, no magic pill, for such complex and difficult psychological problems as PTSD.

The medical journal *Clinical Psychiatry* asked various PTSD experts to name the best initial treatment for PTSD. Psychotherapy experts preferred psychotherapy as the best initial treatment, whereas "the medication experts were much more likely to combine medication with psychotherapy from the start, especially for those with more severe or chronic problems."[89] A combination of the two treatments is the best practice, especially for chronic and severe PTSD, because of the advantages associated with a combined treatment strategy. Combining the two types of PTSD treatments allows each treatment's strengths to offset the other's weaknesses. Psychiatric medications provide relatively quick symptomatic relief, but the effects are only temporary. If a PTSD veteran stops taking the medications, the symptoms will return. On the other hand, a longer period of time is required before the benefits of psychotherapy actually take effect, but once established the benefits are long lasting. Undergoing psychotherapy is like acquiring an education. It takes years of hard work to graduate from college, but even if the college graduate never reads a book again, she is still educated. Once psychotherapy is successful, the benefits will last for years, if not for the rest of the patient's life. Therefore, by taking psychiatric medications, PTSD veterans' emotional symptoms rapidly improve as they begin the slower and more difficult process of psychotherapeutic change. But when the healing and personal growth does finally occur, these benefits are long lasting. Thus a combination of the two types of treatments creates a powerful therapeutic tool for quickly limiting symptoms and at the same time providing permanent benefits. As Professor J. Douglas Bremner of Emory University explains, "there is hope for reversal of symptoms of PTSD.... Both behavioral and medication treatments are hypothesized to act on the brain to reverse some of the neurological changes that are believed to underlie trauma-related psychiatric disorders like PTSD."[90]

One caution needs to be emphasized when planning treatment strategies for PTSD: one size does not fit all. The beneficial effects of psychiatric medications and psychotherapy on any particular individual vary tremendously. What final treatment plan is designed for a PTSD veteran depends ultimately upon his or her individual needs. The best treatment strategies are a product of a strong working partnership between the individual veteran and the treating doctors. Some PTSD veterans refused medications because of bad experiences with medications or street drugs in their past; others resisted the psychotherapy recommendation. Each person is unique; the best treatment plans reflect this uniqueness. For example, a 2008 *TIME* magazine article entitled "America's Medicated Army" described a sergeant who was diagnosed with depression while still in the Army and treated with medications for anxiety and depression. He continued taking the medicines upon returning home. "But PTSD isn't fixed by taking pills.... And I felt like I was drugged all the time." So he stopped taking the medicines and sought psychotherapeutic help from the VA. "He laughs when asked how he is doing. 'I'd like to think,' he says, 'that I'm really damn close back to normal.'"[91]

There are a number of basic medical concepts that combat PTSD veterans considering treatments with medicines needs to understand. First of all they should know that there are two different names for each and every medicine. One is the generic name that reflects the chemical structure of the compound itself; for example alprazolam or fluoxetine. These complex chemical compound names are tongue twisters even for doctors and nurses, plus they cannot be trademarked. Consequently pharmaceutical companies choose an easier to pronounce brand or trade name for each of their medicines that they can then legally protect by a trademark. For our examples, alprazolam's trade name is Xanax; fluoxetine's brand name is Prozac. Doctors and nurses tend to use the brand names instead of the generic names of medicines, so a doctor may say "I am going to write you a prescription for Xanax." Do not be confused when the pills come from the pharmacy in a bottle labeled alprazolam. The pharmacy did not make a mistake; they are simply labeling the medicine by its chemical compound name, not its brand name.

The dosage of any medicine is a critical factor in determining the chemical's effectiveness. Because a medicine provides good relief at a dosage of two pills does not mean that it would provide great relief if one were to take four pills. The ideal strategy for veterans is to take medicines only at the dosage their physician has prescribed. The treating physician is aware of the effective dosages for the medicines he or she is prescribing;

in addition, the physician understands the dangers of poisoning associated with the medicine, technically termed toxicity. If a veteran were to take a larger dose than the one prescribed by the physician, then he or she faces the possibility of toxicity from the overdose. Veterans came to our clinic sick from taking overdoses of their medications in an uninformed attempt to feel better. If veterans ingest a smaller dose than the one the doctor prescribed, then they may not have enough of the chemical compound in their body for it to be effective.

Every veteran should listen carefully to the doctor's explanation of exactly how and when the veteran should take the medicines. Veterans should make every effort to ensure that they understand the details of the physician's directions. Is it four pills every three hours or three pills every four hours? Lack of such an understanding was a problem for our outpatients, especially those who brought their spouses with them for the consultation with the physician. The spouse would pay attention, even taking notes, while the veteran may have disengaged, staring out the window. The wife then supervised the veteran's ingestion of the medications. But what happened when the spouse was out of town for a few days? The veteran had only a vague, incorrect recollection and did not bother to read the directions on the bottle. Veterans became quite ill because they took eight pills of their medicine every three hours (48 pills per day) instead of the prescribed regimen of three pills every eight hours (9 pills per day). There is also the risk of increased severity of side effects from such an overuse of prescribed medicines.

The side effects of prescribed medications are another critical issue for all patients. Every medicine causes side effects, which are the changes in the veteran's body other than the intended therapeutic ones. It is impossible to design a medicine that only targets a specific biological pathology without the chemical also influencing other bodily organs or physiological processes. Some side effects are quite dangerous. It is always a good idea for veterans to ask their psychiatrist or primary care physician about the most common side effects of the medicine the doctor is prescribing. Veterans should also inquire about exactly what the doctor wants them to do if they do experience a negative side effect. Abruptly stopping a medication because of side effects can be hazardous. Any and all changes in a veteran's use of medications should only occur under the supervision of the prescribing physician.

A related concern is the problem of psychiatric medicines interacting negatively with other medicines or other chemicals in the veteran's body. It is a good idea for veterans to make a list of all the medications they take and give it to their physician upon their initial visit. This list should be comprehensive, including any regularly used over-the-counter medications bought at the drug store and any vitamins or herbal products bought at the health food store. Veterans should also inform their doctor about the amount and type of any street drugs and alcohol regularly consumed. The psychiatrist will consider all this information in deciding what type and dose of PTSD medication to prescribe. One final bit of education; it can be very dangerous to mix alcohol with most psychiatric medications, since both types of chemical compounds affect the central nervous system and the brain. At the very least, alcohol dilutes the power of the psychiatric medications. It is a good idea for the veteran to abstain from drinking alcohol while using psychiatric medications.

Once the combat veteran has decided to seek medications as a treatment for PTSD, another question arises. Who should write the prescription? Even though any licensed physician has the legal right to write a prescription for psychiatric medications, it is my considered professional opinion that combat veterans should seek out a psychiatrist, especially one with experience in treating PTSD. Psychiatrists have the training and experience necessary to fully understand psychiatric medications; they know the latest medications, the effective dosages and what to look out for in terms of negative side effects. As mentioned, the veteran should seek out a psychiatrist that has worked with PTSD patients; it is ideal if the veteran can find one that has worked with combat-related PTSD. If the combat veteran is seeking treatment at any VA medical center, he or she will probably be referred to a psychiatrist, because most VA psychiatrists have extensive training and experience treating war related PTSD.

Combat PTSD Medication Types

A. Antidepressants

Currently the most prescribed medications for PTSD are any of the new types of antidepressants know as Selective Serotonin Reuptake Inhibitors (SSRIs). What this means is that these medications increase the amount of serotonin, which is one of the many neurotransmitters that convey nerve signals from one nerve cell to another across the gap that exists between neuron cells. The SSRIs work by blocking the reabsorption of the serotonin back into the neuron. Since serotonin has been associated with increased positive mood in humans, the more of it available the better. Animal studies have provided some of the justification for SSRI use in PTSD treatment. These studies have demonstrated that normal serotonin functioning in the brain is disrupted when the research animals are subjected to severe stress.[92]

In human PTSD treatment research the SSRIs have been the medication most thoroughly studied. The research results demonstrate that the SSRIs reduce PTSD anxiety and also the accompanying symptoms of depression. In fact, evidence of positive outcomes from large-scale human studies led the Food and Drug Administration (FDA) to approve two SSRIs for the treatment of PTSD: they are Paxil (generic: paroxitine) and Zoloft (generic: sertaline).[93] Several other SSRIs are in widespread use even though currently they do not have FDA approval. A few of the more common ones are: Celexa (generic: citalopram), Prozac (generic: fluoxetine) and Luvox (generic: fluvoxamine). All the SSRIs have demonstrated fewer side effects and less potential for toxicity than the older antidepressant medications such as Desyrel (generic: trazadone) and Nardil (generic: phenelzine), both of which could cause heart and liver abnormalities. However, on the plus side, trazadone has been used successfully in the treatment of PTSD insomnia. All the SSRIs also possess the valuable advantage of being nonaddictive. Both the International Society for Traumatic Stress Studies' Task Force[94] and Clinical Psychiatry's Expert Consensus Guidelines recommend the use of SSRIs as a frontline class of medicationsin the war against PTSD.[95]

One disadvantage associated with the use of SSRIs in the treatment of depression has been the time delay before the patient demonstrates clinical improvement. Psychiatrists had to routinely warn depressed patients that it might take three to four weeks before their condition improved; sometimes it would take five to eight weeks. Obviously this is a less than ideal situation given the patient's distress. However, recent human research offers an exciting explanation for the delay period. Treatment with the SSRIs may be promoting the growth of new brain cells in human adults. It takes approximately a month for new brain cells to grow, a process that is known as neurogenesis. The multiple weeks' delay associated with SSRI treatment could be the time required for the growth of new cells in the depressed patient's brain. This exciting development reflects a revolution in human neuroscience because up until just a few years ago the neuroscience establishment thought that neurogenesis could not happen in the human adult brain. It was thought that only children could grow new brain neurons. However, Dr. Ronald

Duman and his Yale University research team demonstrated that the SSRIs promote adult brain cell growth in the hippocampus.[96]

As previously explained, the hippocampus is the brain region that plays a vital role in memory functioning and is quite sensitive to the effects of stress. Dr. Bremner of Emory University was curious to see if the hippocampal shrinkage seen in PTSD patients could be reversed. So he and his research assistant, Dr. Vermetten, treated PTSD patients for one year with the SSRI Paxil (generic: paroxitine). They then measured the patients' hippocampi with an MRI brain scan. They found that their PTSD patients' hippocampal volume increased 5 percent and that the patients' memory ability increased an incredible 35 percent, as measured by cognitive testing. "The patients in this study found that treatment with Paxil led to a significant improvement in their ability to work and function in their lives."[97]

B. Antianxiety Medications

The antianxiety agents are more widely known as the minor tranquilizers. They work quickly in the central nervous system, calming the patient's elevated physiological arousal without affecting clarity of consciousness. Minor tranquilizers, also known by their chemical name benzodiazepines, were used extensively in the treatment of PTSD veterans during the early 1980s; currently their use is controversial. Prescribing psychiatrists found that these medications were quite habit forming, often leading to dependency. This habituation risk was especially high if the veteran had a history of chemical abuse, either with alcohol or illegal drugs. With the development of safer medications like the SSRIs, some psychiatrists, but not all, no longer prescribe the benzodiazepines for PTSD. For many years there were four psychiatrists assigned to our mental health clinic. Two of them were strongly opposed to the use of benzodiazepines for treating PTSD. In sharp contrast, the other two psychiatrists thought that their judicious use could be done safely, but only if the veteran's alcohol and illicit drug abuse were closely monitored.

The most widely prescribed benzodiazepines are: Valium (generic: diazepam), Xanax (generic: alprazolam), Klonopin (generic: clonazepam), and Ativan (generic: lorazepam). These minor tranquilizers are effective in the short term for reducing general anxiety or insomnia, but their long-term use can be problematic. Besides their habituation risk, benzodiazepines may cause depressive symptoms and psychomotor slowing. Abruptly ending their long-term use can be hazardous. After studying the benzodiazepines, the Traumatic Stress Task Force concluded, "They do not appear to have any advantage over other classes of drugs and, therefore, cannot be recommended for use as monotherapy in PTSD at this time."[98]

C. Anticonvulsants

There are two other types of medications that have proven to be helpful in the treatment of PTSD. However, psychiatrists classify them only as adjuncts, which means they are prescribed in addition to, but not as a substitute for, the previously reviewed frontline medications for PTSD. One type of PTSD adjunct medication is the anticonvulsants, which were originally developed to treat seizures. In psychiatry they are called mood stabilizers because they have demonstrated effectiveness in the treatment of the disruptive moods associated with the bipolar disorders. Two of the most common mood stabilizers are Tegretol (generic: carbamazepine) and Depakote (generic: valproic acid). Psychiatrists have accumulated extensive clinical experience that prove how the mood stabilizers could reduce the aggression and impulsiveness of PTSD patients. Of course anticonvulsants can also produce serious negative side effects; therefore, they must be closely monitored.

D. Antipsychotics

The other type of PTSD adjunct medicine is the antipsychotics, which are often called the major tranquilizers. These chemical compounds were developed to treat severe psychotic symptoms such as hallucinations and delusions. A hallucination is a psychotic patient's perception of something or someone that does not exist in reality, for example, seeing or hearing a dead friend. A delusion is a psychotic patient's erroneous belief that is strongly held even in the face of contradictory evidence, for example, a patient's belief that the government is sending him or her top-secret messages through the television set. The use of antipsychotics in PTSD therapy is usually limited to those unfortunate veterans who exhibit these types of severe symptoms or who have not responded well to the frontline medications.[99] The safest antipsychotics are the recently developed ones known as the atypical antipsychotics, because they produce the fewest side effects. A few of the most widely prescribed atypicals are Risperdal (generic: risperidone), Zyprexa (generic: olanzapine), and Seroquel (generic: quetipaine). Even though these medications are safer than the typical antipsychotics, they may cause dangerous side effects, so they too must be closely and continually monitored.

21

Experimental Treatments

This chapter examines several new experimental treatments for combat PTSD. The first section introduces two medicines that show exciting promise for the prevention of chronic PTSD. The other experimental treatment is called virtual therapy, an approach that uses computer-generated video games to artificially reexpose combat veterans to traumatic combat scenarios.

Medications

One medication that shows promise for both the prevention and treatment of chronic PTSD is propranolol, its generic name. It is an older hypertension medicine that is manufactured under a number of different trade names, with Inderal probably the most well known. Propranolol blocks the energizing effects of adrenalin in the body, and thus in a sense, blocks the emergency alarm response (the freeze, fight or flight response). It reduces both the hyperarousal and hypervigilance symptoms of PTSD.[100] Its side effects include but are not limited to hypotension (low blood pressure), nausea, diarrhea, possible depression and possible memory difficulties.[101]

Another hypertension medication that has shown exciting promise in PTSD treatment is prazosin, marketed under the trade names of Minipress, Vasoflex and Hypovase. Prazosin works by blocking the energizing effects of PTSD-generated adrenaline, mainly by relaxing the smooth muscle walls of blood vessels. It also appears to improve the quality of a combat veteran's sleep, even possibly limiting nightmares. Psychiatrists are prescribing prazosin to reduce the nightmares of their combat PTSD veterans. One 2003 research study indicated that prazosin improved sleep, reduced nightmares, and led to a reduction in overall PTSD symptoms among combat veterans.[102] Like propranolol, prazosin also appears to have the potential for preventing chronic PTSD symptoms, if it administered immediately after a trauma. However, the use of both prazosin and propranolol as medical treatments for PTSD must be considered experimental at this time due to the lack of adequately controlled clinical research on PTSD patients. Hopefully their potential for the prevention of chronic PTSD will soon lead to the controlled clinical trials necessary to fully evaluate their therapeutic benefits.

Psychotherapies

Scientists are studying experimental psychotherapies designed to treat combat PTSD. A relatively new type of reexposure therapy takes advantage of the power of computers and video games. This therapy is called *virtual reality therapy* because a computer generates an artificial world, the virtual reality, by combining animated graphics like those in video games with other sensory effects supplied by headphones, odor generators and a vibrating platform. Psychologists, working closely with computer scientists, programmed their virtual reality computers to simulate combat scenarios, first from the Vietnam War and more recently from the Iraq and Afghanistan wars. The combination of the various devices creates a multisensory experience that is vividly lifelike — the patient's virtual world. For example, an Iraq War PTSD veteran sits in a chair on a vibrating platform, wearing a head-mounted visual display device and headphones and holding a steering wheel. Before being hooked up, this veteran described a combat trauma to the clinical psychologist, who then adjusts the computer controls to approximate the veteran's actual combat experience. The computer then generates an artificial recreation of the veteran's combat trauma, perhaps one of driving a Humvee through the streets of Baghdad when an improvised explosive device (IED) explodes near the vehicle. The Iraq veteran not only sees and hears the explosion, but also feels the shock shaking the simulated vehicle and smells the explosion's cordite. Even while within the virtual world, the veteran can discuss with the psychotherapist what he or she is thinking and feeling while reliving the combat trauma. Virtual reality psychotherapy is a modern extension of traditional imaginational reexposure and cognitive therapy combat PTSD treatments. Like the more traditional therapies, the goal of virtual reality therapy is to stimulate veterans' recall of traumatic memories in order to help them adaptively reprocess the trauma and desensitize themselves to these upsetting memories.

The first virtual reality computer program was called Virtual Vietnam. It was developed in 1996 by Dr. Barbara Rothbaum, an experimental psychologist at Emory University, working with Dr. Larry Hodge, a computer scientist at Georgia Tech. They field-tested their early programs with the help of Dr. David Ready, a clinical psychologist at the Atlanta VA Medical Center. They found that PTSD Vietnam veterans "who completed the treatment have shown as much as one-third reduction in severity of symptoms and significantly fewer nightmares, flashbacks, intrusive thoughts, depression and anxiety."[103]

Currently a Virtual Iraq computer program is being tested at San Diego Naval Medical Center and Camp Pendelton as a joint venture between the Office of Naval Research and the University of Southern California's Center for Creative Technologies. Their chief psychologist, Dr. Albert Rizzo, points out that in his virtual combat video the veteran does carry a rifle, but it has been deliberately disabled and cannot fire. The computer video was designed not as a game or a method of expressing revenge fantasies, but as a serious treatment tool. Early trial results indicate that for the first 20 PTSD veterans who received treatment with Virtual Iraq/ Afghanistan, 16 no longer experienced enough symptoms to meet the diagnostic criteria for PTSD. Clinical research is currently underway at Weill Cornell Medical College, Emory University, Fort Lewis and 20 other sites to fully test the Virtual Iraq/Afghanistan program.[104] A major limitation with these virtual reality therapies is that they are quite expensive. Hopefully, future advances in computer simulation will reduce costs. Virtual reality therapy appears to be well suited for our younger generation of combat soldiers, who grew up playing video games. If virtual therapy becomes more accessible and is accepted by combat veterans, it will help reduce the stigma associated with receiving psychological treatment for combat PTSD.

22

CHRONIC PAIN AND PTSD

All soldiers face the risk of death in battle, but for many the prospect of grievous wounds is even more frightening. Combatants are at risk for traumatic amputations, paralyzing spinal cord injuries, horrific burns and brain damage, to name a few. Recent casualty statistics from the United States' Mideast War are shocking. During the first seven months of 2011, military surveys indicate that 134 service members suffered traumatic amputation of limbs due to combat operations. Another 79 combatants suffered multiple amputations, a casualty figure twice as high as the 2010 total. Ninety soldiers wounded during that period lost their genitals due to enemy explosions.[105] A future filled with such devastating wounds is so terrifying that some soldiers think that they would rather die instead. At least then their suffering would be over. Those who do survive such massive injuries must deal with many difficult challenges, not the least of which is chronic pain.

Consider, for example, the published case of Captain Jonathan Pruden, who while driving his unarmored Humvee through Baghdad in July of 2003, took an AK-47 rifle round to his right knee while a roadside bomb shattered his right foot and shredded his arms and legs with 173 pieces of shrapnel. Golf ball-size shrapnel also shattered one of his shoulder blades.[106] The United States military's efforts at improving battlefield survivability have paid off. Captain Pruden was quickly evacuated, stabilized at a battalion aid station and then immediately flown to a hospital in Kuwait, where surgeons worked heroically to save his leg. He was finally transferred to Walter Reed Hospital in Washington, D.C., where he was subjected to 14 more surgeries, none of which removed all the shrapnel in his face. He is now forced to cope with chronic pain. He takes two doses of Oxycontin and Percocet painkillers as needed every day to relieve his right leg pain, which is severe enough to confine him to a wheelchair for most of his day. In fact, the pain is so unbearable that he is considering amputation of his leg, yet he courageously attempts to remain as active as possible and engaged in life.

The problem for Captain Pruden is that even powerful narcotic analgesics such as Percocet do not provide the level of pain relief he desires. For him and many other wounded veterans the daily struggle of coping with pain depletes their psychological resources, frequently leading to the development of depression, self-pity and even suicidal thoughts. If wounded veterans also suffer from Post Traumatic Stress Disorder, then the pain can stimulate memories of their trauma, triggering their emergency alarm reaction, which in turn causes ongoing retraumatization. The negative effects of this continuing pain-triggered retraumatization with injured veterans produces a downward spiral in their Post Traumatic Stress Disorder.

These traumatized veterans enduring chronic pain often become frustrated and angry with their physicians because they think that the perfect analgesic does exist, but the doctor is not prescribing it for them. Veterans eventually feel frustrated and depressed because the doctor is unable to provide the needed pain relief. However, the perfect pain killer — powerful, but producing no side effects — simply does not exist. Part of this dilemma derives from the veteran's mistaken belief that ingesting analgesic medications is the only pain reduction option. Fortunately, however, hope is available in the form of a relatively new medical specialty called pain medicine. This rapidly advancing specialty treats pain, especially chronic pain, as a primary disease in itself, not as simply the side effect of another disease such as cancer or arthritis, which was medicine's usual attitude towards pain in the past.

Pain specialists understand that the pain a patient feels is not entirely due to the amount of tissue damage, but also due to complexities within the psychology of the patient. It should be inspiring for veterans to learn that the original insights within the field of pain medicine were discovered by United States Army doctors during World War II. After the invasion of Anzio, Italy, Dr. Henry Beecher, a battalion surgeon, was treating soldiers on the beach, where he was surprised by how stoic the wounded men were, even those who had sustained devastating injuries. When he asked men whose injuries were as severe as traumatic amputations if they were in pain or needed analgesic medications, fully 70 percent of them answered "no." He noted that these men were not simply numb and in shock, because they complained about the pricks they felt when medics punctured their veins for transfusions. Later when Dr. Beecher was a professor at Harvard Medical School, he asked a group of same-aged civilians with similar injuries to those of the Anzio veterans if they were in pain and desired analgesics. Fully 70 percent of the civilians answered "yes." Dr. Beecher's insights into the differences between these two different patient groups became one of the bedrock concepts in the field of pain medicine. He perceived that the psychological meaning of the wounds was different between the two groups. For the combat veterans their wounds, no matter how severe, were their ticket out of the killing zone that was Anzio beach. They would survive the war. They were anticipating being sent back the United States to recover. In contrast, the civilians had not been worried, like the soldiers had, about dying before their injuries. To the civilians their injuries were devastating interruptions to their life plans, dooming them to years of pain and disability. Dr. Beecher concluded that the psychology of the patient, particularly what meaning the patient gave to the injuries, had a profound effect on the level of pain that patient experienced.[107]

Another World War II Army physician, Dr. John Bonica, was also a major pioneer in the development of pain medicine. He joined the Army in 1944 and was assigned as chief of anesthesiology to Madigan Army Hospital in Fort Lewis, Washington. Hundreds of severely wounded World War II veterans were referred to him for treatment. The dreadful suffering these veterans endured appalled Dr. Bonica. Their courage inspired him to devote himself to learning all that he could about chronic pain. He searched through medical libraries and was disappointed to learn that there existed no textbook devoted to pain as a separate disease; instead he found only chapters on pain in books devoted to other diseases, like cancer. So Dr. Bonica decided to take on the daunting task of writing one. His efforts resulted in the 1953 textbook *Management of Pain.* It is currently in its fourth edition, continued and expanded by other experts who honor Dr. Bonica's legacy; he died in 1977. It is still considered the best textbook written in the field of pain control. He was an innovator who understood that chronic pain is a complex phenomenon that requires a multidisciplinary approach for truly effective treatment. He recruited psychologists and psychiatrists to his hospital's treatment teams to directly treat the depression and fears of his wounded heroes. Dr. Bonica also recognized that the idea of tissue damage as the only cause of pain was incorrect. In his textbook he explains that pain, especially chronic pain, is the result of a complex interaction of many factors including, fundamentally, the psychology of the patient.

There are a number of such mistaken notions involved in the understanding most veterans have of their pain. The following section exposes a number of these myths.

1. *All pain is bad and should be avoided at all costs.* From an evolutionary perspective pain would not exist if it did not provide a survival advantage. Pain usually functions as a valuable alarm, alerting us to any insult to the integrity of our bodies. If a soldier accidentally touches a hot tank engine, the subsequent pain shooting up the arm's nerves to the brain alerts him or her to the injury. The solider immediately withdraws his or her hand, thus limiting the damage resulting from the burn. People may think that being born without the ability to feel pain would be a wonderful advantage. In fact there are children who are unable to feel pain because they were born without certain spinal cord cells that help transport pain signals. Yet their parents quickly learn that their child's pain insensitivity is not a blessing, but rather a true curse.

Consider the case of Gabby Gingras, who was born with this genetic abnormality that results in pain insensitivity. Her parents did not recognize the disorder until Gabby chewed her tongue and knuckles to a pulp during teething. Horribly, she lost one eye and damaged the other because she rubbed her eyes too hard. Gabby's condition is so distressing that her mother, Trisha, stated that she envies other mothers whose children have cancer. "If they go five years and beat it, they're done. With Gabby, it's never going away."[108] There are other cases of pain-insensitive children who have died because they did not feel an ankle sprain that lead to a fatal infection. People cursed with genetic pain insensitivity do not live a normal life span. Pain exists because its alarm function limits post-injury tissue damage.

2. *All pain is the same.* Pain specialists distinguish between two different types of pain based upon time dimensions. *Acute pain* is the discomfort felt immediately after an injury. It forces the person to react to the injury and thus limits the extent of the damage. On the other hand, *chronic pain* is defined as pain that lasts over six months. Chronic pain no longer works as an effective alarm. The injury has been repeatedly broadcasting the same pain message for at least six months. Since it is not sending any new information to the patient, pain specialists strive to teach their patients that chronic pain does not require the reaction that acute pain requires.

3. *The amount of tissue damage determines the level of pain.* Of course a broken leg hurts more than a stubbed toe. But there are patients who have sustained the same injuries and yet report widely different levels of pain. There have been studies of nonpatients whose MRI scans of their backs revealed significant damage and who were not in pain. And as Dr. Beecher learned, the extent of tissue damage is not the only factor that determines an individual's perceived pain level. The psychological meaning of the injury to the patient is another critical factor in the perception of pain equation.

4. *Chronic pain can be cured.* Unfortunately a magic super pill that completely eliminates long-term pain does not exist. Every pain-killing medication has limits to its analgesic effects and they all cause serious side effects. The stronger the pain killer, the more extensive and disruptive the side effects. For example the use of opiumlike narcotics routinely causes constipation in patients and can suppress respiration. Surgeries designed to block or cut the nerves involved in pain transmission have proven to be notoriously ineffective. Many veterans have endured multiple surgeries for lower back pain, yet these procedures produced no consistent pain relief. Frequently the surgeon's only answer to the veteran's persistent back pain complaints is to recommend more surgery.

5. *Patients are powerless in reducing their chronic pain.* Veterans suffering from chronic pain are not as helpless as they may think. Veterans' interpretation of their pain, the meaning they give it, does affect their discomfort level. Other psychological factors, such as the veteran's attitude and motivation, are also powerful weapons in the battle against pain. The healthy attitude is one where veterans accept ownership of their pain and do not passively wait for their doctor to cure them. It is not their doctor's or spouse's problem; it is their pain. Veterans must strive to be well-rounded people, not allowing their pain to define entirely who and what they are.

The concept of motivation affecting a person's pain level will be examined in detail. That psychological factors are critical in pain perception is demonstrated by the fact that an individual's level of motivation to endure pain will affect pain tolerance. Professional football players define painful injuries as an expected occupational hazard; their motto is to "play with pain." These athletes are highly motivated by the large sums of money they risk losing if they allow a painful injury to sideline them. Special

Forces soldiers tend to tolerate painful wounds because they want to return to duty with their units. These warriors are highly motivated by the pride they feel in being a member of an elite fighting unit. Scientists studying pain employ what is know as the cold pressor test to measure a person's pain tolerance. The subject is instructed to place his or her arm into a container full of cold water and ice. Pain tolerance is measured by how long subjects can keep their arm submerged after first alerting the researcher that they now feel pain from the ice water. Imagine taking this test and discovering that you were able to tolerate the ice water for two minutes. Now imagine that the scientist makes you a credible offer of $100,000 if you are able to keep your arm submerged in the ice water for three minutes. Most of us would steel our minds in order to tolerate the ice-cold discomfort for the three minutes because of the exciting reward. The scientist's significant increasing of the payoff increases the subject's motivation, which in turn results in greater pain tolerance. As the psychology of the research participant changes so does his or her pain tolerance.

More compelling evidence for the argument that pain is psychologically based comes from the fact that there exists no purely objective test to measure an individual's pain level. Doctors routinely measure a patient objectively across many dimensions. They can measure a patient's blood pressure, weight, bone density, blood composition, lung capacity, et cetera. Yet none of these measurements will inform the doctor of how much pain the patient is feeling. And it is not because doctors have not tried. Clinical scientists have experimented with various methods in attempts to measure pain, but they have all failed. A doctor is left with only one alternative, asking the patient the purely subjective question: "How much does it hurt?" Pain specialists may attempt to be more objective by asking the patient, "On a scale of one to ten, where ten is the most agonizing pain you can imagine and zero means no pain, what number reflects your current level of pain?" They may provide a paper with a one to ten scale drawn on it (some even have various smiling or frowning faces attached to the numbers) and then have the patient mark the number that reflects his or her current pain level. Yet all of these efforts to bring more objectivity to the effort are still only variations of the basic subjective question: "How much does it hurt?" An individual's personal experience of pain is always a subjective judgment, a behavior that is certainly within the domain of the psychological sciences.

An intriguing question is exactly how does the brain tone down incoming pain signals from the body? Early theories of the central nervous system considered the system of nerves transmitting signals from limbs up through the spinal cord to the brain as a passive communication system, similar to inert telephone wires, which do not react to the signals passing through them. But the central nervous system is clearly much more complex: it is a living system, therefore, it is active. It reacts to pain signals and can, in fact, regulate them. The current theory that best explains the human brain's ability to regulate pain is called the gate control theory. The gate control theory asserts that along the central spinal cord there exist a series of cellular junction points, the gates, that determine whether a pain signal travels upward to the brain or not. These cellular gates can open wider to allow more pain signals to travel through or they can close entirely, thus blocking the pain signal.[109] Neuroscientists think that the spinal cord-based signal pathway system is a two-way street. Theoretically, signals can travel down from the brain through the spinal cord to the body's periphery. Another assertion of the gate control theory is that both psychological factors and physical factors determine whether the cellular gates open or close. For example, how much pain an individual feels after stubbing his or her toe is partially determined by psychological factors such as the individual's current mood. If the toe-stubbing happened on the way to a dreaded court appearance, the injury will generate more pain than if he were to stub his toe on the way to a fun day at the beach. Negative emotions like depression or fear will open the cellular gates, ensuring that more pain signals flow through. How wide the gates open is also influenced by the psychological factor of cognitions, for example, how serious the injury is judged to be. Or as the brilliant neurologist Dr. V.S. Ramachandran expressed it, "Pain is an opinion on the organism's state of health rather than a mere reflexive response to injury."[110]

To demonstrate that top-down control from the human brain to the body's periphery does occur, consider the following thought experiment. Imagine that a woman accidentally touched a hot coil on her kitchen's range; naturally she would immediately withdraw her hand in pain. But now imagine that just as she touched the hot coil, a known serial killer shoves a pistol to her head and threatens to blow her brains out if she were to move her hand. What would she do in this terrifying situation? Yes, her burning hand hurts at first, but her brain would realize that there is a bigger issue at stake, her very life. It would immediately generate emergency signals down to the spinal cord to close the cellular neural gates as tightly as possible, enabling her to keep her hand on the hot coil.

Currently neuroscientists do not fully understand how the descending neural pathways involved in top-down control work, but they do accept that these pathways exist. Many are currently engaged in ongoing research projects in an attempt to answer this intriguing question. One widely discussed theory is that the neural pain gates are closed by endorphins, which means "the morphine within." Endorphins are neurochemicals produced by the pituitary gland in the brain that act as neurotransmitters, which means they are involved in the transmitting of the electro-chemical signals that travel through nerve cells. Neurons, the technical term for nerve cells, are the basic building blocks of the brain and the nervous system. Endorphins have been scientifically demonstrated to be a more powerful painkiller than morphine. In fact it is thought that drugs like morphine and opium obtain their analgesic power because they are chemically similar to endorphin, thus mimicking their functioning in the central nervous system. The theory states that the brain generates endorphins when needed, and then sends them down the spinal cord's descending pathways to close the neural pain gates. Neuroscientists also think that endorphins are involved in the production of euphoriclike emotions such as joy and contentment. Interestingly it has been demonstrated that prolonged continuous aerobic exercise in humans increases the brain's production of endorphins. This fact probably explains the runner's high, that feeling of overall euphoria that runners enjoy after a long run.

A poorly recognized biological fact is that our central nervous system is not an inert system like our home's electrical wiring; it is a sensitive living system and as such is not immune to the pain signals it transmits. The human central nervous system is a vital organ that is changed by the signals traveling through it. When pain signals are broadcast for an extended period of time, the nerves adapt to the experience. Chronic pain can cause peripheral nerve fibers at the site of an injury to become sensitized and irritable. Eventually even the slightest touch will feel excruciatingly painful. It is as if your home wiring system rewired itself so that once a light switch is turned on, the light can never be turned off. Chronic pain becomes a neural disease: the nerves are damaged by the continued transmission of pain signals. As Dr. Sean Mackey, the director of research at Stanford University's Pain Management Center, explains, "Pain causes a fundamental rewiring of the nervous system.... Each time we feel pain, there are changes that occur that tend to amplify our experience of pain."[111]

It is not uncommon for doctors to find that a veteran's initial injury has healed, yet the veteran still complains of intense chronic pain. This pathological outcome becomes a compelling argument against the military's macho creed of being stoic and just enduring pain. The price the soldier can pay is a type of nerve damage resulting in unrelenting discomfort. Veterans suffering from chronic pain must be advised to take their analgesics exactly as prescribed and to apply all the pain management skills they are taught. By following this recommendation veterans decrease the possibility that their nervous system will be damaged by the overload of pain signals. For those veterans who do not like to ingest pills, the following argument can be made. When you have only one-quarter of a pound of pain, then you only need one-quarter of a pound of painkillers to deal with your discomfort. But if you wait until you have a full pound of pain, then you need a pound of painkillers to deal with it. Take the full measure of analgesic medications early on; cut the pain off at the pass. Overall the results will be less pain and fewer pills. There are real medical and biological advantages in closing the spinal neural gates on pain as soon as possible.

Pain is directly connected to psychological factors. Chronic pain frequently causes depression, which is the most common psychiatric co-diagnosis in chronic pain patients. Research studies investigating the co-occurrence of chronic pain and depression have found that up to 100 percent of patients suffering chronic pain meet the diagnostic criteria for depression.[112] A vicious cycle develops: the pain causes depression, which then opens the pain gates wider, leading to even more pain. Recent research from Stanford University, utilizing various sophisticated brain scanning technologies, has demonstrated that the same brain sites are activated in subjects when they are depressed and when they are feeling pain.[113] This means that these brain circuits are actively involved in processing both depression and pain. A recently developed antidepressant medication, Cymbalta, has been approved by the Federal Drug Administration for the treatment of depression as well as for the chronic pain caused by the nerve damage associated with diabetes. Many neurologists and neuroscientists conclude that the effectiveness of Cymbalta for these two disorders provides convincing evidence that the same brain circuits are implicated in negative emotions and chronic pain. The overlap of the two disorders makes it difficult for doctors to distinguish between where the patient's pain ends and the actual discomfort of depression begins. Because of this diagnostic difficulty, every veteran suffering from chronic pain should be evaluated by a mental health professional for the possible existence of depression.

Psychological Treatments of Chronic Pain

Because pain is psychologically as well as physically based, it is a reasonable expectation that effective pain treatments would develop from these two factors in the pain equation. The next section will primarily examine psychological treatments for chronic pain and one physically based treatment. The versatility of a major psychological treatment, cognitive psychotherapy, becomes quite apparent as we apply it to the epidemic problem of chronic pain management.

An underused but effective treatment for reducing chronic pain is regular physical exercise. Unfortunately many veterans suffering from chronic muscular-skeletal pain avoid exercise because they find that the movements hurt. Then they develop fears that exercise may damage them more. The matter is further complicated because in the past doctors tended to recommend plenty of bed rest for chronic pain patients. Physicians currently understand that prolonged bed rest will result in atrophied muscles and reduced endurance in patients, even ones that are fit young adults. Lying in bed all day also significantly increases the risk for heart and lung problems.[114] Pain specialists now think that the discomfort that chronic pain patients feel while moving is due to the loss of physical fitness rather than the original injury or disease.

To reassure themselves, veterans should ask their primary care providers if exercise would benefit their particular condition. Most of the time the answer will be in the affirmative, because physicians recognize the many benefits of exercise for their pain patients. Exercise improves circulation, bringing more vital nutrients to the muscles and joints as well as removing toxic metabolic byproducts. Exercise builds strength, ensuring a solid muscle grid that can support and protect pain-prone backs and joints. It restores normal range of motion for muscles, tendons and ligaments, which helps protect them from strain, thus making it easier for the veteran to accomplish such normal tasks as carrying groceries. Exercise boosts endurance and aids veterans in their weight control, helping to prevent the diseases of obesity, hypertension and diabetes. And as mentioned, exercise has been shown to increase the production and release of endorphins, morphinelike chemicals that are the body's own natural painkillers and mood enhancers.

To maintain physical activity, veterans need to discover an exercise that they find reasonably pleasurable. Rhythmic activities like walking, biking or dancing are recommended over competitive sports like tennis or basketball. Water sports also reduce joint stress in veterans who are overweight or arthritic. Swimming and other water activities are ideal in hot climates like Florida or Arizona because they limit the risk of dehydration and heat exhaustion. Walking is highly recommended because it is more than just an activity; it is the human form of locomotion.

Humans are the primate that was designed to walk upright; our hips and leg bones are made for bipedalism, which is walking on two feet. Army and Marine veterans know how strong and fit they became over the course of a few long-distance hikes. The ability to walk helps an individual keep their personal independence. When a chronic pain veteran can no longer walk to the kitchen or bathroom, the veteran then becomes a nursing problem. Veterans may find themselves confined to a nursing home at a relatively young age — not a pleasant prospect. Veterans who did take up our walking recommendation returned to our clinic smiling as they reported how much better they felt. A few pain specialists think that the main purpose of analgesic medicines is to take enough of the edge off of a patient's pain so that the patient can then exercise. One caution is that veterans with chronic pain should learn how to pace any new activities, incorporating into their schedule regular periods of rest, to reduce the possibility of activity-induced discomfort.

A proven psychological pain management technique is *relaxation training*. We have examined how relaxation procedures can be helpful in controlling the biological arousal symptoms characteristic of PTSD. Refer to the previous chapter on relaxation for the details of this beneficial coping strategy. Basically, by triggering a relaxation response the chronic pain veteran shuts off the emergency alarm reaction. The ensuing decreased energy state is a kind of comfortable low gear that has healing benefits. Dr. Dennis Turk, a psychologist who is a pioneer researcher in the field of pain management, lists the numerous benefits of relaxation.

> It decreases or prevents muscle spasms, reduces and controls muscle tension, and helps control other physiological mechanisms (altered blood flow, changes in brain chemicals) involved in nervous system arousal and pain production. Muscle relaxation may also reduce anxiety and distress, improve sleep, and distract a person from the pain.[115]

There is scientific research that demonstrates that relaxation can be effective in reducing lower back pain as well as the pain of migraine and tension headaches.[116]

Dr. Turk mentioned one simple but effective technique that emphasizes cognitive processes for pain management; it is *distraction*. This management technique literally takes the patient's mind off of the pain. It trains the patient to mentally focus upon ideas, sensations or activities that compete within the patient's brain for attention. Distraction as a pain control skill takes advantage of the fact that the central nervous system circuitry that controls attention are limited capacity processors. They can focus attention on only one topic at a time. Multitaskers who claim that they can answer the phone while writing an e-mail while watching television are fooling themselves. All they are really doing is rapidly switching back and forth from one topic to another. These attention circuits are part of the central nervous system's vast network of filtering mechanisms exclusively devoted to limiting sensations. We unconsciously select, out of the overload of various sensations bombarding our senses, what stimuli are important enough to be noticed. For example a student may at first notice street noise outside his or her room, but after a short time it becomes background chatter, which can be safely ignored. The student's brain filters out the unimportant noise.

By focusing on a distracting stimulus, chronic pain patients monopolize their attention circuits, preventing them from attending to their pain. Patients do not develop a higher pain tolerance; the distraction prevents them from becoming aware of the competing painful sensations. The pain signals do not reach conscious awareness in their brain; therefore, they do not feel the pain. No brain, then no pain. This is the reason why dentists have televisions installed in ceilings over their dental chairs or why nurses will tell a fearful child to look away just before administering an injection. The child's focusing her attention elsewhere reduces the discomfort she feels from the injection. There have been a number of research studies that have demonstrated that distraction significantly reduced children's ratings of their pain.[117] Any pleasant diversion will work if the chronic pain patient feels passionate about it. Reading, listening to music or watching television all are potentially useful. One chronic pain Navy veteran developed a passion for computers. He was pleased to report that if he spent three hours working on his home computer, those were three hours in which he was pain free.

Cognitive Therapy for Pain

The next psychological technique for pain management that will be examined is the powerful one of cognitive therapy. Recall that cognitive psychotherapy is based upon the principle that how one thinks about an event determines one's emotional reaction to the event. How one interprets the pain, the personal meaning one gives to the pain, will determine one's emotional reaction to it. In other words how individuals talk to themselves about their pain will determine the amount of agony they suffer. For example medical centers have had older veterans present at their emergency rooms in a near-panic state complaining of chest pains. Veterans had interpreted the muscular discomfort in their chest as a symptom of an imminent heart attack, and they reacted emotionally as if this interpretation were true. Emergency room doctors physically examine the veterans and order a number of expensive heart scans and blood tests to determine the medical status of the veterans. At times the results of the examination and test results prove to be normal. The puzzled doctors again question the veteran about his activities that day; he reveals that he had been moving heavy ladders that morning while painting his house. The emergency room doctors now recognize the probable source of the veteran's pain. They reassure him that his pain is not due to a heart attack, but rather due to muscle strain from the exertion of moving the ladders. For most mentally sound veterans the doctors' reassurance changes their interpretation of their chest pain, thus they feel great relief. But some highly anxious PTSD veterans are not so easily reassured, necessitating a referral to a mental health clinic. (Review the chapter on cognitive therapy for details.)

Most veterans do not realize how crucial self-talk really is in producing their emotional reactions. The usual assumption is that anyone who talks to her- or himself is mentally deranged. But we all talk to ourselves. That is one way of defining thinking: a self-directed discussion within our heads. Thinking is the internal dialogue that determines our problem-solving strategies. The critical question is not "Do you talk to yourself?" but rather "What exactly do you say?" How do you interpret your pain? What meaning do you give it? If a veteran thinks that chronic pain is a punishment from God, he will have an entirely different emotional reaction to the pain than a veteran who interprets pain as a natural outcome of an injury. The goal for the cognitive psychotherapist treating a chronic pain veteran is to help the veteran change her or his thinking about the pain from an illogical distortion to thinking that is more reasonable. For example if a veteran views pain as an enemy, then he or she must constantly be on guard, tense and battle ready. On the other hand if the veteran can redefine the pain more realistically as a challenge, then he or she does not have to be so tense. Thus the veteran will be more open to learning how to deal with the challenge of pain.

The following are a number of common chronic pain distortions that veterans tell themselves, along with more rational counter arguments.

1. *My pain is extreme; it is just too awful!* This is an example of catastrophic thinking, which exaggerates the intensity of pain. It is the type of self-talk reported by those veterans who, when asked to rate their pain on a one-to-ten scale, answer twelve or even fifteen. They are magnifying an unpleasant situation into a horrific monster. A cognitive therapist would question the evidence that the veteran has for this distorted thinking. If veterans think that they may die from the pain, their therapist would reassure them that no one dies from chronic pain alone. The therapeutic goal is to replace such distortions with less self-defeating and more reasonable thoughts like "My pain will be more tolerable as I learn to deal with it better."

2. *My pain will get worse.* The cognitive therapy counterargument emphasizes that the veteran is assuming the worst possible future. The veteran is reaching an arbitrary conclusion without a thorough and rational evaluation of the probability of its likelihood. Where is the evidence that your pain will inevitably worsen? What if a new treatment is discovered? What if you could learn a technique to reduce your pain?

3. *If my pain continues, I will not be able to stand it.* A cognitive therapist would emphasize how the veteran has already tolerated suffering reasonably well for a considerable length of time. The therapist would also attempt to teach the veteran new coping skills, for example, substituting more adaptive self-talk, such as, "I can enjoy things in life even with some discomfort."

4. *I can't stand the pain anymore.* A cognitive therapist would strive to help veterans understand that when thinking along these terms, they will always be accurate because they are, in a sense, giving up. They are guaranteeing that they will no longer make an effort to cope with the pain, thus sealing their fate. The therapist would challenge this morale-sinking, dispirited self-talk by teaching the veteran to apply more adaptive thinking, such as, "I can take it!" or "I can learn skills to help tolerate the discomfort more effectively."

5. *I still have pain; these pills are useless.* A cognitive therapist would argue that this statement reflects a major cognitive distortion, which is

thinking in only all-or-none categories, without any in-between dimensions. In the real world such absolutes do not exist. The veteran's experiencing even mild pain relief, because of medications, is better than no relief at all.

Scientists have demonstrated that cognitive psychotherapy can provide significant relief of chronic pain. For example researchers at a major university demonstrated that cognitive therapy resulted in a significant reduction of recurrent tension headache pain, from a minimum 43 percent to as much as 100 percent reduction.[118] Scholarly reviews of numerous well-designed scientific studies have concluded that cognitive therapies are effective in reducing pain in adults.[119] Currently scientists have evidence to support the assertion that cognitive therapy reduces musculoskeletal pain, chronic cancer pain, arthritic pain, low back pain, carpal tunnel syndrome pain, and chronic pelvic pain.[120]

Phantom Limb Pain

A strikingly curious phenomenon that wounded amputees have to deal with is phantom limb pain, which is the chronic intense pain that seems to originate from an amputated limb. This strange type of pain is not anything new for the military. The British Lord Nelson lost an arm in battle and later complained that he could still feel it. The American physician Silas Mitchel, while treating the wounded at Gettysburg, coined the term *phantom limb*. He reported that amputees complained that their lost limbs had returned to haunt them. Experts claim that fully 95 percent of amputees experience chronic phantom limb pain and that for most this torment lasts their entire lives.[121] There are cases of men whose cancer forced an amputation of their penis experiencing phantom erections.[122] One veteran had had his arm shot up so badly in Vietnam that surgeons at Walter Reed finally had to amputate it. The veteran then bitterly complained that he wished his arm had never been amputated, because now the arm hurt even worse. He described his phantom limb as being hellishly cramped and clenched across his chest. When he complained to the Walter Reed surgeons, they convinced him that severing the nerves in his stump that led to his spinal cord would end his phantom limb pain. The surgery was carried out, but the veteran's phantom pain persisted. The dilemma for physicians is how to relieve the pain produced by a limb that no longer exists, a ghost limb.

Hope is provided to our warrior amputees by the brilliant neurologist/psychologist V.S. Ramachandran through his elegant clinical research. He is the director of the University of California's Center for Brain and Cognition. Intrigued by phantom limb pain, he studied the major works in the field and examined a number of amputees. Dr. Ramachandran found that when he touched the faces of his blindfolded patients, they reported feeling the touch on both their faces and the amputated limb. Dr. Ramachandran theorized that the brains of the amputees had become disorganized and miswired. The patients' brain areas representing the limb had frozen the memory of the traumatic amputation; these cortical areas "hungered" for new stimulation. He hoped to find an alternative method of presenting the hungered for stimulation to his patients' brains.

Dr. Ramachandran's clever solution was a large topless rectangular box with two lengthwise compartments that had holes in their front. A vertical mirror that faced only one side divided the compartments. The patient was told to put his or her good arm through the front hole of the mirrored compartment and to imagine placing the lost arm in the other. The angle of the patient's seat was such that he or she was able to view the good arm and its mirror image, giving the patient the visual impression of still having two arms. The patient was then told to move the good arm. The mirror reflected the good arm and gave the illusion that the patient was moving both arms, the good one as well as the phantom limb. Amputees happily reported that not only had they seen their lost limbs move, but also that for the first time since its amputation they had felt the limb moving. And most importantly their phantom limb pain vanished.

Dr. Ramachandran's mirrored box supplied visual feedback stimulation to the areas of the amputee's brain that represented the lost limb. The patient's brain was forced to abandon the frozen memory of the painful amputation in order to process this desire for new stimulation. At first the sensation of phantom limb movement accompanied by pain relief worked only while the patient looked at the mirror; however, Dr. Ramachandran found that after extensive practice with his box, patients experienced longer and longer periods of pain relief. After prolonged practice, 50 percent of his phantom limb patients reported that they no longer felt pain in their lost limbs. Scientists have studied these successfully treated amputees with sophisticated brain scans. They discovered that the patients' brains had been rewired; they had reversed their post-amputation misswiring.[123] Dr. Ramachandran had successfully amputated their phantom limbs using only mirrors.

In summary, a cognitive psychotherapist rallies veterans suffering from chronic pain as a result of a battlefield injury out of their despair by challenging their maladaptive thinking. Cognitive therapists teach veterans to restructure their belief that chronic pain is overwhelming, changing it into something much more manageable. At first the therapist identifies veterans' cognitive errors and teaches them how to question their validity. The therapist then teaches veterans how to substitute, in place of the irrational distortions, more reasonable and realistic thoughts. These healthy cognitions help close veterans' neural pain gates and help reduce the accompanying emotional and spiritual demoralization. Finally the therapist trains veterans how to recognize and challenge future maladaptive assumptions on their own. Veterans with chronic pain eventually accept responsibility for their pain as they learn self-control skills that enable them to effectively manage the pain.

23

MILD TRAUMATIC BRAIN INJURY AND PTSD

The success of the United States military's medical care of combat injuries and vastly improved personal and vehicle armor has increased troop survivability in the Iraq and Afghanistan wars. However one consequence of this success is that thousands of recently wounded veterans are returning to America burdened by grievous psychological and physical injuries. Because of the enemy's widespread use of Improvised Explosive Devices (IEDs) and suicide bombers, approximately 22 percent of all our current combat casualties are brain injuries. In contrast the percentage of all casualties that were brain injuries during the Vietnam War was 12 percent.[124] It is estimated that 90 percent of these brain injuries are of mild severity; they are known as mild traumatic brain injuries (mTBIs). Thus the percentage of all our Mideast war combat injuries that are mild brain injuries is approximately 18 percent, but experts acknowledge that the exact figure is unknown.[125] There is a growing concern among United States medical providers about the long-term health consequences of these mTBIs for the veteran and for our society.

Neurologists classify traumatic head injuries as either open or closed head injuries. In open head injuries a powerful blow fractures the soldier's skull or a foreign object, such as an explosion's metal shrapnel, penetrates a soldier's skull. In closed head injuries the combatant's head is violently accelerated/decelerated by striking an object such as the dashboard of a truck suddenly stopped by an explosion; however, the skull's integrity remains intact. The human brain is a vulnerable organ that has the consistency of gelatin, encased in membranes that resemble plastic wrapping. The encased brain floats in fluid within our bony skull. When a soldier's head violently smashes into an object, the floating brain is first compacted against the jagged protrusions of the inner skull (the resulting damaged brain tissue is know as the *coup* injury), and then the brain rebounds against the opposite interior side of the skull (the bruising of the brain tissue [a contusion] at this side of the brain is termed the *counter-coup* injury). In addition, the bouncing and twisting of the upper brain on its narrow brain stem causes tearing and shearing along central fiber tracts know as axons, which serve as the brain's long distance wiring. These microscopic axonal tears disconnect various areas of the brain, decreasing the soldier's ability to process all types of information.

The violent shearing and bruising of the brain may also cause bleeding (the medical term is hemorrhage) either within or outside of the plasticlike membranes. Trapped blood forms a mass, a hematoma, which exerts disruptive pressure on the brain. These contusions, hematomas and axon tears are considered the primary traumatic brain injuries. Secondary injuries are the complex biochemical and neural aftereffects of the primary damage that occur hours or even days after the trauma. Neurologists think that it is probably the interruption of the brain's blood supply that triggers this overproduction of neurochemicals to dose levels that are toxic enough to possibly cause death. It is these secondary injuries that battlefield physicians attempt to prevent or diminish with their emergency treatments after a brain trauma.[126]

Mild traumatic brain injury (mTBI) is defined as brain damage that causes a relatively brief loss of consciousness or an alteration of consciousness, such as feeling confused, disoriented or dazed. Many medical professionals still prefer to call mTBI by its older name, concussion, especially when they are talking with patients and their families. The symptoms of a mild traumatic brain injury can be classified into three categories: (1) cognitive, (2) physical and (3) emotional symptoms.

Since the human brain is our information processor, our built-in computer, it is reasonable to expect that when the brain is injured, the victim will experience information-processing difficulties. The resulting computation problems may include any or all of the following symptoms: amnesia, disorientation, slowed thinking, concentration and problem solving difficulties. Because the brain controls the rest of the body, it is not surprising that brain injuries result in physical symptoms. Possible mTBI physical symptoms include any or all of the following: dizziness, headaches, insomnia, fatigue, nausea, blurred vision, seizures, and gait disturbances. The human brain also initiates and manages all emotions; therefore, brain injuries frequently disrupt the veteran's emotional expressions. Possible emotional symptoms include any or all of the following: irritability, depression, anxiety, loss of initiative and/or emotional control. The specific set of symptoms that any individual veteran suffers depends upon the specific brain sites involved and the severity of the damage. Mild head traumas without loss of consciousness result in a set of mild symptoms that usually last a short time. On the other hand head traumas causing loss of consciousness result in more severe symptoms that can last longer.[127]

The vast majority of victims who suffer a mTBI will fully recover within three to six months. However, for combat veterans the recovery picture is complicated by the fact that many of the traumas were caused by the explosions of enemy ordinance. Explosions create blast waves that subject the brain to cycling waves of intense pressure; the effects of these pressure waves on the human brain are not fully understood. Experts know that blast injuries are not like the brain injuries from the usual civilian trauma of a motor vehicle accident. Blast-induced brain damage exhibits peculiar biological abnormalities not seen in other types of brain injuries,[128] Consequently mTBI veterans tend to suffer from their post-concussion symptoms for longer periods than civilian victims, from 18 to 24 months. Research studies indicate that 10 to 15 percent of veterans suffering from mTBI will experience ongoing symptoms past the usual recovery time period.[129] The specific set of symptoms each veteran encounters depends upon the specific brain sites injured; common symptoms include: headaches, chronic pain, fatigue, amnesia, insomnia, emotional difficulties and changes in vision and/or hearing.

The emotional problems that may persist for the combat veteran diagnosed with mild traumatic brain injury could be those associated with PTSD. Recently there has been a controversy over the question of whether a veteran can develop both mBTI and PTSD from the same traumatic incident. Some physicians accepted the argument that PTSD could not develop after a mild traumatic brain injury. Their argument asserted that the loss of consciousness caused by the head trauma prevented the victim's brain from fully registering the traumatic experience. Lack of proper cognitive trauma registration interfered with recall. Since memory of the traumatic event was considered a necessary symptom for the diagnosis of PTSD, its absence in mTBI meant that the two disorders could not coexist in a patient.[130] The coexistence impossibility argument is based upon a conception of only one type of memory system existing within the human brain.

In fact sophisticated memory research has demonstrated that memory function is not a unitary system, but is composed of at least two major systems: explicit memory and implicit memory. The explicit memory system is involved in the conscious, intentional recall of information concerning the world or our lives. It is the system that reflects what most people mean when they talk of memory, like remembering details from the day you graduated from high school. On the other hand the implicit memory system refers to the effects previous experiences have on current performance without conscious awareness of the learning. The conditioned fear response as evidenced in PTSD is one example of implicit memory. (Review the chapter on fear for information concerning Dr. Joseph Le Doux's work on implicit memory fear conditioning.)

Another example of implicit memory is skill learning, when an individual learns how to perform a complex skill and yet is not fully aware of the sequences of behaviors involved in the task. A bicycle rider will be unable to explain exactly what muscles are involved and how they are used for balancing and riding. The current understanding in psychology is that explicit memory is processed in higher cortical areas of the brain, whereas implicit memory is processed in deeper, more primitive sections of the brain, like the limbic system. Consequently the two memory systems can and often do function independently from one another. Therefore it is possible for a mTBI to damage or disrupt the cortical-level explicit memory system and yet still be registered by the intact implicit memory system, causing the PTSD symptoms. For example, a soldier who was knocked unconscious by an IED explosion while driving a truck through an Iraqi intersection may not recall the event, yet become quite anxious when later riding through intersections, but not understand why he or she feels so frightened. Or if a rapidly responding medical helicopter evacuated the soldier, he or she may later be puzzled over feeling frightened upon hearing the sounds of a helicopter.

In fact there are research results that support the assertion that PTSD and mTBI coexist. Hodge, in a 2008 study of a representative sample of 2525 Iraq and Afghanistan War veterans, found that roughly 5 percent reported loss of consciousness and 10 percent reported an altered mental status like dazed, confused or seeing stars, when injured. Of those suffering loss of consciousness, 43.9 percent met the PTSD criteria; of those who suffered altered mental status, 27.3 percent met the PTSD criteria. Thus mTBI is strongly associated with PTSD. "The data indicate that a history of mild traumatic brain injury in the combat environment, particularly when associated with loss of consciousness, reflects exposure to a very intense traumatic event that threatens loss of life and significantly increases the risk of PTSD."[131] Thus it is quite possible that a combat veteran can suffer brain damage and also suffer ongoing emotional turmoil as a result of the same traumatic incident.

The harsh reality that a blast from an IED or a suicide bomber can be horrific enough to cause both a mTBI and PTSD in an exposed veteran complicates the diagnostic challenge for psychologists and psychiatrists. A thorough assessment is required because the coexistence of the two disorders will make recovery more difficult. First of all, the traumatic injury often occurs during the chaos of an ambush or an IED attack. Many times the veteran's symptoms are ignored or not recognized by the veteran because the effects of the blast were brief. For example, the veteran may have lost consciousness for only a few seconds, or may have been distracted by trying to survive the attack or by aiding other soldiers who were badly wounded. It could be some time before the combatant goes to a medical unit with complaints of fatigue, memory difficulties or the more common headache. Frequently the medical examination performed days after the traumatic event will not find objective neurological evidence of an injury. Even if the soldier is given a brain scan evaluation with the widely available Computerized Axial Tomography (C.A.T.) scan, there still may be no objective evidence of a brain injury because injuries such as microscopic axon tears are not always observable with a C.A.T. scan.[132] Without objective neurological evidence, military physicians often conclude that the problem is psychiatric or perhaps even malingering. This diagnosis only frustrates and irritates the already sensitized combatant.

Another factor complicating accurate diagnosis is the fact that there are a number of symptoms that are common to both mTBI and PTSD. The overlapping symptoms are amnesia, fatigue, depression, anxiety, irritability, and/or insomnia. Currently there are no accepted standards or guidelines that can aid the diagnostician in deciding which disorder accounts for the clinical presentation of the overlapping symptoms. Some experts suggest that the diagnostician should ignore the overlapping symptoms of the two disorders and only consider those symptoms that are unique to each disorder.[133] However since standard diagnostic practice requires the existence of a minimum number of criterion symptoms, then ignoring the overlapping symptoms will lead to inaccuracies due to underdiagnosis.

Part of this diagnostic confusion comes from psychiatry's traditional acceptance of our culture's separation of the mind from the body—what has been termed mind/body dualism. In this tradition PTSD is viewed as due to an emotional trauma (intense fear and horror) to the psyche; in contrast mTBI is viewed as a trauma due to destructive biomechanical forces on the brain. Both approaches use the term "trauma," but with entirely different meanings. As has been explained in the chapter on fear, the concept of a mind/body duality is wrong. The mind and body are united; the psychological mind is nothing more than the ongoing functioning of the biological brain. A better diagnostic strategy is counting the overlapping symptoms common to both PTSD and mTBI towards the required criterion number of symptoms for both disorders. All effective treatment plans depend upon an accurate diagnosis based upon consideration of the complete set of symptoms. This strategy would not only help clarify the duality misconception, but also lead to more effective treatments because now all symptoms would be considered.

Another clinical possibility is that a veteran with a preexisting mTBI could later develop PTSD from a later trauma. "Mild TBI may diminish the capacity to employ cognitive resources that would normally be engaged in problem-solving and regulating emotions after trauma, thereby leaving individuals more susceptible to PTSD."[134] A final diagnostic complication is that often the mTBI veteran has sustained other injuries which produce chronic pain. (Review the chapter devoted to chronic pain.)

Because the diagnosis of the coexistence of mTBI and PTSD is difficult, a reasonable conclusion is that the treatment of these comorbid disorders is also complicated. Veterans with mTBI may require various medical interventions that are outside the scope of this book. The emphasis here will be on psychotherapeutic interventions. Currently there are no research-based treatment guidelines available to advise psychotherapists on the most effective therapy techniques for treating these comorbid disorders. Experts within the Department of Veterans Affairs are currently developing exactly such best practice recommendations. However most experts agree that psychoeducational efforts are critical. The first step is to normalize the symptoms for veterans and their families, establishing for them a positive expectation for the normally rapid recovery. Always the emphasis is on the fact that the brain is a resilient organ that does readjust. Scientific research has demonstrated that, with appropriate treatments and healthy self-care, between 85 and 90 percent of mTBI patients fully recover within a few months.[135] Therapy for the remaining minority needs to address their frustration and fears. Strategies to help compensate for specific limitations are especially helpful. For example veterans may need to learn how to eliminate distractions, such as turning off the television or radio, while concentrating. They may need to learn how to use such memory aids as checklists and organizational calendars effectively. Present-day availability of hand held computers and smart cell phones offer an exciting new opportunity for aiding the cognitively challenged veteran. For example there are now inexpensive software programs for balancing checkbooks and for money management that could be especially helpful.

One concern for psychotherapists of veterans with brain damage is whether cognitive therapies for PTSD will have a negative effect on these impaired veterans. The question centers upon whether TBI veterans can carry out the necessary thinking skills, required for cognitive psychotherapy such as identifying dysfunctional thoughts, without becoming frustrated. Department of Veterans Affairs experts like Dr. E. Summerall point to research results indicating that the same treatments that are effective for PTSD, specifically cognitive processing therapy and medicines like Prozac and Zoloft, are also effective for mTBI.[136] Indeed there exists no evidence that contraindicates the use of cognitive therapies in these cases. In fact there is preliminary evidence that the structure provided by cognitive therapies can be helpful for the cognitively impaired individual with psychological problems. A recent 2010 study of veterans diagnosed with both PTSD and mTBI investigated whether highly modified cognitive processing therapy would be beneficial. Their therapy did not focus upon trauma; instead the focus was on learning the connections between thoughts and feelings, feeling natural emotions and examining those disruptive thoughts that lead to negative emotions. The encouraging results demonstrated significant reductions on measures of PTSD as well as depression in the mTBI veterans.[137] This study demonstrates how mental health professionals treating the brain-damaged combat veteran, who is also burdened by psychological problems like PTSD, must remain flexible; they must be willing and able to modify existing treatments to meet the special needs of their cognitively impaired patients. They must be willing to involve the veteran and his or her family in medical decisions and treatment planning.

The Department of Veterans Affairs has made a major effort at educating its medical staff in recognizing mild traumatic brain injuries and has also established specialized Poly-trauma Centers for the treatment of these injuries as well as any accompanying injuries, like PTSD. The ultimate treatment goal for veterans with mTBI and PTSD is to live as normal a life as possible.

24

SPECIAL COMBAT VETERAN POPULATIONS

All combat troops are valuable and are at risk for PTSD, but it is important to highlight two special groups of combat veterans who are at high risk for PTSD. The first group consists of Army combat medics and Marine corpsmen, who are Navy trained medics assigned to the Marines. Because of their military occupations, these medics have a higher than usual risk for developing combat-related PTSD. The second group consists of prisoners of war (POWs), who, because of their brutal captivity, are also at higher risk for developing PTSD. Both groups are known for their spirit and courage.

Army Medics and Marine Corpsmen

Corpsmen and medics are trained to be the medical first responders on the battlefield. They accompany infantry on their combat patrols in order that they may provide medical care for wounded soldiers or marines. These soldiers have a higher than normal risk for physical and psychological wounds because of their military occupation. First of all, they share with infantry combatants the risk of being killed or wounded by enemy fire while on patrol. In Vietnam the medics were one of the preferred targets for the enemy. The Vietcong or the NVA would deliberately wound an American soldier trapped in a kill zone so that they could then wait for the medic to come forward to treat the injured soldier. The medic would always come, perilously exposing himself in a kill zone in order to save a life. The Vietnamese enemy would then shoot to kill the medic. On top of that primary peril, medics shared with all military medical personnel the genuine risk of being psychologically overwhelmed by the stress of attempting to save the many wounded soldiers. Medics administered medical care with minimal equipment in extremely primitive conditions. They had to cope with treating badly injured soldiers, men they lived with and cared for and who too often died in their arms.

In our current Iraq and Afghanistan wars the job of an Army medic or Marine corpsman is still terribly stressful. The pressures of their job puts them at higher risk for developing PTSD, as illustrated by the tragic example of P.F.C. Joseph Patrick Dwyer. Private Dwyer was an Operation Iraqi Freedom (OIF) Army medic who was photographed by a *Military Times* photographer during the first week of the war in 2003. The now famous photograph showed Dwyer carrying to safety a four-year-old Iraqi boy named Ali, who had been caught in a cross fire and wounded. The photo of Doc Dwyer's heroic concern for an Iraqi child was touted as an example of the U.S. Military's heart and, as such, was published by newspapers all over America. But after his military discharge Doc Dwyer did not feel like a hero; instead he battled his PTSD demons. He became deeply depressed, but did not seek psychological treatment. He abused drugs as his marriage dissolved into divorce. After multiple psychiatric hospitalizations and clashes with the police, he finally became another casualty of the Iraqi War. On June 29, 2008 he died of an accidental overdose of pills and inhalants.[138]

For Army medics and Marine corpsmen struggling with PTSD at our clinic the symptoms of guilt and the subsequent depression caused the most emotional pain. There are a number of sources for their distorted guilt feelings. The primary source was the emotional pain they felt over the wounded soldiers that they were not able to save from death. Every medic or corpsman had tales of that one wounded soldier that they worked so hard to save but could not. Sometimes it was a friend; sometimes it was a soldier who had acted so heroically that in the medic's mind the soldier deserved to live. The wounded soldier or marine might have had traumatically amputated limbs or suffered a sucking chest wound near the heart; no matter how horrible the wound, medics always thought that they should save the casualty. It is this self-demand for perfection that produced the medic's subsequent painful guilt when the casualty died.

Cognitive psychotherapy offered an effective psychological treatment for medics' guilt over their battlefield performance. Their unhealthy guilt was challenged through the following types of questions: "Who can save every patient? At the Mayo Clinic or at Harvard Medical School doctors work in sterile operating rooms, with specially trained teams of nurses and technicians who apply all the advanced medical technology and medications money can buy. But yet they are unable to save every patient, especially those who are as badly hurt as your patients. You set the bar too high for yourself. Consider the conditions you had to work in. You were treating the wounded in dirt and sand, working alone and sometimes under fire yourself, with only the most basic medical equipment and medicines. And on top of every other limitation, your patient was terribly wounded. You wished to save his life, but reconsider the situation realistically. You did your best. What else could you have done?" The therapeutic goal was to help the medics reevaluate their overly perfectionist standards for their performance under the stress of combat.

If a combat medic or corpsman was obsessively stuck on a casualty he or she was desperately treating but who finally died, it could be helpful to inquire if there were any wounded soldiers that he or she had saved. Recounting experiences of stabilizing other severely wounded patients, who were then medically evacuated to the safety of rear hospitals, could help put the medic's losses in the proper perspective. The plan was to help medics realize that by fixating on this one failure they were discounting their successes. Some medics were eventually able to admit that they were not a total failure as a medic. Questioning pathological guilt-ridden thinking within a broader, reality based perspective of achievements helped PTSD medics recognize that they had been too hard on themselves, which reduced their burden of guilt.

A unique source of guilt for medics and corpsmen was over their communication with dying soldiers. For example one Vietnam War medic complained that he had lied to his dying patients. When asked what he had lied about, his answer was that he had told them that they were going to make it, even though he knew the chances of their living were small. The cognitive therapy response followed this line of reasoning: "Think it through. What else are you supposed to say to a soldier who is blown in half or has had his chest torn wide open? Are you supposed to say, 'Man you might as well kiss your butt goodbye, you're a dead man'? Of course not! Your words brought comfort to a horrible tragedy; they enabled the dying man to feel a little hope. It is inexcusable for anyone to deprive the dying of hope. The accuracy of your last words is not the critical point. God forgives such lies." Different forms of this message of forgiveness had to be repeatedly communicated to the medic before he could forgive himself. When he finally was able to rethink and redefine his "lies" into the necessary messages of hope that they actually were, he no longer had to feel guilty over what he had said. (See the chapter on guilt for more information on the cognitive psychotherapy of guilt.)

Depression was another frequent source of emotional pain for medics and corpsmen diagnosed with PTSD. Their extremely negative self-image set the foundation for their depression. All too often they described themselves as "cowards" because of that one time when they did not run into a kill-zone to treat a wounded soldier. One medic gave the following explanation of why he was so disgusted with himself. He had heard a wounded man's calls for help, so he came up the line through thick jungle. He finally spotted the man lying in an open clearing, but the battle was still on going with heavy enemy fire buzzing around the wounded soldier. The Vietcong had baited their deadly trap. They were no longer shooting at the wounded man. Instead they filled the area near him with bullets intended to kill the medic as he exposed himself trying to save the casualty. The medic tearfully recounted how he had frozen in the face of the heavy enemy fire, which he described as a "wall of lead in the air." He just knew that it would be suicide if he came out from behind his tree. The weak calls of help coming from the dying soldier haunted him in his nightmares, making him feel guilty and depressed.

In cognitive psychotherapy this medic's type of distorted thinking is termed *fixation*. He was fixated on only one incident, obsessed about it alone, ignoring others. The previously mentioned medic had been fixated on that one soldier who died while he was treating him. Likewise, the cognitive therapist's challenge is to help this medic broaden his perspective to include all his behavior throughout his entire Vietnam War tour. He was ignoring all the other times when he had placed himself in life-threatening danger to treat the wounded. His negative self-evaluation is another example of primitive all-or-nothing thinking, which follows the logic that if I am not fully courageous all the time, then I must be a coward. It is all-or-none, either-or thinking, which allows no room for anything in between. A soldier is either a total coward or totally courageous. A more sophisticated and reality-based appraisal leaves room for degrees of whatever is being evaluated: a soldier can be eighty percent courageous or another soldier fifty percent cowardly. A therapeutic goal was to teach medics to judge their percentage of courageous behavior, not on one incident, but rather on their total tour of duty. Other therapeutic discussions considered the fact that the United States' military was not like Japan's military in World War II; we have no kamikaze pilots. The United States does not demand that any members of its military commit suicide. In this case, the cognitive therapist questioned, "Why would any unit want their medic to commit suicide?" The depressed medic had to admit that a dead medic could no longer treat all the newly wounded soldiers. Finally the sad fact that the wounded man had been so badly wounded that he quickly died was reconsidered: "How would your death improve that tragedy? Do two deaths make it right?"

Another notable trauma for combat medics and corpsmen was that most of them had wounded people literally dying in their arms. This is one of the many factors that make the job of medic or corpsman such a stressful one. This depressive grief required all the healing power that cognitive psychotherapy provides. (See the chapters on depression and grief for detailed information concerning cognitive therapy treatment of these disorders.) A philosophical argument proved to be therapeutic in these cases. The medics were questioned: "Yes, having a person die in your arms is a tough and sad duty, but isn't it a good thing that at least that man had someone with him when he died? Is it not worse to die alone, with no one to comfort you or to witness your demise?" Combat veterans have a special place in their grieving hearts for those many soldiers who died horribly alone in the stinking jungles of Vietnam or the deserts of Iraq and Afghanistan. These were young people in great pain, calling out for their mothers for comfort, dying alone. The therapeutic goal was for the depressed medics to embrace the idea that their presence at the deaths of their wounded patients was a difficult but extremely honorable duty, something of which they can be justifiably proud.

One final case has important implications for all depressed medics and corpsmen. After months of cognitive psychotherapy one guilt ridden Vietnam medic felt emotionally stable enough to attend an annual reunion of his Army unit. He had avoided the reunion for many years. He returned a happier man, sharing his story. At the reunion a fellow soldier sought him out, warmly shook his hand and sincerely thanked him for saving his life in Vietnam. He was totally shocked by this man's gratitude because he had no recollection of the event. But the fellow soldier was able to vividly recount the firefight with so much detail that eventually the medic was able to recall some memories of the battle. What was so therapeutic for his mental health was this dramatic demonstration that he had saved more lives then he realized. The stunning possibility was that there might be other veterans out there like this fellow who were indebted to him for saving their lives made him smile. All combat medics and corpsmen struggling with PTSD need to consider, when they are feeling low, the uplifting probability that there are more veterans alive today because of their life-saving skills than they realize.

Prisoners of War

The prisoner of war veterans at our clinic were unique men. They all had survived food deprivation to near starvation levels. Many of the POWs had been badly tortured. The Japanese, because of their cultural distain for any soldier who is captured, literally starved their World War II prisoners. The starvation of POWs resulted in these veterans suffering life-long medical and dental disorders. Tragically, the veterans captured by the Japanese died much earlier than the POWs captured by the Germans. The North Korean communists, as part of their brainwashing program, set up gruesome dilemmas where their POWs were caught between two different types of torture. For example an American prisoner was forced to painfully kneel on sharp blocks of wood. When the POW's endurance finally failed and he fell off of the wood, the Korean jailers would severely beat him. In effect the POW had to choose between the pain in his knees or a severe beating, a decision that had negative effects on the prisoner's psychological health. The North Vietnamese communists tortured their POWs so horribly that they were able to break every last one of their prisoners, who were burdened by guilt because of their collapse. The POW captivity experience during the Vietnam War was so extremely brutal that afterwards the American military revised the behavior rules for future POWs. Henceforth American POWs would be allowed to go beyond the traditional limits of name, rank and serial number disclosures. Soldiers are now trained that if captured, they may disclose lies and fabrications of any sort that would enable them to avoid such appalling tortures.

Given the ghastly conditions our POWs endured for so long, the essential psychological question is not, "Why are they having mental problems?" but rather, "Why aren't they all stark raving mad?" The fact that none of the POWs we worked with were psychotic demonstrates the indomitable strength of their human spirit and its capacity to rise above evil circumstances. These hardy men were also highly resilient. They have much to teach us about handling extreme stress. Of course they did not survive tortured imprisonment completely unscathed; they all suffered chronic medical and psychological problems as a consequence of their captivity. Their PTSD symptoms included, among others: survival guilt, repetitive nightmares and major depression. Yet most returned to work, raised families and led full lives in spite of their chronic psychological and medical disabilities. A prime example of the Vietnam War POWs' resiliency is Senator John McCain, who for over six years endured monstrous torture at the hands of the North Vietnamese communists. Even now, decades later, he still cannot raise his arms above his shoulders. Yet, as we all know, he energetically campaigned for and won the Republican presidential nomination in 2008 and currently serves in Congress as an influential United States senator from the state of Arizona.

What are the psychological assets that enabled our clinic's POW veterans to endure and thrive? First of all, one cannot help but be struck by their lack of anger and hate. They had all in some manner come to forgive their captors, which in effect cut their bondage to these evil creatures. Also they all had preserved their sense of humor; they loved to tell jokes and tease each other mercilessly. Furthermore the most prominent psychological asset was their obvious deep affection for each other. No matter what war or what country, they had all learned the fundamental lesson that to survive brutal captivity, they had to care for each other. Every one of the POWs shared passionate stories of how other prisoners had nursed them or had stolen extra food for them when they were sick. They disclosed how they themselves had nursed and feed other POWs back to health or their profound grief when their fellow POW patient died. They shared stories of how they developed various clandestine methods of communication, such as secret tapping codes, so that they could communicate in order to raise each other's morale.

Their dedicated and caring relationships are the reasons why group psychotherapy is the preferred psychological treatment modality for POWs diagnosed with PTSD. Group psychotherapy mimics the POW captivity experience; groups offer individual POW veterans an opportunity to again communicate and interact with their peers. Each individual veteran's recovery benefits from the emotional concern and support of the other POW members. Each individual's healing is enhanced by the opportunity to develop positive relationships with other group members. It was quite educational to observe how the bonds of affection grew among the POW group members, to see how they socialized with each other outside of group, and finally how they supported each other even unto death. They had reached the advanced age when all too often their solemn duty was to attend funerals of former group members. It was both delightful and inspirational to come to know these very special warriors. They taught us convincing lessons on the most effective ways of overcoming extreme stress: to support and truly care for each other and to maintain one's sense of humor.

Resources for the Combat Veteran

For further information on PTSD and related topics visit the following websites:

Department of Veterans Affairs
Washington, D.C. 20011
http://www.va.gov
For the location of the nearest VA facility, visit above website and click on "Locations."

Disabled American Veterans
http://www.dav.org

Military Records
http://www.nara.gov/regional/mpr.html

PTSD Information
(1) http://www.ptsd.va.gov
    Information line: 802-296-6300
(2) http://centerforthestudyoftraumaticstress.org
(3) National Alliance on Mental Illness
     http://wwwnami.org/veterans
    This is an excellent source of links to other veteran-related websites.

Spouses and Families
http://www.vietnamveteranwives.com
http://www.tmkc.netfirms.com
http://www.VetsOutreach.com

Veterans Benefits: Disability, Medical Care, Life Insurance, Sexual Trauma
Toll-free: 1-800-827-1000

Veteran Educational Benefits
http://www.gibill.va.gov/education/benefits.htm

Veteran Health Benefits
(1) http://www.va.gov/health_benefits
    Phone: 202-273-5400
    Toll-free: 1-877-222-8387

(2) For PTSD benefits from Vietnam Veterans of America
    http://www.vva.org/benefits/ptsd.htm

Veterans' Resources
http://www.veteransresources.net

Veterans' Service Organizations
http://www.va.gov/vso/view.asp

Women Veterans
http://www.va.gov/womenvet

The Center for Women Veterans
810 Vermont Ave. NW
Washington, D.C. 20420
Phone: 202-273-6193

NOTES

1. Vanden Brook 2008, 1A, 2A.
2. Cross and Brooke, eds., 1993, 699.
3. Bremner 2005, 27.
4. American Psychiatric Association 1994, 429.
5. Foa, Zinburg, and Rothbaum 1992, 229–230.
6. Gelman 1988, August 29, 64.
7. Kolb 1987, 989–995.
8. American Psychiatric Association 1980, 236.
9. American Psychiatric Association 1994, 427–428.
10. Ursano 1981, 317.
11. Kulka, Schlenger, Fairbank, Hough, Jordan, Marmar, and Weiss 1990.
12. Taniellian and Jaycox, eds., 2008.
13. Jordan, Marmor, Fairbank, Schlenger, Kulka, Hough, and Weiss 1990, 916–926.
14. Bremner 2005, 92.
15. Foa, Davidson, and Frances 1999, 14.
16. Pittman, Orr, Altman, Longpre, Poire, and Macklin 1996, 419–429.
17. Foa, Davidson, and Frances 1999, 14.
18. Foa, Keane, and Friedman 2000, 560.
19. Epictetus 1995, 10.
20. Byrom 1976, 1.
21. Cross and Brooke, eds., 1993, 991.
22. Monson, Price, and Ranslow 2005, 75–83.
23. Janoff-Bulman 1992, 6–7.
24. Cornum 1992, July 13, 15.
25. LeDoux 2002, 326.
26. Kolb 1987, 144, 989–985.
27. LeDoux 2002, 219.
28. Bremener 2005, 193.
29. Benson with Klipper 2000, 99.
30. Jacobson 1938.
31. Luthe,1969.
32. Stoyva 1983, 149.
33. Blackmore and Frith 2005, 134.
34. Yehuda, Golier, Tischler, Stavitshy, and Harvey 2005, 504–515.

35. Bremner, Scott, Delaney, Southwick, Mason, Johnson, Innis, McCarthy, and Charney 1993, 1015–1019.

36. Sapolsky, Uno, Rebert, and Finch 1990, 2897–2902.

37. Bremner, Randall, Scott, Bronen, Seibyl, Southwick, Delaney, McCarthy, Charney, and Innis 1995, 973–981.

38. Gilberston, Shenton, Krasi, Ciszweski, Lasko, and Orri 2002, 1242–1247.

39. Eriksson, Perfilivea, Bjork-Eriksson, Alborn, Nordborg, Peterson, and Gage 1998, 1313–1317.

40. Bremner 2005 253.

41. Zouris, Walker, Dye, and Galarnewau 2006, 246–252.

42. Levin and Nielsen 2007, 489.

43. Bulkeley 1997, 55.

44. Frankel 2004, June 14, A01.

45. Winson 2002, 54–61.

46. Freud 1953.

47. Fromm 1980, 70.

48. Davis and Wright 2007, 123–133.

49. American Psychiatric Association 1994, 428.

50. Whitteman 1991, February 11, 76.

51. Associated Press 1986, April 27, B-8.

52. Evans 1996.

53. Yalom 1995, 1.

54. *Ibid.*, 28.

55. P.P. Schnurr, M.J. Friedman, D.W. Foy, M.T. Shea, F.Y. Hsieh, P.W. Lavori, S.M. Glynn, M. Wattenberg, and N.C. Bernardy 2003, 481–489.

56. Ready, Thomas, Worley, Backscheider, Harvery, Baltzell, and Rothbaum 2008, 571.

57. Foa, Keane, and Friedman 2000, 571.

58. American Psychiatric Association 1994, 425.

59. Wallace 1984, 234–251.

60. Goodman 1986, May 1020.

61. Telushkin 1991, 42.

62. Lifton 1992, 127.

63. Schiraldi 2000, 198.

64. American Psychiatric Association 1980, 237.

65. Figley, ed., 1985, 115.

66. Choca, Shanley, and Van Denburg 1993, 69.

67. Novaco 1976, 1124–1128; Novaco 1978, 135–157; Chemtob, Navaco, Hamada, Grosss, and Smith, 17- 37.

68. Mundt 2009, A48.

69. American Psychiatric Association 1994, 340.

70. Nemiah 1978, 193.

71. Beck 1976, 102–132.

72. Rush, Beck, Kovacs, and Hollon 1977, 17–38.

73. Antonuccia, Danton, and DeNelsky 1995, 574–585.

74. Bockting, Schene, Spinhoven, Koeter, Wouters, Huyser and Kamphuis 2005, 647–657.

75. Baxter, Schwartz, and Bergman et al. 1992, 681–689.

76. Burns 1999, 40.
77. Recent study finds suicide among veterans all too common 2011, 43.
78. Jaffe 2011, August 13, A-6.
79. Beck, 1976, 304.
80. Brown, Ten Have, Henriques, Xie, Hollander, and Beck 2005, 563–570.
81. Lembecke 1998.
82. Greene 1989, 45.
83. Keating 2003, 24.
84. Moniz 2000, November 16, 1A.
85. *Ibid.*, 2A.
86. Kolb 1992, 27.
87. Kolb 2005.
88. Thompson 2008, June 16, 40.
89. Foa, Davidson, and Frances 1999, 12.
90. Bremner 2005, 250.
91. Thompson 2008, June 16, 42.
92. Bremner 2005, 252.
93. Friedman, Donnelly, and Mellman 2003, 58.
94. Foa, Davidson, and Frances 1999, 18.
95. Foa, Keane, and Friedman 2000, 564.
96. Duman, Malberg, and Nakagawa 2001, 401–407.
97. Bremner 2005, 253.
98. Foa, Keane, and Friedman 2000, 565.
99. *Ibid.*, 566.
100. Pitman, Sanders, Zusman, Healy, Cheema, Lasko, Cahill, and Orr 2002, 189–191.
101. Kolb, Burris, and Griffiths 1984, 98–105.
102. Raskind, Peskind, Kanter, Petrie, Radant A, Thompson, Dobie, Hoff, Rein, Straits-Trester, Thomas, and McFall 2003, 371–316.
103. Pueschel 2000, 7.
104. Rizzo, Difede, J, Rothbaum, Johnston, McLay, Reger, Gahm, Parsons, Graap, and Pair 2009, 281.
105. Zoroya 2011, September 20, 9A.
106. Manning 2005, May 11, D1–2.
107. Beecher 1966, 840–841.
108. Sternberg 2005, May 9, A1, A4.
109. Turk and Nash 1993, 113–117.
110. Doidge 2007, 192.
111. Wallis 2005, February 28, 50–51.
112. De Carvalho.
113. Wallis 2005, February 28, 55.
114. *Ibid.*, 57.
115. Turk and Nash 1993, 118.
116. *Ibid.*, 119.
117. Neergaard 2006, October 24, A-5.
118. Turk and Nash 1993, 121.
119. Eccleston 2001, 144–152.
120. Albert Einstein College of Medicine.

121. Doidge 2007, 180–181.
122. *Ibid.*, 184.
123. *Ibid.*, 188.
124. Summerall.
125. Hoge, McGurk, Thomas, Cox, Engel, and Castro 2008, 453–463.
126. Hurley.
127. Stein and McAllister 2009, 771.
128. Cernak and Noble-Haeusslein 2010, 255–266.
129. Chard, Schumm, McIlvain, Bailey, and Parkinson 2010.
130. Shordone and Liter 1995, 405–412.
131. Sica.
132. Basso andNewman 2000, 41.
133. Stein & McAllister 2009, 771.
134. Otis, McGlinchey, Vasterling and Kerns 2011, 148.
135. Hurley.
136. Summerall.
137. Chard, Schumm, McIlvain, Bailey, and Parkinson 2010.
138. Kelly 2008, July 8.

BIBLIOGRAPHY

Albert Einstein College of Medicine. (2011). *Psychological/Mind Body Therapies in Pain Management.* Retrieved August 24, 2011, www.healiingchronicpain.org/content/introduction/conv-mnbdy.asp.

American Psychiatric Association. (1980). *Diagnostic and Statistical Manual,* 3d ed. Washington, D.C.: American Psychiatric Association.

American Psychiatric Association. (1994). *Diagnostic and Statistical Manual,* 4th ed. Washington, D.C.: American Psychiatric Association.

Antonuccia, D.O., W.G. Danton, and G.Y. DeNelsky. (1995). Psychotherapy versus mediation for depression: Challenging the conventional wisdom with data. *Professional Psychology: Research and Practice* 26(6).

Associated Press. (1986, April 27). Dozens of Vietnam vets prefer "jungle life" exile. *Florida Times Union,* p. B-8.

Basso, M.R., and E. Newman. (2000). A primer of closed head injury sequelae in post-traumatic stress disorder. In J.H. Harvey and B.G. Pauwels (eds.), *Post Traumatic Stress Theory: Research and Application.* Philadelphia: Brunner/Mazel.

Baxter, L.R., J.M. Schwartz, and K.S. Bergman, et al. (1992). Caudate glucose metabolic rate changes with both drug and behavior therapy for obsessive-compulsive disorders. *Archives of General Psychiatry* 49.

Beck, A.T. (1976). *Cognitive Therapy and the Emotional Disorders.* New York: International Universities Press.

Beecher, H.K. (1966). Pain: One mystery solved. *Science* 151.

Benson, H., with M. Klipper. (2000). *The Relaxation Response.* New York: HarperCollins.

Blackmore, S.J., and U. Frith. (2005). *The Learning Brain: Lessons for Education.* Malden, MA: Blackwell.

Bockting, C.L.H., A.H. Schene, P. Spinhoven, M.W.J. Koeter, L.F. Wouters, J. Huyser, and J.H. Kamphuis. (2005). Preventing relapse/recurrence in recurrent depression with cognitive therapy: A randomized controlled trial. *Journal of Consulting and Clinical Psychology* 73.

Bremner, J.D., T.M. Scott, R.C. Delaney, S.M. Southwick, J.W. Mason, D.R. Johnson, R.B. Innis, G. McCarthy, and D.S. Charney. (1993). Deficits in short-term memory in post-traumatic stress disorder. *American Journal of Psychiatry* 150.

Bremner, J.D., P.R. Randall, T.M. Scott, R.A. Bronen, J.P. Seibyl, S.M. Southwick, R.C. Delaney, G. McCarthy, D.S. Charney, and R.B. Innis. (1995). MRI-based measurements of hippocampal volume in post-traumatic stress disorder. *American Journal of Psychiatry* 152.

Bremner, J.D. (2005). *Does Stress Damage the Brain?* New York: W.W Norton.

Brown, G.K., T. Ten Have, G.R. Henriques, S.X. Xie, J.E. Hollander, and A.R. Beck. (2005). Cognitive therapy for the prevention of suicide attempts. *Journal of the American Medical Association* 294(5), August 2.

Bryant, R.A. (2001). Posttraumatic stress disorder and mild brain injury: Controversies, causes and consequences. *Journal of Clinical and Experimental Neuropsychology* 23(6).

Bulkeley, K. (1997). *An Introduction to the Psychology of Dreaming.* Westport, CT: Praeger.

Burns, D.D. (1999). *Feeling Good: The New Mood Therapy.* Rev. and updated ed. New York: HarperCollins.

Byrom, T. (1976). *Dhammapada: The Sayings of the Buddha.* Boston: Shambhala.

Cernak, I., and I.J. Noble-Haeusslein. (2010). Traumatic Brain Injury: An overview of pathobiology with emphasis on military populations. *Journal of Cerebral Blow Flow and Metabolism* 30.

Chard, K.M., J.A. Schumm, S. McIlvain, G. Bailey, and R.B. Parkinson. (2010). *Examining the Effectiveness of CPT-C in a Residential Program for Veterans with PTSD and TBI.* Paper presented at the ISTSS 26th Annual Meeting, Montréal, Québec, Canada.

Chemtob, C., R. Navaco, R. Hamada, D. Grosss, and G. Smith. (1997). Anger regulation deficits in combat-related posttraumatic stress disorder. *Journal of Traumatic Stress* 10(1).

Choca, J.P., L.A. Shanley, and E. Van Denburg. (1993). *Interpretative Guide to the Million Clinical Multiaxial Inventory.* Washington, D.C.: American Psychological Association.

Cornum, R. (1992, July 13). *Newsweek.*

Cross, W. L., and T. Brooke (eds.). (1993). *The Yale Shakespeare: The Complete Works.* New York: Barnes & Noble Books arranged by Yale University Press.

Davis, J.L., and D.C. Wright. (2007). Randomized clinical trial for treatment of chronic nightmares in trauma-exposed adults. *Journal of Traumatic Stress* 20(2), April.

De Carvalho, L.T. (2007). The experience of chronic pain and PTSD: A guide for healthcare providers. Created on July 5, 2007. Retrieved August 27, 2011, www.ptsd.va.gov/professional/pages/pain-ptsdguide-patients.asp.

Doidge, N. (2007). *The Brain That Changes Itself: Stories of Personal Triumph from the Frontiers of Brain Science.* New York: Penguin.

Duman, R.S., J. Malberg, and S. Nakagawa. (2001). Regulation of adult neurogenesis by psychotropic drugs. *The Journal of Pharmacology and Experimental Therapeutics* 299(2), November.

Eccleston, C. (2001). Role of psychology in pain management. *British Journal of Anesthesia* 87.

Epictetus. (1995). *The Art of Living.* New York: HarperCollins.

Eriksson, P.S., E. Perfilivea, T. Bjork-Eriksson, A.M. Alborn, C. Nordborg, D.A. Peterson, and F.H. Gage. (1998). Neurogensis in the adult human hippocampus. *Nature Medicine* 4.

Evans, F.B. (1996). *Harry Stack Sullivan: Interpersonal Theory and Psychotherapy.* New York: Routledge.

Figley, C.R. (ed.). (1985). *Trauma and Its Wake.* New York: Brunner/Mazel.

Foa, E.B., R. Zinburg, and B.O. Rothbaum. (1992). Uncontrollability and unpredictability in post-traumatic stress disorder: An animal model. *Psychological Bulletin* 112(2).

Foa, E.B., Davidson, J.R., & Frances, A., (1999). Expert consensus guideline series: Treatment of posttraumatic stress disorder. *The Journal of Clinical Psychiatry* 60 (Supplement 16).

Foa, E.B., T.M. Keane, and M.J. Friedman. (2000). Guidelines for treatment of PTSD. *Journal of Traumatic Stress* 13(4).

Frankel, G. (2004, June 14). Prison Tactics a Longtime Dilemma for Israel. *Washington Post*, A01.

Freud, S. (1953). *The Interpretation of Dreams.* New York: Basic Books.

Friedman, M.J., C.L. Donnelly, and T.A. Mellman. (2003). Pharmacotherapy for PTSD. *Psychiatry Annals*, 33(1), January.

Fromm, E. (1980). *Greatness and Limitations of Freud's Thought.* New York: Harper & Row.

Gelman, D. (1988, August 29). Treating war's psychic wounds. *Newsweek.*

Gilberston, M.W., M.E. Shenton, K. Krasi, A. Ciszweski, N.B. Lasko, and S.P. Orri. (2002). Smaller hippocampus volume predicts pathological vulnerability to psychological trauma. *Nature Neuroscience* 5.

Goodman, W. (1986, May 20). Black soldiers in Vietnam. *New York Times*, Movies Section.

Greene B. (1989). Homecoming. *Esquire Magazine*, February.

Hoge, C.W., D. McGurk, J.L. Thomas, A.L. Cox, C.C. Engel, and C.A. Castro. (2008). Mild traumatic brain injury in U.S. soldiers returning from Iraq. *New England Journal of Medicine* 358, January 31.

Hurley, R.A. (2009). *Neuropsychiatry of Traumatic Brain Injury.* Department of Veterans Affairs video course. Retrieved September 28, 2011, //www.ptsd.va.gov/profes sional/ptsd101/course-modules/traumatic-brain-injury.asp.

Jacobson, E. (1938). *Progressive Relaxation.* Chicago: University of Chicago Press.

Jaffe, G. (2011, August 13). 32 suicides in July a record for Army. *Florida Times Union*, p. A-6.

Janoff-Bulman, R. (1992). *Shattered Assumptions: Towards a New Psychology of Trauma.* New York: The Free Press.

Jordan, B.K., C.R. Marmor, J.A. Fairbank, W.E. Schlenger, R.A. Kulka, R.L. Hough, and D.S. Weiss. (1990). Problems in families of male Vietnam Veterans with post-traumatic stress disorder. *Journal of Consulting and Clinical Psychology* 60(6).

Karnow, S. (1999, June 14). Ho Chi Minh. *Time.*

Keating, S. K. (2003). Debunking the myths. *The American Legion Magazine*, September.

Kelly, K. (2008, July 8). Medic in famous photo dies after PTSD struggle. *Army Times.* Retrieved from http://www. armytimes.com.

Kolb, L. (1987). A neuropsychological hypothesis explaining post traumatic stress disorders. *American Journal of Psychiatry* 144.

Kolb, L.C., B.C. Burris, and S. Griffiths. (1984). Propranolol and clonidine in the treatment of post-traumatic stress disorders of war. In B. Van de Kolk (ed.), *Post-Traumatic Stress Disorder: Psychological and Biological Sequelae.* Arlington, VA: American Psychiatric.

Kolb, R.K. (1992). War in the boonies: Vietnam, 1965–1973. *Veterans of Foreign Wars Magazine,* April.

Kolb, R.K. (2005). An era ends in Vietnam veteran benefits ... and begins. *Veterans of Foreign Wars Magazine*, May.

Kulka, R.A., W.E. Schlenger, J.A. Fairbank, R.L. Hough, B.K. Jordan, C.R. Marmar, and D.S. Weiss. (1990). *Trauma and the Vietnam War Generation: Report of the Findings from the National Vietnam Veterans Readjustment Study.* New York: Brunner/Mazel.

LeDoux, J. (2002). *Synaptic Self.* New York: Penguin.

Lembecke, J. (1998). *The Spitting Image: Myths, Memory and the Legacy of Vietnam.* New York: New York University Press.

Levin R., and T.A. Nielsen. (2007). Disturbed dreaming, posttraumatic stress disorder, and affect distress: A review and neurocognitive model. *Psychological Bulletin* 133(3), May.

Lifton, R. (1992). *Home from the War.* Boston: Beacon.

Lind, M. (2002). *Vietnam, the Necessary War.* New York: Simon & Schuster.

Luthe, W. (ed.). (1969). *Autogenic Therapy.* Vols 1–6. New York: Grune & Stratton.

Manning, A. (2005, May 11). Injured Iraq veterans battle a new enemy. *USA TODAY,* pp. D1–2.

Moniz, D. (2000). Dispelling the myths about Vietnam veterans. *USA Today,* November 16, p. 1A.

Monson, C.M., J. L. Price, and E. Ranslow (2005). Treating combat PTSD through cognitive processing therapy. *Federal Practitioner,* October, pp. 75–83.

Mundt, J.E. (2009). *PTSD in Iraq and Afghanistan Combat Veterans.* Eau Claire, WI: Medical Educational Services.

Neergaard, L. (2006, October 24). Distract kids to ease shot pain. *Florida Times Union,* p. A-5.

Nemiah. J. C. (1978). Psychoneurotic disorders. In A.M. Nicholi Jr. (ed.), *The Harvard Guide to Modern Psychiatry.* Cambridge, MA: The Belknap Press of Harvard University Press.

Novaco, R.W. (1976). The functions and regulation of the arousal of anger. *American Journal of Psychiatry* 133(10), October.

Novaco, R.W. (1978), Anger and coping with stress. In J. Foreyt and D. Rathjen (eds.), *Cognitive Behavior Therapy: Research and Application.* New York: Plenum Press.

Otis, J.D., R. McGlinchey, J.J. Vasterling, and R.D. Kerns. (2011). Complicating factors associated with mild traumatic brain injury: Impact on pain and post traumatic stress treatment. *Journal of Clinical Psychology in Medical Settings* 18(8).

Pitman, R.K., K.M. Sanders, R.M. Zusman, A.R. Healy, F. Cheema, N.B. Lasko, L. Cahill, and S.T. Orr. (2002, January 15), Pilot study of secondary prevention of posttraumatic stress disorder with propranolol. *Biological Psychiatry* 51(2), January 15.

Pittman, R.K., S.P. Orr, B. Altman, R.E. Longpre, R.E. Poire, and M.L. Macklin. (1996). Emotional processing during eye movement desensitization and reprocessing therapy of Vietnam veterans with chronic post-traumatic stress disorder. *Comprehensive Psychiatry* 37.

Pueschel, M. (2000). Virtual therapy program In VA targets PTSD. *U.S. Medicine,* October.

Raskind, M.A., E.R. Peskind, E.D. Kanter, E.C. Petrie, A. Radant , C.E. Thompson, D.J. Dobie, D. Hoff, R.J. Rein, K. Straits-Trester, R.G. Thomas, and M.M. McFall.

(2003). Reduction in nightmares and other PTSD symptoms in combat veterans by Prazosin: a placebo-controlled study. *American Journal of Psychiatry* 160(2).

Ready, D.J., K.R. Thomas, V. Worley V., A.G. Backscheider, L.A. Harvery, D. Baltzell, and B.O. Rothbaum. (2008). A field test of group based exposure therapy with 102 veterans with war-related posttraumatic stress disorder. *Journal of Traumatic Stress* 21(2), April.

Recent study finds suicide among veterans all too common. (2011). *Federal Practitioner,* August.

Rizzo, A., J. Difede, B. Rothbaum, S. Johnston, R. McLay, G. Reger, G. Gahm, T. Parsons, K. Graap, and J. Pair. (2009). VR PTSD exposure therapy results with active duty OIF/OEF combatants. *Medicine Meets Virtual Reality* 17, 281.

Rush, A.J., A.T. Beck, M. Kovacs, and S. Hollon. (1977). Comparative efficacy of cognitive therapy and pharmacotherapy in the treatment of depressed outpatients. *Cognitive Therapy and Research* 1, March.

Sapolsky, R.M., H. Uno, C.S. Rebert, and C.E. Finch. (1990). Hippocampal damage associated with prolonged gulocorticoid exposure in primates. *Journal of Neuroscience* 10.

Schiraldi, G.R. (2000). *The Post Traumatic Stress Source Book.* Los Angeles: Lowell Howe.

Schnurr, P.P., M.J. Friedman, D.W. Foy, M.T. Shea, F.Y. Hsieh, P.W. Lavori, S.M. Glynn, M. Wattenberg, and N.C. Bernardy Randomized trial of trauma-focused group therapy for posttraumatic stress disorder: results from a department of veterans affairs cooperative study. *Archives of General Psychiatry* 60(5).

Shordone, R. J., and J.C. Liter. (1995). Mild traumatic brain injury does not produce post-traumatic stress disorder. *Brain Injury* 9.

Sica, R.B. (1996). *The Neurological Basis of Potential Co-occurrence of Mild Traumatic Brain Injury with Post-Traumatic Stress Disorder,* retrieved September 24, 2011, http://www.aaets.org/article6.htm.

Stein, M.B., and T.W. McAllister. (2009). Exploring the Convergence of Posttraumatic Stress Disorder and Mild Traumatic Brain Injury. *American Journal of Psychiatry* 166 July 7.

Sternberg, S. (2005, May 9). Chronic pain: The enemy within. *USA TODAY,* p. A1, A4.

Stoyva, J. (1983). Guidelines in cultivating general relaxation: Biofeedback and autogenic training combined. In J. Basmajian (ed.), *Biofeedback: Principles and Practice for Clinicians,* 2d ed. Baltimore: Williams & Wilkins.

Summerall, E.L. (2007). *Traumatic Brain Injury and PTSD.* Retrieved September 23, 2011, http://www.ptsd.va.gov/professional/pages/traumatic-brain-injury-ptsd.asp.

Taniellian, T., and L.H. Jaycox (eds.). (2008). *Invisible Wounds of War: Psychological and Cognitive injuries: Their Consequences and Services to Assist Recovery.* Santa Monica: RAND Distribution Services.

Telushkin, J. (1991). *Jewish Literacy.* New York: HarperCollins.

Thompson, M. (2008, June 16). America's medicated army. *Time.*

Turk, D.C., and J.M. Nash. (1993). Chronic pain: New ways to cope. In D. Goleman and J. Gurin, eds., *MIND BODY MEDICINE.* Yonkers: Consumers Union of the United States.

Ursano R.J. (1981). The Viet Nam era prisoner of war: Precaptivity personality and the development of psychiatric illness. *American Journal of Psychiatry* 138(3).

Vanden Brook, T. (2008, November 25). General's story puts focus on stress from combat. *USA TODAY*, p. 1A, 2A.

Wallace, T. (1984). *Bloods: An Oral History of the Vietnam War by Black Veterans.* New York: Random House.

Wallis, C. (2005). The right (and wrong way) to treat pain. *Time,* February 28.

Whitteman, P.A. (1991). Lost in America. *Time,* February 11.

Winson, J. (2002). The meaning of dreams. *Scientific American Special Edition: The Hidden Mind,* August.

Yalom, I.D. (1995). *The Theory and Practice of Group Psychotherapy.* New York: Basic Books.

Yehuda, R., J. Golier, L. Tischler, E. Stavitshy, and P. Harvey. (2005), Learning and memory in aging combat veterans with PTSD. *Journal of Clinical and Experimental Neuropsychology* 27.

Zoroya, G. (2011). Injuries cost more troops their limbs. *USA TODAY,* September 20, p. 9A.

Zouris, J.M., G. J. Walker, J. Dye, and M. Galarnewau, M. (2006). Wounding patterns for U.S. Marines and sailors during Operation Iraq Freedom, major combat phase. *Military Medicine* 17(3).

INDEX